Re-envisioning Chinese Educ

Maintaining education ... hum ...ormation, this book is distinctive in loo... ...uccess ...Chinese education. The editors an... ...contribu..., mo... ...overse... and mainland Chinese scholars, argue that m...ern Chinese education has been built upon a superficial and instrumental embrace of Western modernity and a fragmented appropriation of Chinese cultural heritage. They call for a rethinking and re-envisioning of Chinese education, grounded in and enriched by various cultural traditions and cross-cultural dialogues. Drawing on Chinese history and culture, Western and Chinese philosophies, curriculum and pedagogical theories, the collected volume analyzes (1) why education as person-making has failed to take root in contemporary China, (2) how the purpose of education has changed during the process of China's modernization, and (3) what a rediscovery of the meaning of person-making implies for rethinking and re-envisioning Chinese education in the current age of globalization and social change. *Re-envisioning Chinese Education: The meaning of person-making in a new age* discusses among other issues:

- China's historical encounter with the West and modern Chinese education
- Rediscovering lasting values: Confucian cultural learning models in the twenty-first century
- Rethinking and re-envisioning Chinese didactics: implications from the German *Didaktik* tradition
- The new basic education and the development of human subjectivity: a Chinese experience.

This book will be relevant for scholars, researchers, and policy makers everywhere who seek a more balanced, more sophisticated, and philosophically better grounded understanding of Chinese education.

Guoping Zhao is Professor at the College of Education, Oklahoma State University, USA.

Zongyi Deng is Associate Professor at the National Institute of Education, Nanyang Technological University, Singapore.

Education and Society in China
Series Editor: Gerard A. Postiglione

China's economic rise has been breathtaking and unprecedented. Yet educational opportunities remain highly unequal. China has the essential ingredients to build a great system of education, but educational governance needs an overhaul if China is to realize its goal of dramatically boosting its technological output to world-class levels. As more work by established Chinese and overseas scholars becomes accessible in English to the larger global community, myths will be removed and replaced by more accurate and sophisticated analyses of China's fascinatingly complex educational transformation. This series will provide highly analytical examinations of key issues in China's education system.

Books in the series include:

Re-envisioning Chinese education

The meaning of person-making in a new age

Edited by
Guoping Zhao and
Zongyi Deng

Routledge
Taylor & Francis Group

LONDON AND NEW YORK

Wah Ching Centre of Research
on Education in China
華 正 中 國 教 育 研 究 中 心
The University of Hong Kong 香 港 大 學

First published 2016
by Routledge

2 Park Square, Milton Park, Abingdon, Oxfordshire OX14 4RN
711 Third Avenue, New York, NY 10017

Routledge is an imprint of the Taylor & Francis Group, an informa business

First issued in paperback 2017

British Library Cataloguing in Publication Data
A catalogue record for this book is available from the British Library

Library of Congress Cataloging-in-Publication Data
A catalog record for this book has been requested

ISBN: 978-1-138-81817-0 (hbk)
ISBN: 978-1-138-57592-9 (pbk)

Typeset in Galliard
by Florence Production Ltd, Stoodleigh, Devon, UK

Contents

Contributors

Limin Bai is a senior lecturer in the School of Languages and Cultures, Victoria University of Wellington, New Zealand. She has published extensively on Chinese history, society and education in both English and Chinese, spanning the late Imperial period to contemporary China. Her work on contemporary Chinese society examines education policy and practice from a historical perspective and with a comparative approach.

Yuhua Bu is a professor of education theory in the Department of Education, and researcher of the Institute of the schooling reform and development, East China Normal University, Shanghai. Her research area is education theory, especially in the areas of school reform and classroom teaching.

Thomas D. Curran is a professor in the Department of History, Sacred Heart University, Fairfield, CT. His areas of special interest include twentieth-century Chinese educational and social history, classical Greek history and thought, and the history of the Vietnam War.

Zongyi Deng is an associate professor at the National Institute of Education, Nanyang Technological University, Singapore. His interest areas include curriculum making, curriculum content or subject matter, didactics (or *Didaktik*), educational policy and Chinese education.

Xiaoling Ke is an associate professor in the School of English and Education, Guangdong University of Foreign Studies, Guangzhou, Guangdong. Her research interests include educational philosophy, educational culture in China and curriculum studies.

Wing-Wah Law is a professor in the faculty of education at The University of Hong Kong, Pokfulam Road, Hong Kong. His research interests include education and development, globalization and citizenship education, and education reforms in Chinese societies.

Jin Li is a professor of education and human development in the Education Department, Brown University, Providence, RI. Her research examines primarily the Confucian virtue-oriented versus Western mind-oriented learning models and how these models shape children's learning beliefs and achievement in these two sets of cultures.

Zongjie Wu is a professor of linguistics and language education in the School of International Studies, and Director of the Institute of Cross-Cultural Studies, Zhejiang University, Hangzhou, Zhejiang, 310058, PR China. His research cuts across multiple disciplines with a focus on cultural discourses, especially in the areas of education and the Confucian cultural heritage. The common thread that runs through his work is a philosophical perspective on the relationships of being, knowing, and naming in the context of cross-cultural dialogues.

Jing Xu is a graduate student in Department of Education, East China Normal University, Shanghai, PR China. The areas of her research are children's education, New Basic Education (NBE), and moral education.

Huajun Zhang is an associate professor of education at the Faculty of Education, Beijing Normal University, Beijing, China. Her area of research interest includes Chinese philosophy of education, education and culture in modern transformation, and the humanistic approach to teacher education.

Guoping Zhao is a professor at the College of Education, Oklahoma State University, Stillwater, Oklahoma. Her primary areas of scholarship are philosophy of education, comparative philosophy, and cross-cultural studies of education. She has written extensively on theories of the subject, ethics, spirituality, and democracy and the politics of education.

Foreword

With its focus on education as person-making, this book provides a unique vision of the transformative possibilities of education through a meeting of the Neo-Confucian tradition of self-cultivation and the Western post-humanist tradition of self-formation. It begins by identifying the current crisis in Chinese education, where an obsessive concern with the pursuit of qualifications and competition in the market economy is sweeping young people into forms of learning that may result in examination success, but do little to nurture the development of personality and moral-spiritual selfhood.

Through penetrating historical and philosophical analyses that examine the cultural roots of education in the classics, the experience of individuals who were bridge figures in the transition to modernity and the struggles of a deeply conflicted century of educational reform under changing political regimes, the authors uncover some of the reasons for the current crisis. Their consideration of the changing purposes of education over a century of efforts at modernization sheds further light on this crisis and sets the stage for the main question of the book: What might a rediscovery of person-making contribute to Chinese education, and indeed to education around the world, in the current era of globalization?

In reflecting on what I should write in this foreword, I felt it might be helpful to describe a conversation that has evolved over many years and which this volume carries forward in refreshingly new and insightful ways. William Theodore De Bary's recent publication, *The Great Civilized Conversation: Education for a World Community* (2013) came to mind, as I thought about how this volume builds on De Bary's lifelong dedication to promoting the East Asian classics with new perspectives that are profoundly illuminating. Trained in philosophy, history, comparative education, psychology and sociology, the authors open up new understandings of the vitality and relevance of China's Confucian tradition to the deep concerns of a global community. In the face of a context in which knowledge is largely viewed as a crucial element in economic competitiveness they introduce an alternative approach that sees knowledge as a wellspring of inspiration for person-making, an approach to education that is oriented towards human flourishing and embodies harmony and sustainability.

In the Introduction to this book, editors Zhao Guoping and Deng Zongyi have provided a detailed overview of each of the chapters, ranging from historical perspectives on modernization, through a rediscovery of cultural roots to a re-envisioning of education as person-making. I will therefore offer a narrative of the unfolding conversation I experienced personally in recent years, which may give readers a sense of how, within a community of concerned scholars, the book has arisen and gradually taken shape. Between 2005 and 2010 I was caught up in a research project on China's move to mass higher education, with one of the key questions of our research focusing on what China's universities would bring to the world community from their own heritage and civilization, as they moved onto a world stage (Hayhoe *et al.*, 2011). I felt an urgent sense of the need for a journal that could be dedicated to bringing the voices of Chinese scholars of education into the wider discourse on educational thought and reform around the world and was delighted to discover the *Frontiers of Education in China*. It began its life as a journal of translation in 2006 and since 2009 has published only original articles that go through rigorous peer review.

When I accepted an invitation to serve as advisory editor, one of my first concerns was to identify scholars who could interpret China's rich Confucian tradition to the English-speaking world of education. I soon realized how blessed I had been in the many encounters I had had at international conferences and through other connections with a younger generation of scholars of education. In 1999 I met historian Bai Limin at the Comparative International Education Society (CIES) Annual conference in Toronto, after having been one of several examiners for her doctoral thesis at Melbourne University in 1993. A few years later I wrote a foreword for her book *Shaping the Chinese Child* (2005) and I was delighted she agreed to submit a thoughtful historical comparison of education in Song Dynasty China and Renaissance England to *Frontiers*. Entitled 'Human Capital or Humane Talent? Rethinking the Nature of Education in China from a Historical Perspective', it was published in the first issue of 2010 (Bai, 2010). From historical scholarship I then turned to philosophy and approached Zhang Huajun, whom I had met at a CIES conference while she was doing her PhD in philosophy of education at Florida State University in Tallahassee. Her essay 'Cultivating an Inclusive Individuality: Rethinking the Concept of Quality Education in China' was published in the second issue of *Frontiers* in 2010 (Zhang, 2010). Meanwhile I had learned about the work of Zhao Guoping, another young philosopher of education, through a request to review some of her writings for a Regents Distinguished Research Award at Oklahoma State University in 2008. I was delighted when she submitted an article to *Frontiers* entitled 'Chinese Cultural Dynamics and Childhood: Towards a New Individuality for Education', which we published in the fourth issue of 2010 (Zhao, 2010).

The following year, as I struggled to prepare a keynote lecture for a major intergovernmental roundtable in Hong Kong, celebrating the completion of a 14-year educational reform process after Hong Kong's return to China, these three papers published in *Frontiers* in 2010 proved extremely helpful in thinking about a future for Hong Kong in which the implementation of its educational reform could bring together the strengths of its Confucian tradition and its British colonial heritage. The concepts of humane talent, inclusive individuality and radical creativity created a frame for envisioning the transformative potential of China's educational civilization in the Hong Kong context (Hayhoe, 2012).

Subsequently, an ongoing correspondence with these scholars gave rise to the idea of a special issue of *Frontiers* devoted to the Mission of Education in China. Zhao Guoping had initiated this idea and she took the lead in conceptualizing the design for a two-part panel presentation at the CIES conference in New Orleans in March of 2013. By this time the circle of our conversation had expanded to include Deng Zongyi, a curriculum theorist from Singapore's National Institute of Education at Nanyang Technological University, whom I met while in Singapore in May of 2012, and Law Wing-Wah, a scholar of comparative education and citizenship from the University of Hong Kong. Our five days together in New Orleans, the first time for several of us to meet in person, were both rewarding and energizing. And the special issue of *Frontiers of Education in China* that came out of our panel in December of 2013 might be seen as a precursor of this book (Zhao, 2013).

Since then Zhao Guoping and Deng Zongyi have carried the conversation forward and brought in a number of additional scholars in order to broaden and deepen the dimensions of the dialogue. On the historical front, it is good to see Thomas Curran's chapter on Huang Yanpei's appreciation of Confucian educational traditions in his vocational education programmes during the Republican period, rooted in the wider scope of his volume on *Educational Reform in Republican China* (Curran, 2005), which I was privileged to write a foreword for. It is also a delight to see the chapter by Wu Zongjie, whom I first met at a colloquium in Hong Kong in 2004 (Kwo and Intrator, 2004), and whose call for a radical rethinking of ancient Confucian texts recently inspired two special issues of the *Journal of Curriculum Studies* (Deng, 2011, 2014). As for the chapters by Ke Xiaoling and Li Jin, these are entirely new to me and I can see how they make distinctive contributions to this book in the areas of moral education and comparative child development, which might otherwise have been missed.

Many of the authors in this volume are located outside of Mainland China, which has contributed to the richness of the differing perspectives on what the Confucian tradition has to bring to education in China and the world in a global era. Nevertheless it is fitting that the final chapter should be devoted to the contemporary movement for school reform through Life Practice Education in China, developed by Ye Lan (Hayhoe, 2006) and carried forward by her dynamic associates. Bu Yuhua is both an author of this chapter and of the article about Life Practice Education in the special issue of *Frontiers* on the Mission of Chinese Education (Bu and Li, 2013). Proponents of this influential school of thought are well positioned to explain just how China's indigenous cultural heritage is now serving as a stimulus for a significant reform movement across the country, which is more bottom up than top down. An understanding of how this transformation is coming about in China may in turn stimulate further conversation on the practical implications of this volume for educational reform in the global community.

Ruth Hayhoe
Ontario Institute of Education
University of Toronto

References

Bai, L. (2005). *Shaping the Chinese Child: Children and their Primers in Late Imperial China*. Hong Kong Chinese University of Hong Kong Press.

Bai, L. (2010). Human Capital or Humane Talent? Rethinking the Nature of Education in China from a Historical Perspective. *Frontiers of Education in China*, 5(1), 104–29.

Bu Y. H. and Li J. C. (2013). The New Basic Education and Whole School Reform. *Frontiers of Education in China*, 8(4), 576–95.

Curran, T. (2005). *Education Reform in Republican China: The failure of Educators to Create a Modern Nation*. Lewiston, New York: Edwin Mellen Press.

De Bary, William T. (2013). *The Great Civilized Conversation: Education for a World Community*. New York: Columbia University Press.

Deng, Z. (2011). Confucianism, Modernization and Pedagogy: An Introduction. *Special issue of the Journal of Curriculum Studies*, 43(5), 561–8.

Deng, Z. (2014). Confucianism, Modernization and Pedagogy: Continuing the Conversation. *Special issue of the Journal of Curriculum Studies*, 46(3), 301–4.

Hayhoe, R. (2006). *Liu Fonian and Ye Lan: Influential Educators of Two Generations. In Portraits of Influential Chinese Educators*. Hong Kong: Comparative Education Research Centre, University of Hong Kong (pp. 324–58).

Hayhoe, R. (2012). Hong Kong's Potential for Global Educational Dialogue: Retrospective and Vision. In K. Mundy and Qi. Zha (eds), *Education and Global Cultural Dialogue: A Tribute to Ruth Hayhoe*, pp. 265–88. New York: Palgrave Macmillan.

Hayhoe, R., Li, J., Lin, J. and Zha, Q. (2011). *Portraits of 21st Century Chinese Universities: In the Move to Mass Higher Education*. Hong Kong: Comparative Education Research Centre, University of Hong Kong.

Kwo, O. and Intrator, S. (eds) (2004). Uncovering the Inner Power of Teachers' Lives: Towards a Learning Profession. *Special issue of the International Journal of Education Research*, 41, 4–5.

Zhang, H. J. (2010). Cultivating an Inclusive Individuality: Rethinking the Concept of Quality Education in China. *Frontiers of Education in China*, 5(2), 222–37.

Zhao G. (2010). Chinese Cultural Dynamics and Childhood: Towards a New Individuality for Education. *Frontiers of Education in China*, 5(4), 579–95.

Zhao, G. (2013). Special Issue Editorial. Introduction: Mission of Education in China. *Frontiers of Education in China*, 8(4), 491–7.

Preface

At a time when the 'best practices' in education are restricted to those that account for students' gains in easily observable products, the staggering number of Chinese students – especially in science and engineering – earning graduate degrees abroad and entering the global workforce, and the remarkable performance of Shanghai students in the 4th Program for International Student Assessment (PISA) have led many to believe that the Chinese model of education holds 'lessons' for other countries around the world. Against the global trend of accountability, testing and instrumental rationality in education, this anthology looks at the deeper, more intrinsic meaning of education – education as a pedagogical space for human formation and transformation. In other words, this book is about person-making for human flourishing as the essential purpose or function of education. From this unique yet fundamental perspective, the authors of the book observe that Chinese education is in a state of crisis, and make a case that modern Chinese education has been built upon a superficial and instrumental embrace of Western modernity and a fragmented appropriation of the Chinese cultural heritage. They call for a rethinking and re-envisioning of Chinese education as person-making grounded in and enriched by various cultural traditions and cross-cultural dialogues. Written mostly by overseas and mainland Chinese scholars, this collected volume analyzes (1) why education as person-making has failed to take root in contemporary China; (2) how the purpose of education has changed during the process of China's modernization; and (3) what a rediscovery of the meaning of person-making implies for rethinking and re-envisioning Chinese education in the current age of globalization and social change. A collection of penetrating and thought-provoking analyses and propositions that draws upon history, Western and Chinese philosophies, and curriculum and pedagogical theories, this volume intends to be a unique contribution to the recent literature in Chinese education.

The book is primarily designed for postgraduate students, scholars and researchers in the areas of Chinese education, Chinese studies, international and comparative education. It is particularly relevant for scholars, researchers, and policy makers everywhere who seek a more balanced, more sophisticated, and philosophically better-grounded understanding of Chinese education.

We hope that the book, with its deep insights and provocative ideas, will also be read by scholars outside of education and by the general public who are concerned with the future of education and of culture and society.

Guoping Zhao and Zongyi Deng

Acknowledgements

We are indebted to Professor Ruth Hayhoe for her unwavering support and encouragement throughout the course of this book project. We greatly appreciate her decades-long dedication to East–West civilizational exchanges and for her commitment to Chinese education.

We are also grateful to the following publishers for granting permission to use the following articles:

Higher Education Press (China):

Bu, Y. and Li, J. (2013). The New Basic Education and Whole School Reform: A Chinese Experience. *Frontiers of Education in China*, 8(4), 576–95.

Deng, Z. (2013). On Developing Chinese Didactics: A Perspective from the German *Didaktik* Tradition. *Frontiers of Education in China*, 8(4), 559–75.

Law, W.-W. (2013). Globalization, National Identity, and Citizenship Education: China's Search for Modernization and a Modern Chinese Citizenry. *Frontiers of Education in China*, 8(4), 596–627.

Zhang, H. (2013). Individuality Beyond the Dichotomy of 'Small Self and Big Self' in Contemporary Chinese Education: Lessons From Hu Shi and Liang Shuming. *Frontiers of Education in China*, 8(4), 540–58.

Zhao, G. (2013). Introduction. *Frontiers of Education in China*, 8(4), 491–7.

Taylor & Francis:

Wu, Z. (2014). 'Speak in the Place of the Sages': Rethinking the Sources of Pedagogic Meanings. *Journal of Curriculum Studies*, 46(3), 320–31.

Guoping Zhao and Zongyi Deng

1 Introduction

Guoping Zhao and Zongyi Deng

With China's rapid geo-political and economic rise in recent years, education in China has attracted considerable attention all over the world. Education has been seen as the 'secret' to China's economic transformation. The number of Chinese students entering the global workforce having studied abroad, especially in the fields of science and engineering, and the remarkable performance of Shanghai students in the 4th Program for International Student Assessment (PISA), have led many to believe that the Chinese model of rigorous education holds lessons for other education systems around the world. Thomas J. Baker, for example, in his book (2013), *Exploring Chinese Education: Triangulation Theory*, offers a set of 'lessons' from China's education system in response to China's high performance in the PISA test.

Yet, behind the facade of educational 'success' is a public concern in Chinese communities across the world that education in China is in a state of crisis. Relentless criticism can be heard on social media, and it seems to come from all corners of Chinese society, including some of the most influential public intellectuals, such as the winner of the 2012 Nobel Prize in literature, Mo Yan (莫言). In his scathing article, *The Hypocritical Education*, Mo notes that when a few Chinese newspapers opened forums on current conditions in Chinese education, they immediately drew tremendous attention, with criticism flooding in. Besides the criticism that Chinese education has become commodified and schools are run like businesses and that instructional methods are outdated and rote learning still predominates, much of the criticism questions the value orientations governing Chinese education. Critics claim that China's basic education is concerned only with test scores and that higher education has become merely job training (基础教育是分数教育, 大学教育是职业教育; Lao, 2013). Teachers are seen as interested only in social status and monetary gain rather than genuine knowledge production and consumption, and students are seen as only being interested in good scores and the benefit of social mobility such scores can bring them, rather than having a genuine passion for and interest in learning. Learning is seen as purely exam-oriented and students' knowledge base as inadequate to meet their life challenges.

If we apply Biesta's theory of the purposes of education (Biesta, 2009) to the criticisms of Chinese education, we see that the criticisms encompass all three functions/purposes: the function of qualification – education should provide students with the knowledge, skills, abilities, and dispositions to fulfil their future job challenges (p. 39); the function of socialization – education should teach students to 'become members of and part of particular social, cultural and political "orders"' (p. 40); and the function of subjectification – education should allow students to become unique, individual subjects (p. 40). For many critics, Chinese education has failed to teach the skills and abilities deemed necessary for China's growing economy. It has failed to help students develop creativity and critical thinking skills; thus students are incapable of innovative work. Qian Xuesen's (钱学森) famous question, 'The Chinese are so smart and hardworking; why are we not producing innovative talent?' (中国人那么聪明，那么勤奋，为什么培养不出创新性的拔尖人才？), is often mentioned in discussion of the dire situation. On the other hand, many critics emphasize that students are not taught a basic sense of morality and how to be responsible citizens. Materialism dominates the social climate, and success is often judged only by the amount of money an individual makes. Social media are never short of reports of official corruption, dishonest business conduct, counterfeit products, and poisonous foods, incidents that indicate widespread disregard for law and reason and are seen as a sign of the failure of Chinese education. In a recent higher education conference, Beijing University professor Qian Liqun 钱理群 commented that Chinese universities are now producing 'polished egoists' (*jingzhi de li ji zhuyi zhe* 精致的利己主义者), who are more adept at and interested in using the system for their own benefit[1] than in becoming responsible social members who can fit in and contribute to society.

But above all, critics argue that Chinese education has mostly failed as a process of person-making and that this failure has contributed to the rapid deterioration of morality and spirituality in China. Underneath all the complaints about Chinese education, it seems, is the concern that Chinese education does not provide the conditions under which students can develop and become well-rounded, self-aware, and ethical and spiritual beings. Instead, in going through the Chinese educational system, students' critical and creative potential is deeply stifled and their very being is subjected to alienation. The real issue, therefore, is that Chinese education has been so instrumentalized, either for political or economic reasons, that it is devoid of the basic purpose of person-making – in the sense of self-cultivation or self-formation. When education does not participate in nurturing the flourishing of the human person, it contributes to its degeneration. In the words of Zi Zhongjun (资中筠), a well-known scholar from the Chinese Academy of Social Sciences, 'Chinese education now, from kindergarten on, teaches extreme materialism and instrumentalism, which completely wipe out creativity and imagination. . . . Education is destroying people! . . . If Chinese education does not change, our Chinese race will degenerate!' (Zi, 2012).

However, the idea of person-making is at the heart of the Confucian heritage of educational thinking. It has long been held that self-cultivation is the precondition for cultivating the critical and creative potential of the individual and enabling him or her to fulfil social responsibilities and functions. From a Confucian perspective, becoming a responsible citizen, or a functional and capable worker, cannot be separated from becoming an ideal and genuine human person; and cultivating a responsible citizen starts with cultivating the inner self, the ideal person – the *Junzi*. Thus in Confucianism, the value of education is first to 'help the person succeed in fulfilling or living up to what makes him a human being' (Lee, 2000, p. 16). With the cultivation of an inner sagehood, the person can realize and fulfil his responsibility of outer 'kingship' in bringing peace and harmony to the world. Since Confucianism provides the cultural and philosophical foundation for Chinese education, person-making is at the core of Chinese educational thinking.

The centrality of self-formation is also deeply entrenched in the Western tradition of educational thinking. Since the time of Kant, modern Western education has been tasked with educating/nurturing the kinds of individuals who are rational, autonomous, law-abiding, and capable of critical and independent thinking, the kinds of subjects deemed necessary for the project of modernity. The realization of a nation's inspiration for democracy and for economic and technological advancement is premised on the realization of the potentials of the human subjects as rational and autonomous beings. Thus modern education as person-making 'is about producing rationally autonomous individuals' (Wain, 1996, p. 351) and is a process of 'liberation' that is distinguished from domination, indoctrination or domestication.

Despite education in China having been 'modernized' through the adaptation of a school system from the West since the beginning of the twentieth century, together with Western curricular structure, theory, and practice, and despite numerous efforts having been made in recent years to rejuvenate the Confucian tradition of educational thinking, the concept of person-making, either in the Confucian or Western sense, has failed to take root in educational theory and practice in China. Thus it is a matter of recovering and reclaiming education's intrinsic role in person-making that this book proposes to re-envision Chinese education as a process of person-making.

Written mostly by overseas and mainland Chinese scholars, this collected volume analyzes (1) why education as person-making has failed to take root in contemporary China; (2) how the purpose of education has changed during the process of China's modernization; and (3) what a rediscovery of the meaning of person-making implies for rethinking and re-envisioning Chinese education in the current age of globalization and social change. Drawing on Chinese history and culture, Western and Chinese philosophies, education and curriculum theories, contributors of the book pursue the analyses and discussions in relation to curriculum, teaching and learning, citizenship education, and educational reform.

The book is organized into three parts. Part I, *Modernization and Chinese education: historical perspectives*, consists of four chapters that critically examine problems facing education in China today from historical perspectives – concerning East–West encounters and China's modernization over the late nineteenth and twentieth centuries. These four chapters, with different emphases, serve to explain why education as person-making has failed to take root in contemporary China, and shed light on how the meaning of person-making has changed over time.

Guoping Zhao (Chapter 2) presents a broad historical overview of China's encounters with the West, with a focus on the ways of Chinese reformers in borrowing from the West and exploiting Chinese cultural traditions to revitalize the nation. The overview unveils the historical and cultural landscape in which contemporary Chinese education is embedded and operates – characterized by the 'importation of a superficial and distorted form of modern Western civilization' (p. 17) and the 'fragmentation of China's cultural traditions' (p. 25). As such, education in China lacks solid philosophical and cultural grounds upon which a concept of the new Chinese person can be articulated, and from which substantial and coherent resources can be drawn for the educational purpose of person-making.

Wing-Wah Law (Chapter 3) examines various approaches to cultivating Chinese citizens during different historical epochs as China went through modernization and national revival at the interplay between nationalism and internationalization. The examination reveals that Confucianism has long been exploited for cultivating the obedience and loyalty of Chinese citizens. This is achieved by selecting certain Confucian values and norms, and rejecting others, to strengthen state control and foster social conformity. China's social, political and educational milieus, Law argues, 'have never been conducive to making free and autonomous persons' (p. 35). Citizenship education in China has always been employed as a socialization vehicle, directed towards citizen-making rather than person-making.

Set against the backdrop of China's encounters with the West, Limin Bai (Chapter 4) examines the changing meaning of *Gewu zhizhi* 格物致知 ('investigating things and extending knowledge') over the eighteenth and nineteenth centuries. As an embodiment of the Neo-Confucian vision of person-making, *Gewu zhizhi* provided a powerful framework for Chinese intellectuals to integrate Western modern scholarship with traditional Chinese learning, and to balance scientific studies of natural phenomena with the pursuit of moral self-cultivation. However, such integration and balance was gradually lost following China's humiliating defeat in the Opium war (1839–1842) due to a break with the Confucian tradition. Bai points to the shared humanistic values in the Confucian approach to education and in the Renaissance ideal of liberal education, and argues for the significance of the search for a common humanity in our rethinking of the purpose and practice of Chinese curriculum

Comparing the thoughts on individuality of Hu Shi (1891–1962) and Liang Shuming (1893–1988), Huajun Zhang (Chapter 5) seeks the root cause of the absence of person-making in terms of cultivating individuality in China's contemporary education and proposes a return to the traditional emphasis on self-transformation. The comparative analysis identifies the instrumentalist mode of thinking that dominates China's contemporary educational practices as the problem and suggests that the dichotomy between the 'small self and big self,' a notion that has been present throughout modern Chinese history, exacerbates this instrumentalism, paralleling the loss of China's tradition of self-cultivation. Zhang proposes self-transformation as a way to build connections between 'the small self' and 'the big self,' thus overcoming the dualism of the individual and the others ('the small self' and 'the big self').

Part II, *Rediscovering China's cultural roots of education*, presents five chapters devoted to re-discovering ideals and values embedded in Confucianism and Chinese folk culture for education as person-making. The contributors of these chapters, in varying degrees, challenge instrumentalism prevalent in contemporary educational thinking in China. Exploring different aspects of Chinese educational tradition, including The Imperial Civil Examination (*keju* 科举) (Chapter 6), Confucian moral education (Chapter 7), the virtue-oriented Confucian learning model (Chapter 8), and Huang Yanpei's vocational education ideas (Chapter 9), these chapters rediscover the Chinese cultural roots of education, and make a case that education for person-making provides the essential precondition not only for the development of intellectual capacities like critical thinking and cross-cultural competence, but also for the cultivation of responsible, committed, and participatory citizens.

Zongjie Wu (Chapter 6) rediscovers the authentic pedagogic vision for person-making embedded in the Imperial Civil Examination (*keju*) – which has been blamed for its undue emphasis on memorization and regurgitation of the classic texts, and seen as the very antithesis to the Confucian vision of education centred on cultivating the gentleman (*junzi*). Based on an analysis of an eight-legged essay written by a candidate in the Examination, Wu shows that the Examination embodied a Confucian way of meaning-making grounded in the indigenous consciousness of classical texts, through establishing a language by means of which learners 'could speak/act in the place of the sages' (p. 98). Furthermore, he argues that such a Confucian way of meaning-making can not only contribute to the development of a deep understanding of the world, and of the moral virtue to act properly in society, but also yield possibilities for learners to achieve practical competence and skills in the modern world.

Set against the backdrop of current revival of Confucianism in China, Xiaoling Ke (Chapter 7) explores the implication of Confucianism for contemporary moral education. Based on an analysis of the notions of person-making and citizen-making in the Confucian tradition, she argues that person-making in terms of self-cultivation is the precondition for citizen-making because citizens are not obedient and passive but capable of independent thinking, taking initiative, and assuming social responsibility. Therefore, moral education in China needs to 'embrace the original Confucian person-making (inner sagehood) and citizen-making (outer kingliness), and guard against the appropriation of Confucianism to serve ideological purposes' (p. 117).

Based on decades of empirical research, Jin Li (Chapter 8) presents the virtue-oriented Confucian learning model (vis-à-vis Western-mind-oriented model) that has lasting effect on Chinese children's learning experience. Deeply entrenched in the Confucian-heritage cultures, this model is centrally concerned with learning to be a person or person-making, including cultivating the moral and social self, fulfilling one's roles and responsibilities, making social contribution, and committing to doing or action. She contends that grounding in the Confucian cultural heritage is an indispensable condition for the development of children's cultural identity and self-confidence, as well as learning and growth in other cultures. However, Confucian cultural values have been 'tarnished' over 150 years of China's tumultuous history. Rediscovery and restoration of these values thus becomes an urgent and important task.

Through examining a set of important writings of Huang Yanpei (1878–1965), Thomas Curran (Chapter 9) shows how even a prominent advocate of vocational education came to realize the need for a broader approach to education directed towards person-making. As China suffered multiple crises from the 1920s to the 1940s, there was a shift in Huang's educational thinking – from an emphasis on job training to the cultivation of personhood. Huang articulated a vision of Chinese personhood – in terms of a set of virtues and values – rooted in Chinese history and culture, and argued that the country's folk culture constitutes a rich resource for educating Chinese students to become well-rounded and morally-refined individuals.

There are three chapters in Part III, *Re-envisioning Chinese education as person-making*, that, in one way or another, engage in the endeavour of rethinking and re-envisioning Chinese education as person-making. The writers of these chapters highlight the need for a new concept of the human subject as a necessary starting point for such endeavour, grounded in and enriched by various cultural traditions and cross-cultural dialogues. Cultural traditions – both Chinese or Eastern and Western – provide rich educational resources for person-making.

To search for such a new concept, Guoping Zhao (Chapter 10) outlines the changes in the concept of what it is to be a Chinese or the Confucian man as the result of cultural and civilizational dialogues in Neo- and New- Confucianism. She then examines the new developments in Western post-humanist philosophy of human subjectivity to show the resonance and convergence with the Chinese tradition. Based on this East–West dialogue, she embarks on the project of re-configuring the notion of what it is to be the new Chinese person, and argues that this notion provides an essential point of departure for re-envisioning education as person-making – 'cultivating the new Chinese person for the flourishing of human beings and for a vibrant society' (p. 180).

Zongyi Deng (Chapter 11) engages in a project of rethinking and re-envisioning Chinese didactics within the current social, cultural and educational context of schooling in China. Tracing the historical development of Chinese didactics, he argues that the development has been profoundly influenced by Kairvor's theory of pedagogics and, as a result, a concern for the formation of self is largely neglected in current theory and discourse on didactics. He calls attention to the German *Didaktik* tradition which, largely unknown in China, is undergirded by a philosophical concept of human formation through participating in the world and culture. Deng expounds three basic tenets of the German *Didaktik* tradition – (1) the concept of *Bildung*, (2) a theory of educational content, and (3) the idea of teaching as a learner–content encounter – and discusses the implications of these tenets for rethinking and re-envisioning the purpose, content and methods of teaching in Chinese didactics.

In the last chapter (Chapter 12) Yuhua Bu, Jing Xu and Zongyi Deng describe the New Basic Education (NBE) project that entails re-envisioning the purpose of education and translating the new purpose into school reform, classroom practice, and school management in the midst of China's social, economic and educational changes at the turn of the twenty-first century. The project is animated by an image of active, self-aware human beings, and underpinned by a corresponding new educational theory of human development that emphasizes school transformation along with students' personal development and heightened self-awareness. They further detail how schools can be restructured and transformed for the development of such active individuals.

We hope that this anthology will be of interest to international readers who are interested in Chinese education, the status of which has been recently brought to the international foreground. Unlike other books in English that focus on describing the recent developments of education in China and explaining China's educational 'success' (e.g., Baker, 2013; Ryan, 2013; Tan, 2012), this book provides a deep and yet critical analysis of the current conditions of Chinese education. Confronting the so-called educational crisis, it engages in a rethinking and re-envisioning of Chinese education based on cross-cultural analyses and historically and philosophically informed investigation.

While taking education's responsibility for the current deterioration of morality and spirituality in China and education's role in person-making seriously, authors of this book are also fully aware that education is always situated in its sociocultural and political environment and often times the larger environment exerts an effect beyond education's own making. It has been discussed on social media (which is significant in China considering the control of press and lack of free expression in formal publications) that the Chinese 'degeneration' in recent history has been a result of the more than half a century's continuous sociocultural and political oppression. It has been recognized that while Daoism has encouraged the 'natural' and free flourishing of human beings, and Confucianism has attempted to enlighten Chinese minds and hearts and cultivate Chinese spirituality and morality – and these cultural resources will never die out – the operation of a reversed survival mechanism, that is, the killing of the courageous and the critical, and the survival of the coward and the conformist, the decades-long crushing of Chinese intellectuals' independent thinking and autonomy, and the blind indoctrination of the Chinese people and control of information have suffocated the Chinese mind and heart and stunted the free and natural development of the Chinese person. Now the deep-seated Chinese spiritual pursuit to become a dignified human person infused with the Mencian 'righteous energy' (*hao ran zhi qi* 浩然之气) and Zhuangzian 'spirit of the cosmos' (*tiandi jingshen* 天地精神) has become a distant and lost dream. The fear instilled in people for decades through political terror, public humiliation, and physical torture and elimination has crushed and damaged the Chinese spirit. While this is a much deeper, more fundamental issue warranting future research and exploration, we argue that, in the context of the current Chinese government's proposition of national revival (*minzu fuxing* 民族复兴), if education is to play any important part in the survival and revival of the Chinese race, if China is to regain the strengths of its civilization, it is essential that education take on its responsibility of person-making. To reinvigorate the Chinese race, education must participate in creating the space for human flourishing. It is education's role as person-making to generate a respectful environment where students can be nurtured and encouraged to come to terms with themselves in their never-ceasing becoming. They must be respected and encouraged in their freethinking, imagination and their development of rationality and sensitivity, so that they can eventually shine forth with their creativity, multiplicity and irreducibility.

In short, this book provides not only a critical analysis of what has happened but also a normative proposition of what should happen in the face of China's current challenges and aspirations. Through a collective analysis of the issues and problems concerning person-making and arguing for rethinking and re-envisioning Chinese education, we invite educational scholars, researchers, and policy makers, in China or overseas, to search for a critical yet balanced, more sophisticated, historically and philosophically better-grounded understanding of education in China.

Note

1   Available online at: http://news.sina.com.cn/c/2012-05-03/040724359951.shtml

References

Baker, T. J. (2013). *Exploring Chinese education: Triangulation theory*. Colorado Springs, CO: CreateSpace Independent Publishing Platform.

Biesta, G. J. (2009). Good education in an age of measurement: On the need to reconnect with the question of purpose in education. *Educational Assessment, Evaluation and Accountability*, 21(1), 33–46.

Lao, J. (2013). 中国最大的问题是教育 *[China's biggest problem is education]*. Available online at: http://bbs.creaders.net/politics/bbsviewer.php?trd_id=829966&blog_id=140079 (accessed 22 February 2013).

Lee, T. H. C. (2000). *Education in Traditional China: A History*. Leiden: Koninklijke Brill NV.

Mo Yan (2012). 虚伪的教育 *[The Hypocritical Education]*. Available online at: http://21ccom.net/articles/lsjd/jwxd/article_2012120772486.html (accessed 25 August 2013).

Ryan, J. (ed.) (2013). *Education Reform in China: Changing Concepts, Contexts and Practices*. New York: Routledge.

Tan, C. (2012). *Learning from Shanghai: Lessons on Achieving Educational Success.* Dordrecht: Springer.

Wain, K. (1996). Foucault, Education, The Self and Modernity. *Journal of Philosophy of Education*, 30(3), 345–60.

Zi, Z. J. (2012). 中国教育不改变, 人种都会退化 *[Humankind will degenerate if Chinese education doesn't change]*. Available online at: http://comments.caijing.com.cn/ 2012-08-03/111990775.html (accessed 25 August 2013).

Part I

Modernization and Chinese education

Historical perspectives

2 China's historical encounter with the West and modern Chinese education

Guoping Zhao

Introduction

The past more than 150 years of Chinese history is a history of East and West encounter, and of the remarkable struggles of the Chinese to revive their nation and civilization. The Opium War of the 1840s forced open the Middle Kingdom and exposed its weakness and vulnerability to the world. China's subsequent defeat in the Sino-Japanese War (1894–1895) further devastated the nation, crushing its sino-centric mentality. The particular nature of the encounters, the collective memory of China's humiliation, and the lesson China learned – that *luohou jiuyao ai da* 落后就要挨打 (being backwards leads to being beaten up) – I suggest, have been the decisive factors shaping the course of Chinese modernity. They fashioned the modern Chinese approach to the West and to China's cultural heritage and underpinned the formation and transformation of modern Chinese education. The impact of the encounters is still palpable today.[1]

In this chapter, I trace the modern history of East–West encounters, the strategies of Chinese reformers in borrowing from the West to revitalize the Chinese nation, and the ups and downs of Confucianism in China's cultural landscape in an attempt to understand the broad historical and socio-cultural conditions of modern Chinese education, and how it has failed as a process of person-making. Education, as Biesta (2009) has argued, has historically served three functions in different contexts: socialization, qualification, and subjectification. While it is important and inevitable that education be entrusted with the task of producing qualified workers and socialized members of a certain social order, I argue that the ultimate purpose of education lies in subjectification, in the sense that education exists to encourage and cultivate the full development of the human person. In other words, education is person-making. In the West, particularly in modern times, the person-making function of education has focused on cultivating modern subjects who are rational and autonomous, capable of critical thinking and creative imagination. In China, on the other hand, particularly in the Confucian tradition, person-making has historically emphasized cultivating other-oriented human beings. What distinguishes education as person-making from the other functions of education is that the cultivation of the human person is not for instrumental purposes. Human beings are not cultivated only to serve social, economic or political ends; rather, they are cultivated to become what they can be – the ideal, complete and fully developed, flourishing human beings. While education as person-making does not serve instrumental purposes, it nevertheless has far-reaching social, cultural, political and economic implications. The qualification and socialization functions of education are premised on the person-making purpose because the kind of human beings coming out of education eventually defines the kind of society, state or economy there can be.

The educational process of person-making relies heavily on profound and rich philosophical and cultural grounds from which a sound idea of the human person can be articulated. Person-making in modern Western education has relied on the modern philosophy of the subject as it had relied on Confucianism in traditional Chinese education. I argue that modern Chinese education has failed as a person-making process because in rejecting China's cultural roots and embracing a 'pseudo-Western version of modernity' (Curran, 2005, p. 426), education has lost the solid philosophical and cultural grounds from which a new concept of the Chinese person can emerge. The urgent practical goals of 'saving China' and striving for wealth and power (*fuqiang* 富强) using Western means, I suggest, have led modern Chinese reformers into 'a quasi-Western cultural sphere' (Curran, 2005, p. 426) and instigated a deconstructive attitude towards the Chinese cultural heritage. What has come out of China's modernization process in the cultural landscape is a mixture of residual, entrenched or mutated cultural habits and selectively adopted and transmuted, modern Western ideas and practices. Such a mixture creates the context within which Chinese education is operating, but education cannot draw from the mixture, for the purpose of person-making, a meaningful articulation of what it is to be a new Chinese person.

In the following, I first introduce Confucianism and Confucian education in pre-modern China and its struggle as a process of person-making. Then I trace the modern encounters of China with the West and how a pseudo-Western modernity was adopted, and Confucianism, along with the entire Chinese cultural tradition, was gradually fragmented in the modernization process. Lastly, I describe the current cultural landscape in China, since the historical struggles, and suggest that if we want to revitalize Chinese civilization and restore education's purpose of person-making, we need to fully understand and appreciate what the West can offer and what we can draw from our own cultural heritage.

Confucianism and person-making in pre-modern Chinese education

While Chinese civilization has a long and rich history, with varied schools of thought providing streams of (sometimes contradicting) ideas, almost from the beginning of Chinese civilization, Confucius was accepted as the single most important source of Chinese political ideology and educational ideas (Lee, 2000). At the core of Confucianism is an image of the ideal human person, one that is formed as another-oriented, ethical being striving for harmony and peace in the world, rather than the enclosed, self-realizing individual often idealized in the West. The other-orientedness of the person is situated in a variety of human relations, but the most essential relation, as Confucius sees it, is that of father and son. This relationship also gives significance to the relationship between emperors and subjects – a relationship of care, responsibility, loyalty and obedience. For Confucius, to strive for harmony in the world means first of all to strive for harmony within the social and familial relations through self-cultivation. The ultimate moral responsibility of a person, therefore, is *xiushen* 修身 (self-cultivation), which is the foundation of all worldly endeavours. Through an eight-staged endeavour, the person reaches his goal of self-perfection and social harmony: *gewu* 格物 (investigating things), *zhizhi* 致知 (extending knowledge), *yichen* 意诚 (straightening the will), *xinzheng* 心正 (rectifying the mind), *xiushen* 修身 (cultivating the self), *qijia* 齐家 (regulating the family), *zhiguo* 治国 (governing the state), *qitianxia* 平天下 (harmonizing the world).[2] These Confucian doctrines have been the foundation of China's political ideology and its educational ideal for thousands of years.

For Confucius, therefore, education is, first of all, person-making. 'The value of education was to help the person succeed in fulfilling or living up to what makes him a human being' (Lee, 2000, p. 16). This intrinsic value and purpose is the most important aspect of traditional Chinese education. As Lee notes, 'A human being committed to a search for personal moral perfection, without forgetting that his personal moral growth has social implications, is considered by Confucian, and in fact Chinese, educational thinking as the ideal person' (Lee, 2000, p. 9). In Neo-Confucianism, de Bary maintains, Confucian education further strives to cultivate individuals that have 'a sense of self-worth and self-respect not to be sacrificed for any short-term utilitarian purpose; a sense of place in the world not to be surrendered to any state or party; a sense of how one could cultivate one's individual powers to meet the social responsibilities that the enjoyment of learning always brought with it' (de Bary, 1996, p. 33).

At the same time, education for Confucians is also socialization and qualification. Since Confucians see the perfection of the human person as the foundation and necessary first step of social and political applications, the Confucian education ideal ties together all functions and purposes of education. The establishment of traditional Chinese educational institutions and China's civil service examination system also serve to help disseminate a 'unifying code of ethics . . . [and offer] a vehicle for upward mobility' (Curran, 2005, p. 119). The educational system was there to make a person an integral part of Chinese culture and society. Education was also a means of producing qualified scholar-officials to govern the country for the emperors. As Curran observes, traditional Chinese education 'was an institution that, for a very long time, had helped to bind together the diverse segments of Chinese society' (p. 119). It helped maintain Chinese civilization.

Throughout the thousands of years' history, however, the pre-modern Chinese education's person-making purpose has also been challenged and it is not unusual to find historical times when education was used by ruling elites purely for the instrumental purpose of social control, enforcing obedience and conformity while eliminating critical and independent thinking,[3] or by literati themselves only for the purposes of employment, financial security and social mobility. Nevertheless, within the Confucian educational doctrines there is always room, sometimes unrealized potential, for the nurturance of critical and independent thinking, as it is how the human person is conceived in Confucianism. The Confucian men are not all obedient and conformist subjects. As far as education serves the purpose of person-making, the educated intellectuals should be able to act as independent 'moral advisors to the throne and the conscience of the people' (Curran, 2005, p. 30). Since Confucian political ideology is based on an ethical code of sage/father-king, rulers' exercise of power was only justified by their moral conduct. 'The orthodoxy made ample room for literati to present an independent critique of state policies and play an assertive role in the evolving intellectual life of the country' (p. 29). Far from blindly submitting to the rulers, the intellectuals have the responsibility to critique and advise the rulers who are not acting as caring and responsible kings of their people.

Throughout its long history, Confucianism, as well as all of Chinese civilization, has also encountered daunting challenges from the outside world, such as Buddhism from India and Christianity from Europe, brought in by Roman Catholic missionaries in the seventeenth century. With remarkable resilience and internal strength, Chinese civilization always rose up again through cultural renovation and assimilation. Challenges coming from the outside world were seriously studied and gradually absorbed or assimilated into Chinese civilization, at times leading to mutual transformation, as is the case of Chan Buddhism (*chanzong* 禅宗) and Daoism. Neo-Confucianism can be seen as a fruitful renewal of Confucianism in the face of Buddhist challenges.[4] Through this renewal, Neo-Confucianism was able to provide a renovated, and yet richer, articulation of the Chinese person, or the Confucian man, based on which education was able to fulfil its purpose of meaningful person-making.

During the whirlwind process of Chinese modernization, Confucianism, along with the whole Chinese traditional culture, was tested, challenged, rejected, or revived. However, at the dawn of Chinese modernity, it was no longer the case that acculturation and renovation necessarily ensued, and genuine civilizational engagement and dialogue took place. The Opium War brought a challenge of unprecedented magnitude and, for the reformers, it was evident that the ultimate survival of China was at risk. As Bai comments, the military defeat 'took away the easiness' the earlier Ming scholars had had in their encounters with the West and a new, instrumental and utilitarian attitude emerged among the reformers (Bai, Chapter 4). They saw their task as appropriating the most effective means for solving urgent practical problems. Such a typical attitude was expressed in an 1896 letter to Zhang Zhidong 张之洞 (1837–1909)[5] in which Liang Qichao 梁启超 (1873–1929)[6] declared that as of now 'the ultimate objective of all learning ... should serve an immediate practical purpose.'[7] A sense of life and death urgency, a felt need for immediate utility, profoundly affected the Chinese approach to Western civilization and shaped the course of Chinese modernity.

From *Zhongti Xiyong* 中体西用 to the Socialist/ Communist China: The importation of a 'pseudo-version of Western modernity'

From after the Opium War to the present, the Chinese have attempted to borrow from the West for the survival of China and to revitalize Chinese civilization. The borrowing approaches have been varied, but except for the earliest attempt, the approaches that have had the most impact on the course of Chinese modernity, unfortunately, were often formed as a result of the traumatic experiences of China's recent history. They were therefore mostly practical and utilitarian, and eventually led to the importation of a superficial and distorted form of modern Western civilization, or in Curran's words, a 'pseudo-version of Western modernity' (Curran, 2005, p. 426). Such importation has had significant consequences for Chinese modern education. Without introducing and appreciating the deep underlying foundation of modern Western accomplishments, the modern Chinese learning from the West was superficial and incoherent. More importantly, such borrowing failed to enrich and transform the cultural and philosophical ground from which a new understanding of the Chinese person could emerge for education.

The first response of Chinese reformers to the military defeat was captured in Zhang Zhidong's 张之洞 phrase *zhongti xiyong* 中体西用 (using Western technology as a means to strengthen the Confucian Chinese substance) in the 'Self-Strengthening Movement' after the Opium War. For early reformers, the superiority of Western civilization lay mainly in its practical means and instruments (*qiwu* 器物), which enabled its dominance in the world. For China to procure wealth and power, then, it needed only to embrace the West's practical means without attending to their deeper philosophical underpinnings. In the Confucian tradition, practical and technical means were never of high status; therefore, the reformers believed that adding practical skills and knowledge to the knowledge base while keeping the substance of Chinese culture intact would be sufficient to save the country.

But China's subsequent defeat in the Sino-Japanese War in 1895 and the aftermath of the Boxer Rebellion smashed the deep-seated confidence/ arrogance of the Chinese literati, galvanizing a new wave of more comprehensive reforms modelled on the West. As Yu Yingshi 余英时 notes, culturally, Japan had been borrowing from China since the Tang dynasty and Chinese intellectuals had considered Japan one of China's 'cultural satellites in the East Asian world' (Yu, 1993, p. 136). Since the Meiji Restoration in 1868, however,

Japan had turned away from Chinese civilization and had started transforming itself on the Western model and had become increasingly Westernized. In this context, therefore, the humiliating defeat at the hands of the Japanese was particularly devastating for the Chinese. 'It was a catastrophe of this magnitude that finally awakened Chinese intellectuals to the painful truth that China had been marginalized not only in the world but in East Asia as well' (Yu, 1993, p. 137).

Within two weeks of the end of the war, Kang Youwei 康有为 (1858–1927),[8] joined by more than 1200 examination candidates in Beijing, presented to the Qing emperor the famous 'Ten Thousand Word Memorial' advocating an 'immediate' and 'whole-sale' reform (Yu, 1993, p. 128). Kang Youwei 康有为, Liang Qichao 梁启超, and Chen Duxiu 陈独秀 (1879–1942)[9] believed that both Western science and Western political systems, dubbed by Chen Duxiu as Mr. Science and Mr. Democracy (德先生 賽先生), were essential to China's survival, so they asked not only for an adoption of Western technological means but also for an across-the-board institutional reform including political and educational changes. In 1901, a countrywide modern school system was established; in 1905 the civil service examination system was abolished; and in 1912, the Qing monarchy was overthrown and a Western-modelled Republic of China was established.

Chinese scholars, especially those who had visited foreign countries, started translating and importing Western social, political and economic texts to China. In 1898, Yan Fu 严复 (1854–1921), a pioneering scholar in translating Western texts, published *Tianyan Lun* 天演论 (*The Theory of Natural Evolution*), his translation of Thomas Henry Huxley's *Evolution and Ethics*. This paraphrastic, selective translation made an enormous impact at the time on the already alarmed minds of Chinese intellectuals and left a long-lasting mark. With an emphasis on the concepts of 'the weak as the prey of the strong' and 'survival of the fittest', Yan's Social Darwinism became the dominant Chinese framework for understanding and making sense of the world and China's place in it. Yu Yingshi 余英时, however, called Yan's translation, along with Tan Sitong's 谭嗣同 (1865–1898) *A Study of Humanity*, 'a psychological aftermath of the war' (Yu, 1993, p. 138) and an expression of the traumatic experience of the historical times rather than an accurate explication of Huxley's ideas.

Many have pointed out the inaccuracies in Yan's translations. Fu Sinian 傅斯年 (1896–1950), who studied history, linguistics, experimental psychology, mathematics and other subjects in England and Germany for seven years (1919–1926), commented that Yan 'was paraphrasing and not translating and his translation sacrificed accuracy for accessibility.'[10] Qian Zhongshu 钱钟书 (1910–1998) also criticized Yan's work as being 'limited by his vision and interests' and as distorting the Western texts to express his own political concerns.[11] Since Yan's major concern was to build a strong and wealthy Chinese nation, he ignored the ideas of democracy or individual freedom, a central part of Huxley's original text. He Lin 贺麟 (1945) observes that when Yan introduced British utilitarianism with the purpose of encouraging the Chinese people to search for wealth and power, . . . he neglected democratic ideas stressing laissez-faire, tolerance, liberty, and equality, along with ideas about social reform, social welfare, and the practical improvement of living conditions.

(p. 21)[12]

Like He Lin, Benjamin Schwartz (1964) held that Yan was more interested in the pursuit of the wealth and power of the state and the importance of group solidarity than in individual liberty. Citing Schwartz, Huang (2003) comments that 'Yan did not understand the Western concept of the individual and mistakenly regarded individual liberty as just a means with which to create a wealthy and powerful state' (p. 33). These scholars further pointed out that Yan was using the Chinese intellectual framework to understand Western thinkers' reasoning, and his excessive use of 'traditional ethical–philosophical categories and terms [. . .] failed to convey various specifically English ideas or nuances' (Huang, 2003, p. 33).

Nevertheless, Yan's mis/interpretation of Western thought has been tremendously influential throughout China's modern history. Yan's contemporaries as well as the later May Fourth leaders, including Liang Qichao 梁启超, Cai Yuanpei 蔡元培 (1868–1940), even Hu Shi 胡适 (1891–1962), who had lived in the US for years and had a good command of the English language, all admired Yan's 'accurate translation' and acknowledged how much they had benefited from it.[13]

Another major translator of the time, Lin Shu 林纾(琴南) (1852–1924), similarly misinformed the Chinese about Western ideas. Qian Zhongshu called their works 'literary creations' rather than authentic translations.[14] Even Cai Yuanpei, the liberal educator who was mainly responsible for shaping modern Chinese education in the Republican era, seemed to not be able to fully appreciate the Western ideas in their own right. In introducing the key concepts of the French Revolution, for example, Cai asserted that the meanings of liberty, equality and fraternity were no different from the ancient Chinese notions of righteousness, reciprocity and benevolence (Curran, 2005). Citing the modern historian Tian Zhengping, Curran (2005) comments,

There is no evidence . . . that Cai had given any thought to the exercise of individual freedoms in either the political or economic realms. He did not attempt to articulate a natural law-based concept of individual rights. Nor did he mention freedom of speech, ownership of private property, or any other individual liberties . . . that Tian associates with the bourgeoisie for whom Cai is supposed to have spoken. Rather, when he spoke of liberty, what he appears to have had in mind was a version of human freedom that could easily be interpreted in a utilitarian context – a free man, . . . cannot be compelled to yield to the will of those who would oppress him.

(p. 192)

But not all Chinese scholars of the time misunderstood or mis-introduced Western thought to China. Versatile scholars who were brilliant in their grasp of both Chinese and Western civilization, such as the editor of China's first educational journal, *Jiaoyu Shijie* 教育世界 (*Education World*), Wang Guowei 王国维 (1877–1927), attempted to enlighten the Chinese with genuine Western ideas. Chen Yinke 陈寅恪 (1890–1969) once commented that Wang's work could 'change the trend of the time and show the followers the way' (Chen, 1996, p. 6).[15] Wang Guowei also criticized Yan Fu for his inaccurate and culturally loaded translation – how Yan selectively emphasized utility and evolution and omitted ethics even in the title of his translation (Huang, 2003). In fact, Wang was critical of the many translations and importations of Western thought of the time, including the articles discussing Kant and Rousseau's philosophy published in magazines and newspapers edited by Liang Qichao. He claimed that those authors knew little about scholarship besides their political purpose.[16] He was appalled by Zhang Zhidong's *Zhongti Xiyong* policy that rejected Western philosophy while adopting its science and technology. He maintained that philosophical study is the foundation of all practical studies, including education. Based on his systematic understanding of modern Western thinking, he called for a new education that makes its ultimate purpose to cultivate the 'complete person' based on the Kantian idea of a rational free being with intellectual, moral and aesthetical capacities.[17]

But Wang's scholarly insights and deep grasp of Western civilization (and those of many others like him) were only occasionally appreciated.[18] The political and cultural climate of the time was moving towards radicalization (Yu, 1993), sustained by and devoted to a distorted version of modern Western civilization. At the same time, Confucianism was frequently used by conservative and reactionary governments to invoke obedience and loyalty from their subjects. This use of Confucianism only further alienated the intellectuals and provided ammunition for their attacks against Chinese tradition.

Finally, during the May Fourth era beginning with the New Culture Movement in 1917, a radical attitude against the traditional Chinese culture emerged among the various opponents. Radical intellectuals saw their role as terminators of the 'old' and 'sick' Chinese culture and creators of the new. Lu Xun 鲁迅 (1881–1936), Qian Xuantong 钱玄同 (1887–1939) and others harshly criticized Confucianism and Daoism and proposed a total denunciation of Chinese tradition. In Qian Xuantong's words, 'In order for China to not perish, for Chinese to become the 20th century's civilized race, the fundamental solution is to completely wipe out Confucianism and Daoism, along with the language that conveyed them.'[19] Confucian and Daoist thought was attacked, 'Confucian stores/shrines' smashed (砸烂孔家店), and the entire Chinese historical and cultural tradition questioned. In denouncing the old and welcoming the new, the radical intellectuals invariably turned to what they perceived as Western ideas and values for 'ultimate [. . .] justification' (Yu, 1993, p. 130). Followers of Dewey (Hu Shi 胡适, Tao Xingzhi 陶行知 1891–1946) and the Soviet Union (Chen Duxiu 陈独秀) introduced Pragmatism and Marxism/

Communism to China, with the latter receiving particularly overwhelming and long-lasting attention. According to Yu Yingshi, 'The enormous and long-enduring influence of social Darwinism [. . .] paved the way for the wholehearted acceptance by May Fourth intellectuals of the Marxist iron law of social evolution as self-evident truth' (Yu, 1993, p. 134). Both Communist and Nationalist parties embraced Soviet Communism. While some intellectuals steadfastly upheld traditional cultural values, such as the family system, and viewed Western individualism, materialism and utilitarianism as shells without substance and morals, their approach was similar to Zhang Zhidong's *zhongti xiyong* (中体西用), utilizing Western means while keeping the substance of Chinese culture intact.

The radical intellectuals were eager to reform the Chinese people in order to transform Chinese culture and identity. Urgent calls were repeatedly made for education to take the responsibility for creating the 'New Youth' (新青年), the 'Young Chinese' (中国少年). In their minds, the new Chinese would be citizens who were equipped with Western political and technical knowledge, having cleared themselves of their cultural heritage, and were willing to sacrifice themselves for China's nation building. Without a coherent articulation of what the New Youth or Young Chinese should be, or how they were to be grounded, and in what sense they were to change and build a new Chinese identity, however, the call for the new Chinese was empty, often simply emotional and essentially ineffective. But their failure only provided additional ammunition for their attack on China's cultural traditions. Curran notes that in the early twentieth century, Chinese social criticism was replete with complaints. Reformers realized that for all their efforts they had failed to

> transform the attitudes and expectations of the people whom they had chosen to target for cultural renewal through modern education. . . . Thus, one reaction to the reforms was a scathing critique of conventional attitudes that reformers believed to be an enduring, perhaps unshakeable, legacy of China's traditional educational culture.
>
> (Curran, 2005, pp. 463, 427)

The unasked question was, how had education been conceptualized to transform people? If there are enduring conventional attitudes and mentalities – the so-called national character (*guominxing* 国民性) or *cultural garbage* 文化糟粕 – if people indeed are irrational, selfish and short-sighted, what had been done to transform them and to what end? Appropriating only the means and technologies of Western civilization, the reformers were unable to conceptualize a 'new' Chinese that was significantly different from the 'old'.

After 1949, the Communist central government in Mainland China initiated a long-term effort at both rooting out the traditional Chinese culture and denouncing the evil of the Western capitalist influence. For a long time the only thing left from the destruction was the socialist ideology, presumably inherited from the German philosophers and political theorists Marx and

Engels. But the socialism popularized in China was mostly imported from the Soviets, a version of Marxism that disregards its essential humanist concern for human freedom and dignity. The government proposed the need for 'Socialist New Persons' (社会主义新人) and urged that the purpose of education was to produce such new persons who would conform to the Communist ideology and be willing to sacrifice themselves for the government's agenda. However, the instrumental use of these 'Socialist New Persons' led only to a profound loss of the self among many Chinese.

After the Cultural Revolution, among the ruins of the Chinese civilization and personal dignity and well-being, a passionate search for meaning and a burning quest for *Zhuti Xing* 主体性 (subjectivity) emerged and prevailed among Chinese youth and intellectuals, who were suffering from a deep sense of disillusionment. It has been observed that in the 1980s one could 'hardly open a journal without confronting a discussion of subjectivity.'[20] Western philosophies such as existentialism, which proposes a search of meaning and freedom on the ground of nothingness, became particularly popular. Many Western philosophical and literary texts were translated and fervently embraced.

But soon the government cracked down on 'Capitalist liberalism'. After the Tiananmen Square massacre, and with the subsequent concerted move towards a market economy, the quest for meaning and subjectivity died out and the pursuit of money and wealth became the main channel for the Chinese energy. The market economy adopted in China has nothing to do with a natural-law-based concept of individual rights and liberties, nor with ideas of fairness and justice associated with ownership of private property. A heightened, purely instrumental mode of thinking soon permeated China. Chinese education lost its function of person-making and, as has been observed, China's basic education has become concerned only with test scores and higher education has become merely job training. The government, while frantically guarding against Western cultural influences, encouraged unequivocally the importation of Western science and technology (器物 once again). Under Hu Jintao's 胡锦涛 leadership, *kexue jiuguo* 科学救国 (using science to save China) and *kexue xingguo* 科学兴国 (science for China's prosperity) once again became the national strategy for China's nation building and revitalization. Most recently, since Xi Jinping's 习近平 rise to power, he has also advocated the so-called 'China Dream,' a dream that strikingly resembles the century-long Chinese aspiration for wealth and power and desire to rise up among world powers in the struggle for the survival of the fittest.

In this long history of East and West encounters and China's efforts to survive and return to its past glory, it seems we have started on a path of inevitable radicalization and what we have adopted is mainly a superficial and distorted version of modern Western civilization. The particular context of the East and West encounters and the psychological trauma they caused shaped the modern Chinese approach towards civilizational borrowing. There is a lack of careful investigation and analysis of what should be learned and adopted and what should be denounced and avoided. The frequent misreading of Western thought, the obstinate belief in 'the law of the jungle', has made it difficult for the radical intellectuals to fully appreciate what the West can offer and what we Chinese can learn to strengthen our own civilization. Needless to say, fear and the perceived threat of Western thought to the 'Communist' regime have further prevented genuine learning from the West. The result of such a selective and superficial adoption of modern Western ideas and practices, therefore, was that a profound philosophical and cultural transformation did not take place and education was unable to draw from modern Western thinking in conceptualizing the new Chinese person deemed so essential for bringing China out of its defeat and back to its past glory.

The fragmentation of Confucian tradition in China and modern Chinese education

At the same time as a modern Western façade was adopted, the Confucian tradition was also undergoing a gradual process of exploitation, rejection and finally, fragmentation. After more than a century's destruction, Confucianism, and the traditional Chinese culture as a whole, no longer provides a substantial and coherent resource for the cultural and spiritual lives of the Chinese. There are no longer consistent cultural grounds from which to draw a concept of the new Chinese person, and education has gradually lost its person-making function and become purely instrumental.

After the turn of the twentieth century, the Qing court embarked upon an educational reform to adopt a new school system based on Western models. It was believed that Western success came from a form of schooling 'that had a proven record of success' (Curran 2005, p. 423). The reformers' hope was that the new system would transform the Chinese people and bring about new generations equipped with practical skills deemed essential for 'the defense of the nation and China's future' (p. 423).

Zhang Zhidong was the key figure responsible for the curriculum in the first modern school system, established in 1901. Under the *zhongti xiyong* framework, the curriculum was heavy on Confucian classics and ethics, with history, Chinese and foreign politics, science and technology as subsidiary courses (Yuan, 2001). From 1904–1905, however, China again witnessed war between Japan and Russia over privileges in China and Korea about which China had no say. This situation prompted the Qing court to further its educational reforms (Yuan, 2001). The traditional school system and civil service examinations were subsequently dismantled and the new school system expanded, but the court made sure that students were taught the Confucian virtues in such a way that, instead of becoming independent moral agents, they would continue to be submissive to the monarchy. In March 1906 the court issued 'The Aims of Education', 'which included teaching students "to be loyal to the monarch", "to worship Confucius", "to care about public good", "to have a martial spirit", and "to value practical studies"' (*zhongjun, zun kong, shanggong, shangwu, shangshi* 忠君, 尊孔, 尚公, 尚武, 尚实) (Yuan, 2001, p. 200).

In January 1912, the Qing monarchy was overthrown and the Republic of China was established. The first Republican education minister was the famous liberal educator Cai Yuanpei 蔡元培. Soon the Qing 'Aims of Education' were abolished and Confucian classics removed from the curriculum. Courses on moral self-cultivation were maintained, but the content was greatly changed. According to Curran (2005),

> The reformist approach rested upon a distinctly untraditional assumption regarding the purpose of education: it must serve the practical needs of a modernizing society by training the population at large to contribute to the nation's material development.... It was also to serve the goal of cultivating the moral character of the individual [so that] every individual was prepared voluntarily to sacrifice his immediate self-interest to the goal of national development.
>
> (p. 127)

Education was mainly for the purpose of nation building and students were to be transformed into the means for such an endeavour, rather than into complete or ideal human beings. An instrumental and utilitarian approach to education started to prevail.

Not only was the curriculum greatly changed, but education as a whole was also increasingly seen as technical and methodological practices and its success was measured only by the extent to which 'new' and 'advanced' Western educational methods were adopted. The dialogical pedagogy demonstrated in Confucius' *Analects* (Wu, 2011) and the traditional learning method emphasizing repetition and absorption of classics were seen as outdated and, consequently, rejected. Between 1912 and 1931, educational reformers sifted through a flood of new educational theories and practices from the West, attempting to adopt the 'newest' ones, and eventually a 'developmental' education model was eagerly embraced. Discounting the deep philosophical assumption about the 'free child' embedded in developmental pedagogy, reformers introduced and embraced this pedagogy 'for no other reason than that the foreign models were associated with the wealth and power of their countries of origin' (Curran, 2005, p. 126). Dewey's, Monroe's and McCall's theories of child-centred pedagogy were treated as teaching methods and scientific experiments. Curran observes, 'As China approached and then entered the 1920s, Cai [Yuanpei] and others gave increasing attention to "the science of education and the technical aspect of the profession"' (Curran, 2005, p. 210).

Throughout the Republican era, conservative governments also made attempts to restore the status of Confucianism in the curriculum, mainly for the political purpose of control. Yuan Shikai 袁世凯 (1859–1916) in the 1915 and Chiang Kai-shek 蒋介石 (1887–1975) in 1929 'strove to restore Confucianism to its former orthodox position, . . .[while] endeavoring to combat liberal and democratic theories emanating from the West' (Yuan, 2001, p. 205). When

Yuan Shikai took over the Republic, he issued his own 'Principle of Education', which highlighted *Fa Kong Meng* 法孔孟 (following the instruction of Confucius and Mencius). 'Yuan elaborated on what this meant: "[Confucius] takes 'not offending against superiors and not creating disorders' as the root of humanity"' (Yuan, 2001, p. 205). Similarly, Chiang's ministry of education required that *Dangyi* 党义 party doctrines, which included Confucianism, be an obligatory course for all students (Yuan, 2001). Between 1932 and 1933,

> Chiang's Ministry of Education stipulated that the goal of the course in citizen training was to . . . teach pupils 'to show filial obedience to parents' as well as 'to obey the instructions of parents, elders and officials' and 'to obey collective decisions' which meant 'obedience to those in power.'
>
> (Yuan, 2001, p. 210)

In 1938, Confucian classics such as *The Spring and Autumn Annals (Chunqiu* 春秋) and *The Book of Rites* (*Liji* 礼记) were made the core of the textbooks on 'citizen training' and 'civics'.

Both Yuan and Chiang emphasized the Confucian doctrine of *bu zai qi wei, bu mou qi zheng* 不在其位, 不谋其政 (a noble man does not consider things outside his position), to control students' liberal activities and participation in political affairs. 'By reviving Confucianism, they hoped that schools would continue to nurture students to be obedient subjects', Yuan (2001, p. 205) observes. Thus Confucianism became mainly a means of political control.

Against this conservative backlash, the radical revolutionaries 'conducted a merciless attack upon the conservative values embedded within the New Policies educational code, condemning the traditional curriculum, including its Confucian core, for the support it provided to the monarchy' (Curran, 2005, p. 182). The 'New Culture Movement' began against, or partly as a response to, Yuan's reactionary effort and later merged with the May Fourth Movement. Confucianism, along with traditional Chinese culture, was fiercely denounced. After 1949, under the Communist rule, Confucianism was completely eliminated from the school curriculum, and if that was not enough, during the Cultural Revolution, 'an explosive attempt [was made] to bring about a complete transformation of curricular knowledge and the elimination of persisting values from the Confucian knowledge tradition' (Hayhoe, 1987, p. 197).

In recent years the government made a few attempts, alluding to an intention to revive Confucianism, and 'Confucius colleges' 孔子学院 (mainly teaching Chinese language) have been founded by the Chinese government across the globe to export and show the world China's 'soft power', but such a use of Confucianism is as superficial as it is misleading.

To the extent that people are carriers of cultures, even after a century of destruction, Confucianism, along with the entire Chinese cultural tradition, does not simply disappear, but it is completely fragmented in Mainland China. The fragmentation of China's cultural traditions in Chinese social, political and educational arenas is significant. After a century without the option of explicit recourse to Confucianism and Daoism, the Chinese have lost their cultural and spiritual home. Education is also unable to draw from its own cultural resources to articulate a concept of the new Chinese person that is rooted in its own soil and yet revitalized to face contemporary challenges.

The aftermath of a historical legacy

The more than 150 years of modern Chinese history, which saw the adoption of a pseudo-version of Western modernity and the fragmentation of Chinese cultural traditions, eventually brought us a mixture of entrenched and degenerated cultural remnants and a façade of Western modernity – the unfortunate aftermath of China's historical legacy. Such is the current Chinese cultural landscape, and it has serious consequences for Chinese education, particularly education as a process of person-making.

Since Western civilization has been appreciated mostly as scientific and technical means, even political tools, and little attention has been paid to its philosophical underpinnings, Western civilization has been dissected. We adopted only its external manifestations and disregarded its internal logic and course of development. We overlooked the fact that modern Western achievements in science, economics and political systems are only the logical results of a deeper and broader development in the philosophical understanding of human beings and their relationship with the world. Western science and technology, for example, long perceived and adopted by Chinese reformers merely as skills and means, became possible only because a yet deeper and more fundamental revolution had taken place during the Enlightenment with great epistemological and ontological significance. Without Descartes' locating the origin and certitude of knowledge in human consciousness, without Kant's proposition that rational and autonomous human beings ought to impose order on the natural and human worlds, and without Locke's and Hobbes' idea that free and rational men are capable of taking care of their own lives and that governments can be legitimately established only through voluntary contract with the governed, there would be neither science nor democracy, at least not in the forms they have taken. The early modern thinkers strived to establish a new social order, but only through revolutionizing the Western understanding of the human person and upholding human agency and value at an unprecedentedly high level. The dominant philosophy of Western modernity, the so-called philosophy of consciousness or philosophy of the subject, originates from and is built upon the idea that humans distinguish themselves from other species by their consciousness, rationality, and thus freedom.[21] Science, technology and democracy are grounded in such a philosophy and if there are any advantages or problems with science, technology and the Western social and political order, they need to be understood and analyzed in light of their origin and underpinnings.

The same applies to economic systems. We thought capitalism was market controlled and profit driven and thus that the economic reform inspired by it meant reducing government control and allowing people to pursue profit. What has been little understood is that the emergence of Western capitalism was situated in a broad social, cultural, spiritual and philosophical movement that fundamentally transformed the way the individual, his work and his responsibility to himself and to God was conceived (Weber, 1905). This movement provided the normative context for its moral principles and justifications of economic conduct. Capitalism is about much more than 'all for money' or 'all for profit'. That is why modern capitalist societies are no less normative than traditional societies. Without such groundwork, or an alternative groundwork, the current Chinese 'capitalist' economy may only be described as a form of 'primitive capitalism', or perhaps more accurately, a mixture of primitive and crony capitalism.[22]

Thus we have not fully appreciated what appear to be the advantages and strengths of Western civilization. Bits and pieces have been introduced and adopted, but the entire foundation is missing. We still think the only rule that governs Western international policy making is the incontestable 'law of the jungle', despite repeated failed predictions.[23] Even the Communist central government's adoption of Marx's communism demonstrates the lack of a full appreciation of its origins and underpinnings. We are not aware that Marx's communism is located in the context of the history of the philosophy of the subject and that Marxism is a development as well as a critique of, and response to, this philosophy. To truly benefit from or to be able to coherently adopt Marxism, or democracy, or science or technology, for that matter, knowing only what Marxism or democracy is and how to do it is not enough; we need to understand coherently where they come from, how they have come to be, where they are likely to go, and their strengths and pitfalls. We need to understand deeply both where they are and where we are so we can examine, compare, and judge whether, or in what ways, something from them can be introduced or implanted into Chinese soil and with what consequences – we need a true, meaningful civilizational engagement and interchange.

On the other hand, the overall rejection of traditional Chinese culture and the Confucian educational tradition has not resulted in the expected total elimination of Chinese ways of thinking and action. Even after the Cultural Revolution, there is abundant evidence of entrenched cultural habits and expectations in people's beliefs and behaviours that form a 'cultural continuity' (see Curran, 2005; Duara, 1995; Grieder, 1981; Hayhoe, 1987). It seems that, even when the cultural values and ideologies are deliberately silenced or rejected, the values, habits and expectations still operate in people's minds and behaviours. However, without being articulated, cultivated, or consciously strengthened or modified, these cultural remnants can flow, expand or extend beyond the boundary of the cultural project. What is left from the destruction and fragmentation of traditional Chinese culture, then, are entrenched, mutated and even degenerated cultural habits, either in the conscious or the subconscious, but always observable from the outside.

As Metzger (1977) cogently argues,

> Discrete changes in doctrine and overt behavior do not necessarily reflect changes in psychologically deep-seated attitudes. It is one thing polemically to denounce 'the three bonds' and 'the five relationships', another to uncover and alter partly unconscious beliefs about the nature of authority and selfhood.
>
> (p. 195)

The explicit denunciation or conscious dismissal of the cultural tradition does not mean the entrenched beliefs and attitudes automatically disappear; it does mean, however, that the lack of deliberative reworking and reflection on the cultural elements will lead to their unconscious persistence or mutation. For example, while Communist China is premised on a very different political ideology, many Chinese still expect moral rulers who will protect and take care of people as their own children. While a careful analysis may pinpoint the problem and the danger associated with such an expectation and its inconsistency with the Communist ideology, such deliberative reflection did not happen. Similarly, while Communism advocated the overthrow of all saviours and the proletariats becoming their own masters, the Chinese still called Mao Zedong 毛泽东 (1893–1976) their Rising Sun, *da jiuxin* 大救星 (great saviour), without any sense of contradiction. Ruth Hayhoe (1987) also points out that 'a complete change in the content of high status knowledge, with the Confucian texts fully and finally repudiated, did not disturb the traditional structure of knowledge' (p. 207).

Without clear articulation, justification or renewal of traditional doctrines and beliefs, and when thoughtful cultivation and discipline of the hearts, minds and behaviours of people are paralyzed, the deeply seated habits mutate and even degenerate in coping with life challenges, especially in a social environment dominated by materialism and instrumentalism. I argue that this may have been part of the reason why there has been such a conspicuous moral decline over the last decades, about which the government-initiated, morale-elevating movements of *wujiang, simei, sanreai* 五讲 四美 三热爱 (five talks, four beauties and three loves), or *barong baru* 八荣八辱 (eight honours and eight disgraces), have done nothing to help. On 24 October 2013, the Chinese 'bystander problem' made headline news in *The Washington Post*:

> When a 26-year-old woman in Beijing leaned a little too hard against a roadside barrier and got her neck stuck between two of the railings, Chinese bystanders did what they're increasingly notorious for doing: nothing. Security camera footage showed over a dozen people gawking and taking photos of the woman, who stood helpless on the side of a busy Beijing street in broad daylight for 30 full minutes before anyone tried to help. Finally, someone called the police, who pulled her out and rushed her to the hospital, where she was pronounced brain dead on Thursday.[24]

Recognizing that China's bystander problem is 'pervasive but complex', multiple theories have been advanced to make sense of this problem. It has been pointed out that Confucianism brought a social code that encourages 'kindness to people in our network of guanxi, family and friends and business associates, but not particularly to strangers, especially if such kindness may potentially damage your interest,' but also that 'Japan and Korea are similarly Confucian but lack this notorious bystander problem'.[25] I argue that this is a clear demonstration of the deterioration of the traditional moral code that was supposed to emanate from the inner circle but reach out to the larger society.

The deterioration of the Chinese moral sense is particularly poignant when the strength of the Chinese sense of morality, the Mencius *bu ren ren zhi xin*, 不忍人之心 (a heart that cannot stand others' suffering), is totally uncultivated and people become so cruel out of fear or out of self-interest. That is the most devastating aspect of the current moral decline. Hannah Arendt's *Eichmann in Jerusalem: A Report on the Banality of Evil* (1977) has awakened Westerners to the lack of a principle-based, reason-directed morality. The Chinese Confucian Other-oriented self and deep empathy for others was a strength, but now we are observing some of the most appalling cruelty against humanity in China in recent history.[26]

In the aftermath of this historical legacy, therefore, we are essentially living in cultural poverty, without any substantial cultural, moral and spiritual resources. Even though the communist government recently has advocated a 'Chinese Characteristics Socialism' (中国特色的社会主义) or 'Chinese Characteristics Path' (中国特色的道路), its theorists have not been able to articulate exactly what those terms convey. What Chinese characteristics are they referring to? How is China still a socialist country? And how can the perceived Chinese characteristics and socialism be integrated into a unique path for China? Its poverty of theory, as well as poverty of thought, makes its slogan of *san ge zixin* 三个自信 (three confidences) nothing more than a slogan.

It is within such a cultural landscape that modern Chinese education is operating, but the mixture, the poverty we are living in, cannot provide the necessary, philosophically and culturally rich grounds for education to draw upon for the purpose of person-making. We are unable to benefit from the critical insights offered by Western modernity for the education of rational, critical thinking and autonomous persons. We also lost ground in educating moral persons who are deeply connected with other human beings and with the world. In this climate of pure instrumentalism, perhaps Qian Liqun 钱理群 is right – our best universities are producing refined or polished egoists who are adept at using the system to pursue their own interests at all cost,[27] but they are clearly recognizable neither as Chinese nor as Western.

To revitalize Chinese civilization and reinvigorate the educational purpose of person-making, therefore, we need to go beyond our superficial understanding of Western civilization and start to deeply, carefully and coherently study Western thought as a whole, so we may gain insights that can help us reconsider what it is to be a human subject in the contemporary world.

We also need to explore ways to recover elements of traditional Chinese culture, not to return to its original shape, but to renew it, revitalize it and transform it with the insights from the West. We need to rebuild our spiritual and cultural home, and the particular ways Chinese live in and relate to the world. With that, education may be able to reengage with the purpose of cultivating the full development of a human person.

Notes

1 Recently the president of the Chinese Association for Historical Studies, Zhang Haipeng 张海鹏, published a newspaper essay discussing the trenmendous, 'centurial' impact of the Sino–Japanese defeat. See *Guangming Daily* 光明日报, 25 June 2014. Available online at: http://column.cankaoxiaoxi.com/2014/0625/405853_2.shtml

2 《礼记·大学》: 物格而后知至；知至而后意诚；意诚而后心正，心正而后身修，身修而后家齐，家齐而后国，国治而后天下平。 (When things are investigated, knowledge is extended; when knowledge is extended, the will becomes sincere; when the will is sincere, the mind is rectified; when the mind is rectified, the personal life is cultivated; when the personal life is cultivated, the family will be regulated; when the family is regulated, the state will be in order; and when the state is in order, there will be peace throughout the world) [Translated by Wing-tsit Chan, in *A Source Book of Chinese Philosophy* (Princeton: Princeton University Press, 1963), pp. 86–7.]

3 Recently, Yong Zhao (2014) has argued, in *Who's Afraid of the Big Bad Dragon? Why China Has the Best (and Worst) Education System*, that the *keju* (civil service examination) system was designed, with its centrally administered system, to only reward obedience, conformity, compliance, respect for order and homogeneous thinking. As much as I agree with him that such has often been the case, I also warn that it is not necessarily the rule and that it has happened only when education was used for instrumental reasons and lost its genuine person-making purpose in the Confucian sense.

4 See Fung Youlan 冯友兰 (1942), 'The Rise of Neo-Confucianism and Its Borrowings from Buddhism and Taoism', trans. by Derk Bodde, Harvard Journal of Asiatic Studies, 7(2), 89–125.

5 One of the 'Four Famous Officials of the Late Qing' (四大名臣) who advocated limited or controlled reform. Zhang served several impostant postings in the Qing court and was the leading figure of Chinese educational reform.

6 Arguably the most important intellectual leader of China in the first two decades of the twentieth century. Liang was part of the group of advisers behind the Hundred Days of Reform (summer 1898), in which the young emperor attempted to renovate the imperial system. When the reform was halted by empress dowager Cixi, Liang fled to Japan, but his iconoclastic journalism affected a whole generation of young Chinese.

7 Liang Qichao, '上南皮张尚书论改书院课程书' (A letter to his excellency Zhang of Nanpi County on reforming shuyuan curricula). See Curran, 2005, p. 176.

8 Prominent and influential political thinker and reformer of the late Qing dynasty; mentor of Liang Qichao. His ideas inspired the Hundred Days of Reform.

9 Revolutionary socialist; co-founder of the Chinese Communist Party in 1921, serving from 1921 to 1927 as its first General Secretary.

10 傅斯年, '译书感言' (My opinion about translating books), 《新潮》 1919. 3. Trans. Huang, 2003, p. 32.

11 钱钟书, 谈艺录 (*Records of Discussing Art*) (北京：中华书局, 1984). Trans. Huang, 2003, p. 32.

12 贺麟, 当代中国哲学 (Contemporary Chinese philosophy) (南京：胜利出版社, 1945), 21. Trans. Huang, 2003, p. 33.
13 See Huang's discussion of Liang Qichao, Hu Shi and Cai Yuanpei's praise and admiration of Yan's translation, expressed in Liang Qichao 梁启超, '绍介新书〈原富〉', 《新民丛报》第1号 ('Introducing a new book: *The Principles of Prosperity*', (New citizen journal, no. 1); Cai Yuanpei 蔡元培, '五十年来中国之哲学' (Chinese philosophy in the last fifty years) and Hu Shi 胡 适, '五十年来中国之文学' (Chinese literature in the last fifty years), in 最近五十年 (The last fifty years), ed. The House of *Shenbao* (Shanghai: The House of *Shenbao*, 1923).
14 钱钟书, '林纾的翻译.' Trans. Huang, 2003, p. 32.
15 '陈寅恪评价王国维的学术地位时指出': 其著作可以转移一时之风 气, 而示来者以轨则也。'[1] 陈寅恪. 王静安先生遗书·序[A].刘桂生等.陈寅恪学术文化随笔[C].北京:中国青年出版社, 1996.6,6.
16 王国维.论近年之学术界[A].姚淦铭等.王国维文集(第三卷)[C].北京:中国文史出版社, 1997.
17 王国维.述近世教育思想与哲学之关系[A].姚淦铭等.王国维文集(第三卷)[C].北京:中国文史出版社, 1997.
18 While these scholars diverge from the trend, they had little impact on shaping the course of Chinese modernity. For example, Qian Zhongshu, widely appraised as a scholar with a brilliant grasp of both civilizations, limited his work on comparative literature; Wang Guowei killed himself not long after the Qing monarchy was overthrown. Chen Yinke, a brilliant historian, was fiercely non-political throughout his life. In general, these scholars are appreciated as individual academics with great talents, rather than influential reformers.
19 In a letter to Chen Duxiu, 14 March 1918: '我再用大胆宣言道：欲使中国不亡，欲使中国民族为二十世纪文明之民族，必以废孔学，灭道教为根本之解决，而废记载孔门学说及道教妖言之汉文，尤为根本解决之根本解决。' Available online at: http://theory.people.com.cn/n/2013/0110/c49163-20156495-2.html
20 Chris Jochim, 'Just say no to "no self" in Zhuangzi', in *Wandering at Ease in the Zhuangzi*, Roger T. Ames (ed.), (State University of New York Press, 1998), p. 40.
21 The Western emphasis on human rationality did not start with the Enlightenment. Many of the ancient Greek thinkers, including Aristotle and Seneca, considered the human capacity for reason the most essential part of humanity. The difference between the modern and pre-modern thinkers, if there is an identifiable difference in this regard, I would suggest, is that the ancient Greeks still believed in teleology or the idea of providence but modern thinkers have elevated the rational, free self to the level of God, as particularly expressed in modern German philosophy.
22 Crony capitalism is the economic system where resources and opportunities are often carved up by those who have close ties with the government, instead of success being determined by a free market and the rule of law.
23 Chinese generals and military consultants have been predicting the motives and trends in world military affairs based on this principle and have failed, sometimes hilariously. See Niu Xinchun 牛新春 (President and researcher, China Institute of Modern International Relation Studies), 'Collective Blindness: Reflection on Chinese Scholars' Prediction on Iraq and Afghan Wars.' Modern International Relations, 2014(4). Available online at: http://21ccom.net/articles/qqsw/zlwj/article_2014 0703108807.html Also see his interview at: http://bbs.creaders.net/military/bbs viewer.php?trd_id=975543
24 Available online at: http://washingtonpost.com/blogs/worldviews/wp/2013/10/24/chinas-bystander-problem-another-death-after-crowd-ignores-woman-in-peril/
25 See note 24.
26 One example of this cruelty and analysis can be found in Lin Zhao's 林昭 case. Available online at: http://blog.creaders.net/hetan/user_blog_diary.php?did=180035
27 Recently, in a higher education conference, Beijing University professor Qian Liqun 钱理群 made a striking comment: 'Our universities, including Beijing University, are

now producing 'polished egoists', highly intelligent, worldly, sophisticated, good at performing and cooperation, more adept at using the system for their own purposes.' Qian predicts that if these people are eventually in the position of power, they will be more dangerous than the regular corrupted officials we now see. See: 北大教授钱理群：北大等大学正培养利己主义者 Available online at: http://news.sina.com.cn/c/2012-05-03/040724359951.shtml

References

Arendt, H. (1977). *Eichmann in Jerusalem: A Report on the Banality of Evil.* New York: Penguin Books.

Biesta, G. (2009). Good Education in an Age of Measurement: On the Need to Reconnect with the Question of Purpose in Education. *Educational Assessment, Evaluation and Accountability*, 21(1), 33–46.

Chan, W. (1963). *A Source Book of Chinese Philosophy.* Princeton: Princeton University Press.

Chen, Y. (1996). 'Preface: Wang Jingan Testament.' In *Chen Yingke's Academic and Cultural Essays*, Liu Guisheng and Zhang Buzhou (eds.). Beijing: Chinese Youth Press.

Curran, T. D. (2005). *Educational Reform in Republican China: The Failure of Educators to Create a Modern Nation.* Lewiston, New York: Edwin Mellen Press.

De Bary, W. T. (1996). Confucian Education in Premodern Asia. In Tu Wei-ming (ed.), *Confucian Traditions in East Asian Modernity* (pp. 21–33). Cambridge: Harvard University Press.

Duara, P. (1995). *Rescuing History from the Nation: Questioning Narratives of Modern China.* Chicago: The University of Chicago Press.

Fung, Y. 冯友兰 (1942). The Rise of Neo-Confucianism and its Borrowings from Buddhism and Taoism, trans. by Derk Bodde. *Harvard Journal of Asiatic Studies*, 7(2), 89–125.

Grieder, J. B. (1981). *Intellectuals and the State in Modern China: A Narrative History.* New York: The Free Press.

Hayhoe, R. (1987). China's Higher Curricular Reform in Historical Perspective. *The China Quarterly*, 110, 196–230.

Huang, K. (2003). The Reception of Yan Fu in Twentieth-century China. In Cindy Yik-yi Chu and Ricardo K. S. Mak (eds), *China Reconstructs* (pp. 25–44). Lanham, MD: University Press of America.

Jochim, C. (1998). Just Say No to 'No Self' in Zhuangzi. In Roger T. Ames (ed.), *Wandering at Ease in the Zhuangzi* (pp. 35–74). New York: State University of New York Press.

Lee, T. H. C. (2000). *Education in Traditional China: A History.* Leiden: Koninklijke Brill NV.

Metzger, T. A. (1977). *Escape from Predicament: New-Confucianism and China's Evolving Political Culture.* New York: Columbia University Press.

Niu, X. (2014). Collective Blindness: Reflection on Chinese Scholars' Prediction on Iraq and Afghan Wars. *Modern International Relations*, (4). Available online at: http://21ccom.net/articles/qqsw/zlwj/article_20140703108807.html (accessed 22 November 2014).

Schwartz, B. (1979/1964). *In Search of Wealth and Power: Yen Fu and the West.* Cambridge, MA: Belknap Press of Harvard University Press.

Wang Guowei (1997a). On the Academic Community of Recent Years. In Yao Ganming and Wang Yan (eds), *Collected Works of Wang Guowei* Vol. 3. Beijing: Zhongguo Culture and History Publisher. 王国维.论近年之学术界[A].姚淦铭等.王国维文集(第三卷)[C].北京:中国文史出版社, 1997.

Wang Guowei (1997b). On the Relationship between Recent Educational Thought and Philosophy. In Yao Ganming and Wang Yan (eds), *Collected Works of Wang Guowei* Vol. 3. Beijing: Zhongguo Culture and History Publisher. 王国维.述近世教育思想与哲学之关系[A].姚淦铭等.王国维文集(第三卷)[C].北京:中国文史出版社, 1997.

Weber, M. (1905/2012). *The protestant ethic and the spirit of capitalism* (S. Kalberg, trans.). New York, NY: Routledge.

Wu, Z. (2011). Interpretation, Autonomy, and Transformation: Chinese Pedagogic Discourse in a Cross-cultural Perspective. *Journal of Curriculum Studies*, 43(5), 569–90.

Yu, Y. (1993). The Radicalization of China in the Twentieth Century. *Daedalus*, 122(2), 125–50.

Yuan, Z. (2001). The Status of Confucianism in Modern Chinese Education 1901–49. In G. Peterson, R. Hayhoe and Y. Lu (eds), *Education, Culture, and Identity in Twentieth-century China* (pp. 193–216). Hong Kong: The University of Hong Kong Press.

Zhao, Y. (2014). *Who's Afraid of the Big Bad Dragon? Why China has the Best (and Worst) Education System*. San Francisco: Jossey-Bass.

3 Cultivating Chinese citizens

China's search for modernization and national rejuvenation

Wing-Wah Law

Introduction

Since its military defeat by Western powers in the 1840s, China has worked steadfastly to modernize itself at home and revive the Chinese nation abroad. In the early 2010s, President Xi Jinping exhorted Chinese to pursue 'China's dream' and realize these longstanding national goals. For nearly two centuries, Chinese leaders have adopted different approaches to prepare Chinese citizens for, and engage them in, China's development in changing international and domestic contexts.

This chapter's broad-brush, historical approach explores the cultivation of post-1840s Chinese citizens at the interface between nationalism and internationalization in their pursuit of modernization and national revival. Through a reflective and critical analysis of Chinese classical and public texts (e.g., policy documents, curriculum standards, commentaries), it shows the different views of, and approaches to, cultivating Chinese citizens that China's leaders have advanced in response to changing domestic and international contexts since the mid-nineteenth century.

Herein, modernization refers to a country's transition from an agricultural to an urban industrialized society. In China's case, this process is not necessarily unilinear and may not adopt Western values and institutions (e.g., democracy), as modernization theory predicted in the 1950s (Pan, 2009). Though contested, nationalism and internationalization presuppose the nation-state as the basic unit. Internationalization refers to bilateral or multilateral relations between nations (Marginson, 1999), while nationalism emphasizes individuals' identification with the named political community of which they are legal citizens, and the commonalities broadly differentiating them from other peoples, e.g., historic territory, culture, legal rights and duties, and a common economy (Smith, 1991). Kellas (1998) identified three types of nationalism: ethnic nationalism, based on a common descent; civic or social nationalism, based on social ties and culture; and, state/official nationalism, encompassing 'all those entitled to be citizens, irrespective of their ethnicity, national identity and culture' (p. 67). These distinctions aid in the understanding of the stages of nationalisms in China's nation-(re)building since the nineteenth century; to different extents, distinct nationalisms (e.g., ethnic and state), can coexist within stages.

Education has two opposing functions, subjectification and socialization, that cause tension between person-making and citizen-making (Biesta, 2009). The former refers to processes of individuation, helping people 'become more autonomous and independent in their thinking and acting,' and the latter to citizen-making processes socializing people to 'become members of and part of particular social, cultural and political "orders"' (pp. 40, 41). As a vehicle of socialization, citizenship education contributes to citizen-making (Cogan, 2000 p. 13) by equipping individuals with 'knowledge, skills, and values needed to function effectively within' a polity with local, national, regional and global levels (Banks, 2008, p. 129). It confronts the tension between creating cohesive, governable, conforming citizens and those capable of employing critical and independent thought when scrutinizing and electing governments (McCowan, 2009). Citizenship education, however, is not static; rather, it is a dynamic social construction, contextualized in its social, political and cultural settings and continuously reinvented in response to changing domestic and global contexts (Law and Ng, 2009), and thus balances conformity and individualization. In school, citizenship education can be conducted in specific subjects (e.g., civic/citizenship education), integrated into several subjects (e.g., geography and history), provided as a cross-curricular theme, and/or promoted in extracurricular assemblies or events (Schulz, Ainley, Fraillon, Kerr and Losito, 2010).

A newly-emerged debate in contemporary Chinese education literature concerns the possibility of making free and autonomous persons through Confucian traditions. Using a linguistic perspective, Wu (2011, 2014) contended that 'authentic' traditional Confucian pedagogical discourse could be learner-led and help learners to make meaning and develop autonomy in learning; such pedagogical discourse, however, has gradually faded since the early 1800s. Hayhoe (2014) commended Wu's rediscovery of early Confucian learners' 'vision of autonomy' (p. 315), and further illustrated the Confucian legacy in contemporary China by tracing how three important contemporary Chinese educators (born between 1912 and 1941) learned from their teachers and themselves. Learning autonomously and self-learning, however, do not necessarily make free, independent and autonomous persons or citizens. The content, processes and outcomes of person- and citizen-making, as shown below, are contextual.

China's sociopolitical, cultural and educational contexts, this chapter argues, have never been conducive to making free and autonomous persons or citizens; that is, the necessary conditions literally have not existed. In different epochs, different regimes adopted different orthodoxies by selecting (ergo, deselecting and/or rejecting) certain cultural ideals, values and norms from China and other (including Western) countries to facilitate state governance and foster social conformity for social and political stability. State-run and state-funded education transmitted state-supported orthodoxies to people and sustained the symbiotic relationships between the state, governance orthodoxy and education. In effect, the Chinese state used education, particularly citizenship education as a socialization tool, emphasizing citizen-making (e.g., preparing individuals to live in a collectivist society and work towards a common cause prescribed by state orthodoxy) rather than person-making (e.g., developing unique personal traits and characteristics). If the Chinese state wants to foster active and autonomous persons and citizens for national rejuvenation in an increasingly competitive, globalized twenty-first century world, its governance orthodoxy, education and citizenship education must be more politically and ideologically open and accommodative, to help students develop global, national and local identities and function as active, responsible citizens of a multilevelled, multicultural, globalized world.

Confucian-oriented, moral cultivation approach (pre-1800s)

Since 221 BCE, agrarian imperial China had eschewed other philosophies to make Confucianism its main state governance orthodoxy, and adopted a Confucian-based approach to person- and citizen-making. Confucianism is a broad, multifaceted and ever-evolving tradition (Gan, 2009), and includes conflicting and mixed concepts about state-society relationships and state governance (Law, 2011). Some Western political concepts echo ideas found in such Confucian texts as the *Classics of Rites* and *Mencius*; e.g., a country belongs to its people (*tianxia weigong* 天下为公), from whom all power is derived (*mingui junqing* 民贵君轻), and by whose consent it is wielded (*de minxin de tianxia* 得民心得天下).

Imperial Chinese regimes, however, did not welcome such concepts, and selectively endorsed those Confucian ideas that helped foster an obedient citizenry to pursue collectivistic goals (i.e., social stability and harmony) in a paternalistic, hierarchical society, rather than develop unique personal characteristics and traits. First, the state-supported Confucian tradition took a narrow approach to person-making, stressing the moral, rather than cognitive or affective, development of individuals with similar ethical qualities. Confucianism emphasized cultivating individuals' moral integrity, and considered moral goodness the highest level of human nature, and to comprise five constant virtues (*wu chang* 五常): benevolence (*ren* 仁); rightness (*yi* 义); propriety (*li* 礼); wisdom (*zhi* 智); and, trustworthiness (*xin* 信). Gentlemen (*junzi* 君子) possess these moral qualities, while demeaned people (*xiaoren* 小人), seek profit (Mencius 2003, Book VII, Part A). The concept of moral cultivation (*xiushen* 修身) encouraged people to develop their moral selves by improving their nature and attaining moral standards. Confucius' *Analects* (c. 551–479 BCE) (1992) base moral cultivation on two main principles – observing rites, and practicing self-control in speech, thought and behaviour. They suggest numerous moral cultivation methods, including self-examination, self-censure, prudent speech and conduct, respect for teachers, faithfulness, loyalty and reciprocity (L. F. Chen, 1986). Thus, moral cultivation can be regarded as a means of socializing individual citizens into socially acceptable types of communication, manners and behaviours.

Second, the state-supported Confucian tradition emphasized fostering obedient, not autonomous, collectivist citizens, able to cooperatively live, function and sustain China's traditional social and political stability, based on the interdependence and interconnectedness of the Mencius' (2003) five basic human relationships (*wulun* 五伦), that is, those between: ruler and subject; father and son; husband and wife; elder and young brothers; and, friends. Save for the last, which was social, these relationships were hierarchical and non-egalitarian, with the first three being considered cardinal (*sangang* 三纲). In traditional Chinese society, these relationships were not about the individual self (differentiating individuals from others), but about the relational (assimilation with significant others) and collective selves (inclusion within one group in contrast to other groups) (Sedikides and Brewer, 2001). In China's paternalistic society, *wulun* largely defined how self connected to others – either through personalized bonds of connection, or through shared, impersonal identification with the larger community.

This powerful sociopolitical hierarchy eroded the Confucian-educated (*shi* 士) literati's moral integrity and courage to speak truth to power. Some classical Confucian texts (e.g., *Book of Rites*) suggested they should not compromise their moral integrity for money and should prefer death to disgrace. They lived, however, in the same *wulun* hierarchy as commoners, and not many dared criticize or denounce their superior's wrongdoings as their career wholly depended thereon; Neo-Confucianism, developed during the Song dynasty (960–1279), attempted to revive the moral qualities and standards that had been declining among the literati (Zhuge, 2001).

Third, the state-supported Confucian citizen-making tradition realized the collectivistic self by fostering its moral, relational and/or collective selves for social harmony and stability, which could be preserved by prioritizing the common good over individuals' needs and conforming to the sociopolitical status quo defined in these super-ordinate/sub-ordinate relationships. Even more important were two interrelated keys to Chinese citizens' moral cultivation: loyalty to the ruler (*zhong* 忠) and filial piety (*xiao* 孝). The classic *Filial Piety* espoused using filial piety 'to govern the country' (*xiao zhi tian xia* 孝治天下), paralleling son-to-father loyalty with people-to-ruler loyalty (Confucius and Cengzi, 1993; also see Ke, Chapter 7; Curran, Chapter 9). Despite its emphasis on moral integrity (*shi*), Neo-Confucianism continued to teach these two key moral codes (Yu, 2004). Moral ruler and commoners, according to Confucius's (1963) *Great Learning*, could maintain social harmony by helping manage families, govern the nation, and secure domestic peace (*xiushen qijia zhiguo pingtianxia* 修身齐家治国平天下). This is an important Confucian management and governance principle.

Confucian values survived centuries of dynastic change to become the core of ethnic nationalism in imperial China, moulding Chinese into moral individuals and collectivistic selves. Their role in civil servant recruitment examinations (605–1905) perpetuated them for over two millennia. Person- and citizen-making through moral cultivation, however, subsumed individuality into collectivity, over-emphasized moral development and social conformity, and neglected the cultivation of rational and autonomous individuals and citizens. This suggests that Confucian tradition was oriented more towards social conformity than subjectification in person- or citizen-making, ignored development and technological progress, and could not transform agrarian imperial China into a modern, urban society. This pursuit was further limited by imperial China's Sinocentric worldview, which viewed other peoples and cultures as 'barbarian' (*yi* 夷) and inferior (Yin, 2002). Thus, China began to suffer foreign aggression in the mid-nineteenth century, when confronted by more technologically and militarily advanced European countries.

Supplement approach in Imperial China, late nineteenth to early twentieth centuries

Imperial China's military defeats at the hands of Western powers and Japan were seen as a national insult and became the impetus for its modernization and global national revival (Lovell, 2011). In the late nineteenth century, China reformed its education system to stress Western technology (for national development) and essential Chinese values (to develop moral and collectivistic selves).

The defeats forced the late Qing dynasty to admit China's economic and technological backwardness, question its ethnic nationalism, rethink the utility of Confucian education for national development and revival, and re-examine Confucianism's suppressive approach to person- and citizen-making (Law, 2013b). Specifically, Confucianism's three cardinal human relations and five constant virtues were likened to 'eating people' (*chi ren*, 吃人) (Lu, 1982) and called a 'poison' to individuality development (Tan, 1981, p. 299). Confucian education was even criticized for making China a 'factory' producing obedient citizens who obeyed, rather than resisted, superiors (Y. Wu, 1985 p. 311), and reformists and intellectuals strongly advocated its elimination (Law, 2011). The resulting national and cultural identity crisis shattered people's 'long-unchallenged understanding of China's place in the world' (Wang, 1977, p. 9) and made the core cultural values and beliefs informing Chinese identity 'irrelevant or worse in the new world' (Gray, 1990, p. 3).

In the late nineteenth century, China was encouraged to study Western learning and methods, but warned of the dangers of Westernization (Zeng, Zhang and Li, 1986). Various approaches were proposed to revive China and save it from foreign aggression (Law, 2011), most centring on the suitability of Chinese and Western traditions and institutions for development and citizen-making, and recognizing the importance of science and technology for overcoming China's economic and technological backwardness. They also shared three assumptions: that importing Western methods and systems would introduce Western values into China and its education; that Confucianism's hierarchical paternalism contradicted Western values; and, that the triumph of Western learning and technology implied the victory of Western values over Confucian.

In 1898, Emperor Guangxu officially adopted the supplement approach to China's development – imitating Western methods, but strictly maintaining Chinese (i.e., Confucian) values (Cameron, 1974). This approach was based mainly on top official Zhang Zhidong's (1901) dichotomization of 'Chinese learning for morality [and] . . . Western learning for utility' in national development and modernization (*zhong ti xi yong* 中体西用). Zhang suggested that traditional Chinese learning, based on classical and historical writings and rooted in filial piety and loyalty to the emperor, would rectify students' moral conduct, while Western learning could consolidate Chinese students' knowledge and train them in Western military, educational, commercial and political systems.

In the early 1900s, the supplement approach was applied to state-run education for making the collectivistic self, in order to strengthen China and resist foreign aggression (Law, 2011). A primitive Western-style public education system was established that expanded the focus and function of education to include economic development. To facilitate national development and modernization, Western academic and vocational subjects and academic disciplines were incorporated into Chinese education. However, the Qing state insisted its schools teach Confucianism's Four Books, Five Classics and values, rather than Western political values and traditions (Yuan, 2001) to maintain China's ethnic and cultural identity, and foster the moral, relational, collective and collectivistic self in person- and citizen-making, and students' love of the nation. Moral cultivation was offered in all curricula; primary students studied Confucian classics and Chinese poetry, and secondary students learned personal attitudes and behaviours, women's virtues, and social, political and court customs. Underlying this were Confucian moral cultivation concepts for managing and governing self, family and the nation, and, especially, loyalty to the emperor (B. Z. Sun, 1974).

Thus, although the Qing state based its public education on Western models, it did not adopt Western approaches to person- and citizen-making; instead, it maintained Confucianism as its state orthodoxy and promoted Confucian-oriented ethnic nationalism to differentiate its people from those of other nations; Confucian citizen-making, which subordinated citizens' moral, relational and collective selves to sustain imperial rule, was also preserved. The Qing dynasty had little time to prove the approach, however, because it was overthrown in 1911 by the Kuomintang (KMT) under Sun Yat-sen, later the Republic of China's first president.

Synthesis approach in the Republic of China, 1912–1949

Sun's KMT established, in 1912, the Republic of China (ROC). The ROC faced a turbulent international environment, including two world wars and the capitalism/communism schism, as well as internal struggles for national revival, and the dichotomy between Western and Chinese learning. In response, its government espoused a synthesis approach, selectively integrating Western and Chinese values and traditions in its nation-building and citizen-making.

The ROC adopted Sun's (1984) Three People's Principles (TPP) as its state orthodoxy and prescription for modernizing and reviving the Chinese nation. The principles–nationalism (*minzu* 民族), democracy (*minquan* 民权) and people's livelihood (*minsheng* 民生) – reflected Sun's selective attempts to combine Chinese and Western political traditions in a state structure consisting of five democratic institutions integrating the Western tri-partite governance model (legislative, executive, judiciary) with two traditional Chinese political powers – examination power (appointment) and control power (impeachment) (Meissner, 2006). However, the KMT monopolized political power and never realized this structure.

As an integral part of its modernization project, the KMT-led government adopted three-level, American-style public education, comprising primary, secondary and university education of six, six and four years' duration, respectively. ROC Minister of Education Cai Yuanpei still, however, attempted to blend Chinese and Western learning by equating three Confucian virtues – righteousness (*yi* 义), reciprocity (*shu* 庶), and benevolence (*ren* 仁) – with the French concepts of liberty, equality and fraternity (Levenson, 1968).

Understandably, during its founding years, the KMT focused on building a modern republic and fostering a modern citizenry, rather than on developing individuals. In preparation for their future participation in China's modernization and exchanges with other peoples, public school students were required to learn both Chinese (starting from grade one) and English (from grade seven), and to become scientifically literate by studying general science in primary school and core scientific disciplines in secondary school.

Moreover, unlike imperial China's emphasis on *wulun*, the ROC promoted a more accommodative citizenship education component in its state-prescribed curriculum to prepare students to live in a modern republic and develop multiple (global, national and local) identities in a multilevelled world. Its 1912 primary and secondary education regulations and curricula targeted students' personal conduct and habits, love and sense of responsibility for community, society and nation, and understanding of China's structure and development (Ministry of Education, Republic of China, 1991a, 1991b). In 1923, the ROC promulgated its first comprehensive primary, junior secondary and senior secondary Civics curriculum outlines (Curriculum and Teaching Materials Research Institute, 2001), which featured a multilevel model of citizenship education (self, family, school, community, society, nation, world) at all three levels; some textbooks (e.g., Miu, 1912) stressing loyalty to the nation, rather than to the ruler, were tolerated.

The government created curriculum and school conditions conducive to fostering autonomous citizens in a modern republic. First, from 1912–1926, schools enjoyed their 'greatest degree of freedom' from central government regulation (Yuan, 2001, p. 194). Second, the 1923 junior secondary Civics subject emphasized autonomy and responsibility; respect for freedom, rights and responsibilities; the nature and importance of local self-governance; representative government; and political and electoral rights. Third, in many areas of China in the early 1920s, the ROC allowed secondary students to learn and practice self-governance by forming and participating in student self-government organizations (Culp, 2007).

The ROC's goal of fostering autonomous citizens and building a democratic China, however, began to collapse in the late 1920s, after Chiang Kai-Shek (an influential KMT leader) succeeded Sun and replaced his accommodative citizen-making framework with one of low political tolerance. First, to fight the spread of communism, the KMT required all curricula and textbooks to reflect its interpretation of the TPP and banned 'unacceptable' teaching materials (Ceng, Zhang and Li, 1986) – similar to imperial China's ban on all schools of thought but Confucianism. Second, it stressed seven Confucian values (loyalty, filial piety, benevolence, love, trustworthiness, rightness and peace) as fundamental for national revival, and another four (propriety, rightness, integrity and sense of shame) as schools' common motto (Curriculum and Teaching Materials Research Institute, 2001). Third, students were taught the TPP, Sun's and Chiang's thoughts, and to respect the KMT's flag and anthem; famed Chinese literary figure Lu Xun (1973) likened this to indoctrinating students with feudal values.

This suggests that, during the early years of the ROC, the adoption of the TPP and the synthesis approach to nation-building and citizen-making shifted the basis of Chinese society from Confucianism's five basic human relationships to a structural model linking self to diverse societal levels (family, school, nation, world); it also perpetuated appeals to ethnic and state nationalism that differentiated ROC citizens from their imperial Chinese predecessors and foreigners. Despite this, much as in imperial China, the ROC's citizenship education and education in general, tended more towards social conformity than subjectification. In the 1930s and 1940s, the KMT even attempted to build a personality cult around Sun and Chiang, making citizen-making education a tool for social conformity and the suppression of individuality and autonomy (Law, 2011). The KMT's attempt to construct a modern Chinese republic ended in 1949, when the Communist Party of China (CPC) forced it to decamp to Taiwan.

Rejection-replacement approach in Maoist China, 1949–1978

After founding the People's Republic of China (PRC) in 1949, the CPC under Mao Zedong adopted a rejection–replacement approach to nation-building and citizen-making, rejecting both Confucianism and capitalism in favour of communism/socialism. The CPC, this section contends, undermined the fostering of unique, individual selves to create a communist utopia, and cultivated ideo-politically collectivistic selves by tying people's relational and collective selves to the socialist cause.

Like the KMT, the CPC developed its version of state nationalism to differentiate Chinese from their pre-1949 counterparts and make them proud of and loyal to CPC-led socialist China. Unlike the KMT, it rejected Western thought and capitalism as exploitative, imperialist tools, eschewed the TPP and condemned Confucian and traditional Chinese culture as feudal impediments to modernization. In their stead, Mao's CPC adopted a foreign political ideology, communism/socialism, as its state orthodoxy for building a new socialist China. Mao's China was self-contained, breaking diplomatic ties with enemies (i.e., Western capitalist countries) and developing close links to friends (i.e., the Soviet Bloc). In the 1950s, the CPC, with Soviet help, adopted the ubiquitous Leninist party-state structure and the centrally-planned Stalinist economic development model by nationalizing the means of production (Ishikawa, 1986). It emphasized proletariat/bourgeoisie class struggle, eradicated market forces and private sectors, downplayed the rule of law, and denounced Chinese culture (Law, 2006). Its ideological emphasis on dualistic divisions between enemies and friends, capitalism and communism, and feudal and socialist China defined the Chinese people's collective and collectivistic selves, domestically and internationally (Law, 2011).

For the CPC, developing a new socialist China and offering a viable alternative to capitalism required transforming the Chinese people's feudal or imperialist thoughts to create 'new socialist persons' possessing seven political qualities: absolute selflessness; obedience to the CPC; class consciousness; diligence in studying communist, the CPC and Mao's political writings; loving and integrating labour and production; versatility towards China's changing needs; and, being red and expert (T. H.-E. Chen, 1969). To be 'red' was to allow socialist ideology to shape and guide their lives; to be 'expert' was to possess the knowledge and skills needed for economic and socialist undertakings (Baum, 1964).

Despite its rhetorical emphasis on students' needs and differences in some 1950s education policy documents (collected in Curriculum and Teaching Materials Research Institute, 2001), the CPC-led state used education to nurture and equip 'new socialist persons' to be collectivistic, rather than individual, selves, living and functioning to serve a new socialist China. It positioned education politically to serve the proletariat, integrate needs with production and equip students with socialist consciousness and culture (Mao, 1977). Education was tasked with preparing students to be red experts for a new socialist society, and helping them to acquire Chinese and foreign (mostly Russian) language proficiency and basic scientific literacy for socialist modernization.

In 1957, Mao (1977) specified an important political socialization task for education: equipping students to be labourers possessing a socialist consciousness and culture. Ideological and political lessons taught an ideologically dualistic worldview (capitalism vs. communism, enemies vs. friends), communism's superiority to capitalism, China's socialist systems and policies, and Mao's thoughts. Senior secondary students were required to learn dialectical and historical materialism (Marxist views on science and nature, and on history, economy and society, respectively); role modelling, such as evoking the spirit of Lei Feng (a model citizen praised by Mao), fostered CPC-prescribed student values to generate devotion to, and self-sacrifice for, China's socialist undertaking.

At the societal level, the state launched various large-scale political campaigns to make 'new socialist persons' and sustain Mao's leadership by suppressing individuality and political deviance. In the early 1950s, the thought rectification movement forced intellectuals to accept Marxism–Leninism and Maoism. Between 1957 and 1958, anti-rightist campaigns targeted those deemed opposed to socialism and CPC leadership. During the Cultural Revolution (1966–1976), politics took command. Confucianism was severely criticized. Red Guards (mainly secondary and university students) travelled the country to eradicate the 'four-olds' (old (feudal) ideas, cultures, customs and habits) by criticizing scholars, artists and scientists and destroying temples and religious and cultural artefacts. For ideological reasons, children and students criticized, denounced and attacked parents and teachers deemed counter-revolutionary. People were tried by the masses, not by law. Mao's personality cult reached its zenith, his words and instructions replacing textbooks and teaching materials in humanities and the social sciences (M. R. Chen and Hu, 1993).

The radical rejection-replacement approach was unsuccessful, however, in reviving the Chinese nation globally, improving China's economy, and creating a communist/socialist utopia; instead, it severely harmed China in virtually all areas (including education). Ethnic nationalism was suppressed, Chinese people de-rooted from their traditional culture, and the sociopolitical hierarchy of the five basic human relationships destroyed. Individual autonomy and individuality were anathema to China's centrally-planned economy, education and society; where people studied, lived and worked was mostly determined by the state, and people largely dressed alike. Education, including citizenship education, became a means of promoting social conformity and suppressing subjectification. To transform Chinese people into idealistically collectivistic selves (new socialist persons) with shared political qualities, normal human relationships were distorted and ideo-politically 'incorrect' thoughts and behaviours suppressed. After Mao's 1976 death, this ceased, and the CPC Central Committee (1986) condemned the Cultural Revolution as a period of disaster, chaos and lawlessness.

Pragmatic approach in post-Mao China since 1978

In the late 1970s, the CPC-led state, under Deng Xiaoping's leadership, reversed most Maoist policies, and began to adopt an accommodative, pragmatic approach to nation-building and citizen-making, using any measures, methods and learning deemed useful, whether Western or non-Western in origin. In 1978, under Deng, the CPC's party line changed from class struggle to economic modernization and introduced a policy of reform and opening to the world. Deng's successors proposed their versions of Chinese socialism: Jiang

Zemin's (1989–2002) 'Three Represents' theory; Hu Jintao's (2002–2012) scientific development outlook; and, Xi Jinping's (2012–present) promotion of 'China's dream'. These versions were largely adaptations of Deng's and became the content of state nationalism for addressing new issues and concerns at different stages of China's nation-rebuilding. The pragmatic approach, this section argues, has afforded post-Mao China a less restrictive modernization framework and situated modern Chinese citizenry in a globalized, rather than ideologically dualistic, world. It has also created new tensions in person- and citizen-making, between the pursuit of modernization and the preservation of cultural heritage, and between internationalization and ethnic nationalism.

Redefining socialist citizenship and identity in a global age

The pragmatic approach has engendered significant changes, affords Chinese people more freedom in many aspects of their life, and constitutes a state nationalism that helps Chinese people identify with post-Mao China. First, since the late 1970s, China has expanded its diplomatic links to include capitalist countries, and intensified its engagement in the global economy and international community. It signalled its national strength and rising global status (to its people if not the world) by hosting the 2008 Beijing Olympic Games, the 2010 Shanghai World Exposition, and the 2014 Nanjing Youth Olympics (Law, 2010).

Second, China gradually reintroduced market forces and private sectors to revive its socialist economy, despite serious ideological challenges from CPC conservatives. As a result, China has become the world's second largest economy and a rising global power. Today's socialist market economy allows Chinese people more autonomy over their lifestyles and careers, and to own properties, invest, or go abroad as students or tourists.

Third, civil society, the third realm between state and economy, has also re-emerged, with people able to discuss and criticize the government publicly and in cyberspace (Law and Xu, 2013). This does not mean the CPC-led state tolerates dissidents' views; it still arrests and imprisons dissidents for political reasons, as with 2010 Nobel Peace laureate Liu Xiaobo, who was sentenced, in 2009, to an 11-year imprisonment.

Fourth, to address issues and problems arising from new state-market-society relationships (e.g., corruption, social crimes, moral decline), the state has gradually re-established China's legal system as an external force, appealing to traditional Chinese values (e.g., harmony, shame, honour), rather than socialist ideals, to shape and guide people's thinking and behaviours (Law, 2006). In the 2000s, the state began to downplay creating a communist utopia and to emphasize turning China into a moderately prosperous society by 2020, and a great global nation by the mid-twenty-first century. In 2011, the CPC Central Committee (2011) unprecedentedly recognized China's 'excellent traditional culture' as a strong foundation for an advanced socialist culture, and a cornerstone of China's common spiritual home.

These changes in state–economy–society relationships inform the new state nationalism, which, unlike Mao's version, accommodates ethnic nationalism. They have also redefined the socialist framework for how individuals in post-Mao China relate to others, with or without personal bonds, within and outside of China. However, China's political system has changed little. The CPC continues to uphold socialism as state orthodoxy and to espouse democratic centralism's monopoly on political power. It also continues to suppress deviant views, and does not tolerate popular challenges to its political leadership and administrative dominance.

Readjusting the tension between 'red' and 'expert' in education

The changes to, and continuities in, Chinese people's relationships with the state, economy and society have refracted into, and are reflected by, the new state-prescribed curriculum for state-run and private schools. This pragmatic approach, this section argues, has broadened the orientation of individual, relational, collective and collectivistic selves by situating them in China's quest for nation-building and global revival, in competition with other countries in an increasingly connected and interdependent world. This has modified the tension between 'red' and 'expert' in nation-building and citizen-making. Unlike Mao's era, during which school curricula had an ideologically dualistic worldview, post-Mao China has begun to prepare students to live and function in a moderately prosperous China and in an increasingly competitive globalized world, as reflected in state-prescribed curriculum standards for primary and junior secondary education subjects, promulgated after reforms in 2001 and 2011 (Law, 2014).

Post-Mao China has changed its school curriculum orientation from preparing students for domestic development, to helping them cope with interconnected and interdependent emerging global and domestic challenges and contexts. First, the 2001 and 2011 curriculum reforms expanded schooling aims and stressed the importance of enabling students to 'meet the needs of the time', 'progress with the times', and cope with the changing demands of a volatile, knowledge-based global economy (Ministry of Education 2001, 2011d). Second, they urged students to develop a broader knowledge base in the humanities, sciences and social sciences, and to master generic skills and competences (e.g., collaboration, exploration, problem solving and independent thinking). Third, they required students to master transnational skills, including foreign languages (particularly English) and information technology. Started in 2001, students' English language learning now begins in grade three in most areas, and in grade one in more developed areas, such as Shanghai. Additional foreign languages (Japanese and Russian) are encouraged as electives in senior secondary schools, where conditions permit.

Although the reforms stressed education's citizen-making task, its socialist citizenship education framework has been broadened. Post-Mao China has adopted a more accommodative, less ideological, multilevelled or multidimensional framework for citizenship that encourages students to understand themselves and society and develop multiple identities, and fosters affiliation to global, national and local communities (Law, 2014), extending students' relationships from the nation to the personal–social and global domains.

The personal–social domain of citizenship education concerns making individual and collective selves, with students expected to: learn about personal strengths, growth and development; foster a good social manner in school and in public; understand the importance of competition and collaboration in human relations; and, cope with the complexities of a more open society by developing healthy habits and avoiding addictive behaviours (Ministry of Education, 2011b). The revised citizenship curriculum encourages developing a global outlook and awareness by studying important international organizations, respecting other cultures, and understanding common global problems (Ministry of Education, 2002).

Between its personal–social and global domains, lie citizenship education's local and national domains. Locally, the revised citizenship curriculum asks students to know and appreciate community features, including transportation, economy, cultures and lifestyles. Nationally, it promotes a post-Mao state nationalism, asking students to know and respect the national flag, anthem and emblem, and to have a basic knowledge and understanding of China's geography, its ethnic diversity and unity, recent national policies, economic and social developments, the characteristics of socialist political, legal and social systems, socialism with Chinese characteristics, and, above all, the CPC's role in China's achievements (Ministry of Education, 2011a, 2011c).

CPC leaders have also sought to infuse so-called socialist values into all levels of education (and society) to address issues of national moral decline since the market reforms of the 1980s (e.g., money worship, hedonism, extreme individualism). In 2001, the CPC Central Committee under Jiang Zemin introduced the *Implementation Outline on Ethic Building for Citizens*, defining citizens' basic qualities as: patriotism; observance of the law; courtesy; honesty; solidarity; friendship; diligence; frugality; self-improvement; devotion to one's job; and, contribution. In the mid-2000s, Hu Jintao launched a nationwide campaign to promote 'eight honors and eight disgraces' (a set of dos and don'ts). In the early 2010s, Xi Jinping promoted a similar set of 'core socialist values' at three different levels: prosperity, democracy, civility and harmony at the national level; freedom, equality, justice and the rule of law (*fazhi* 法治) at the societal level; and patriotism, dedication, integrity and friendship at citizen level. Despite slightly different terms at different times, both used the same underlying moral principles to address moral and social issues in the cultivation of collectivistic selves for nation-rebuilding purposes. Compared to Mao's time, they are less about a socialist utopia, and more about a strong, modern and civilized China; although the CPC labels them socialist values, it is difficult to see how they relate to socialism.

Bringing Chinese culture back for reinforcing students' Chinese national identity

Besides making state-supported values less ideological, the pragmatic approach has allowed socialist China to return Chinese culture and ethnic nationalism to China's society and its nation-building/citizen-making curriculum. Despite adopting an accommodative citizenship education framework and encouraging Chinese people to engage with the world, the CPC-led state wants Chinese identity to be a distinctive element of their collective selves.

Accordingly, it has promoted ethnic nationalism by preserving Chinese culture and harnessing its soft power at home and abroad. In the opening ceremonies of the 2008 Beijing Olympic Games, the 2010 Shanghai World Exposition and the 2014 Nanjing Youth Olympic Games, China portrayed itself as the world's oldest civilization and its citizens, whether Han or one of 55 ethnic minorities, as a unified people with a common history and language, and a shared pride in China's achievements. The Nanjing Games' opening ceremonies showcased China's major cultural, scientific and commercial achievements: Chinese characters; the water-powered armillary sphere; bronze products; Chinese porcelain; and, its Silk Road trade with the Mediterranean, and Maritime Silk Road trade with Europe. Law (2010, 2013a) showed that hosting such events strengthens the cognitive and affective domains of surveyed students' global, national and local identities, by helping them understand and become closer to the world, their nation and the host city.

In a similar vein, more Chinese or China-specific elements have been incorporated into state-prescribed school curricula and promoted in schools: in the 1990s, traditional stories, figures and heroes reappeared in text-books; the 2001 curriculum reform emphasized education in Chinese culture and traditions (Ministry of Education, 2001); and, the 2011 reform provided concrete guidelines for fostering students' identification with China, and their pride in being Chinese, China's achievements and the CPC's leadership (Law, 2014). For example, grades one to nine Chinese language students take calligraphy lessons, music students learn Chinese traditional and ethnic music, and junior-secondary general science students study China's recent aerospace achievements.

Moreover, the CPC-led state makes rigorous use of education to promote Chinese culture to the world, establishing over 380 Confucius Institutes and 500 Confucius Classes in universities and schools in 105 countries (Ministry of Education, 2013). Confucius Institutes promote Chinese language, culture and tourism, and collaborate with overseas universities and schools. They are heavily subsidized by the Chinese government and used as cultural diplomacy platforms to gain China 'a more sympathetic global reception' (Pan, 2013, p. 30).

Traditional Chinese culture is no longer seen as an impediment to China's modernization and revival, but as an essential national identity element of a modern Chinese citizenry, an asset to be preserved, developed and promoted through various channels (including education) at home and abroad.

Reducing political and moral burdens on students?

The CPC-led state's changed approach to nation-building and citizen-making can further be seen in proposed modifications to moral and behavioural regulations for primary and secondary students, which the state has used to shape and guide students' daily personal and social behaviours since the early 1980s. In 1981, it issued separate regulations for primary and secondary students, supplementing and elaborating on them in 1991 and 1994, respectively. In 2004, the Ministry of Education further revised and combined the two codes in its *Regulations for Primary Students and Secondary Students*, which are often displayed in classrooms or conspicuous campus locations.

The 2004 regulations favour developing collectivistic selves over nurturing autonomous selves and citizens. They comprise 70 items (over 2,000 words) intended to help students develop 'correct ideals and beliefs' and good habits, and to reinforce their concepts of nation, morality and being law-abiding. The codes have a prescriptive orientation, listing 103 'don'ts' (e.g., no fighting, cheating, jaywalking), and even more 'dos' (e.g., politeness, civility, loving China, its people and the CPC) (Ministry of Education, 2004).

In August, 2014, the Ministry of Education proposed further integrating and simplifying of the regulations into one guideline, *Regulations for Primary Students and Secondary Students (Draft for Consultation)* (2014, revised; *Regulations*, hereafter), which summarized extant moral and behavioural codes into nine items, further divisible into three categories: 'three loves' (the nation, learning and labour); 'three stresses' (civilized behaviours, integrity and law-abiding); and, 'three protections' (personal safety, personal health and the environment) (Ministry of Education, 2014). The *Regulations* encourage students to be (a) good social citizens by loving the nation, obeying laws and regulations, demonstrating civilized behaviour, evincing integrity, offering community services, and protecting public facilities and properties; (b) a responsible student by respecting teachers, loving learning and exploration, being diligent and attentive in class, completing assignments on time, and keeping the campus clean and tidy; (c) a good family member, by respecting parents and sharing housework; (d) a decent person, in good physical shape and with healthy life habits; and, (e) a responsible protector of the environment, by preserving the natural ecology, recycling, lowering their carbon footprint, and conserving food, water and electricity.

Compared to the 2004 versions, however, the *Regulations* reduce moral and political strictures on students' behaviours in five ways: reducing 70 items and over 2,000 words to nine items and about 300 words; reducing the number of 'don'ts' from 103 to eight; incorporating more elements relevant to students' daily lives (e.g., limiting time spent online, avoiding plagiarism); replacing abstract concepts (e.g., consciousness of innovation, social morality and self-respect) and those beyond the cognitive, affective and/or physical abilities of schoolchildren (e.g., fighting injustice (*jianyi yongwei, ganyu douzheng* 见义勇为，敢于斗争)) with calls to learn self-care and how to seek help; and, surprisingly, deleting 'fervently loving the CPC', while adding 'having the courage to express opinions' (*yongyi fabiao jianjie* 勇于发表见解).

At the time of writing, it is unknown whether these proposed changes will be in the *Regulations'* final version; they seem to hint, however, that the CPC-led state might be moving to reduce students' moral and political burdens.

Conclusion

This chapter has used a historical approach to trace China's major strategies for nation-(re)building and citizen-making: imperial China's Confucian-oriented approach (pre-mid-nineteenth century); the late Qing Dynasty (late nineteenth and early twentieth centuries); the ROC's synthesis approach (1912–49); Mao's rejection-replacement approach (1949–1976); and, the pragmatic post-Mao approach (from 1976). Except for the first, all approaches related (to different extents) to China's tensions between preserving cultural heritage as part of ethnic nationalism and the pursuit of modernization, and between learning from itself and from other (particularly Western) countries. Except during the 1910s and 1920s, China has consistently rejected Western liberal political and democratic traditions of state governance and person- and citizen-making.

Citizenship and general education promote two opposing concepts: social conformity and subjectification (Biesta, 2009; McCowan, 2009). In China, the four approaches, as shown earlier, did not create educational and societal conditions conducive to making free and autonomous individual selves and citizens; rather, they constrained it, and favoured cultivation of collectivistic selves for a common cause. Since the mid-nineteenth century, state-run Chinese education has had the important development task of equipping students to modernize and rejuvenate China domestically and globally. In the early 2010s, Xi called this 'China's Dream' and exhorted Chinese people and students to pursue it. In most periods of China's history, education has been an ideological and political instrument for socializing students into different political and social values prescribed by different ruling regimes; however, these were used more to perpetuate paternalistic state governance and maintain social stability and ruling class dominance, than for developing unique, individualistic and autonomous citizens.

China's development trajectory further shows that, the more China pursues modernization and internationalization, the more it must learn from and compete with other countries in an increasingly interconnected and interdependent world. However, it also shows that China's reliance on a state-supported or state-initiated value system as state orthodoxy for nation-(re)building and citizen-making, low tolerance for thoughts and beliefs that might challenge its orthodoxy and political leadership, and educational orientation towards social conformity, were common to all four approaches. If China is to cultivate free and autonomous selves and citizens and help them to develop multiple identities and function as active citizens in a multilevelled, multicultural world, it must make its state-supported orthodoxy and education more ideologically and politically open and accommodating. This could be a mission for Chinese education in the twenty-first century; its realization, however, depends on the willingness of Chinese leaders to tolerate views that are inconsistent with state orthodoxy, and that may even challenge their leadership. The provision of these conditions is more important for fostering free, independent and autonomous persons and citizens than, as Wu (2011, 2014) has suggested, rediscovering and reviving 'authentic' Confucian pedagogy in Chinese education.

It remains to be seen whether 'fervently loving the CPC' will be re-incorporated into the new *Regulations*. However, its proposed deletion, together with the proposed addition of having the courage to express one's opinions, have significant political implications for the development of civil society and the making of autonomous citizens in contemporary China. Encouraging students to express their opinions (which might differ from those of the majority, or even of the authorities) and not pressurizing them to love and blindly support the ruling party through fear and intimidation, could be an important starting point for educating them to be autonomous selves and citizens in twenty-first century China.

References

Banks, J. A. (2008). Diversity, Group Identity, and Citizenship Education in a Global Age. *Educational Researcher*, 37(3), 129–39.

Baum, R. D. (1964). 'Red and Expert': The Politico-Ideological Foundations of China's Great Leap Forward. *Asian Survey*, 4(9), 1048–57.

Biesta, G. (2009). Good Education in an Age of Measurement: On the Need to Reconnect with the Question of Purpose in Education. *Educational Assessment, Evaluation and Accountability*, 21(1), 33–46.

Cameron, M. E. (1974). *The Reform Movement in China, 1898–1912*. New York: AMS Press.

Ceng, Z., Zhang, J., and Li, Q. (eds). (1986). 中国教育史简编 *[The History of Chinese Education]*. 江苏：江苏教育出版社 [Jiangsu: Jiangsu Education Press].

Chen, L. F. (1986). *The Confucian Way: A New and Systematic Study of The Four Books*. London: KPI.

Chen, M. R. and Hu, X. Z. (1993). 学科中心课程在我国的历史命运 [The Historical Fate of Subject-oriented Curriculum in China]. In Y. H. Yang (ed.), 中国课程变革研究 *[China's Curriculum Reform]* (pp. 390–416). 西安：陕西人民教育出版社 [Xian: Shaanxi People's Education Press].

Chen, T. H.-E. (1969). The New Socialist Man. *Comparative Education Review*, 13(1), 88–95.

Cogan, J. J. (2000). Citizenship Education for the Twenty-First Century: Setting the Context. In J. J. Cogan and R. Derricott (eds), *Citizenship for the 21st Century: An International Perspective on Education* (pp. 1–20). London: Kogan-Page.

Communist Party of China Central Committee (1986). 关于全党必须坚决维护社会主义 法制的通知 [*Circular Concerning the Whole Party's Determination to Defend the Socialist Legal System*]. 北京：中共中央 [Beijing: Communist Party of China Central Committee].

Communist Party of China Central Committee (2011, 26 October). 关于深化文化体制改 革推动社会主义文化大发展大繁荣若干重大问题的决定 [Decision Concerning the Major Issues of Deepening Cultural System Reforms, Promoting the Great Development and Prosperity of Socialist Culture]. 人民日报 [*People's Daily*], pp. 1, 5–6.

Confucius (1963). *The Great Learning and the Doctrine of the Mean* (J. Legge, trans.). Hong Kong: Hequan Book Company.

Confucius (1992). *The Analects* (D. C. Lau, trans. bilingual ed.). Hong Kong: Chinese University Press.

Confucius and Cengzi (1993). 孝经 [*The Classic of Filial Piety*] (R. X. Liu and Z. H. Lin, trans.). 济南：山东友谊书社 [Jinan: Shandong Youyi Book Club].

Culp, R. (2007). *Articulating Citizenship: Civic Education and Student Politics in Southeastern China, 1912–1940*. Boston, MA: Harvard University Asia Center.

Curriculum and Teaching Materials Research Institute (ed.) (2001). 20 世纪中国中小学 课程标准·教学大纲汇编：思想政治卷 [*Collection of Curriculum Standards and Teaching Guidelines of Primary and Secondary Schools in the Twentieth Century: Ideological and Political Education*]. 北京：人民教育出版社 [Beijing: People's Education Press].

Gan, C. S. (2009). 儒学概论 [*An Introduction to Confucianism*]. 北京：中国人民大学出 版社 [Beijing: China Renmin University Press].

Gray, J. (1990). *Rebellions and Revolutions: China From the 1800s to the 1980s*. New York: Oxford University Press.

Hayhoe, R. (2014). Hopes for Confucian Pedagogy in China? *Journal of Curriculum Studies*, 46(3), 313–19.

Ishikawa, S. (1986). China's Economic System Reform: Underlying Factors and Prospects. In N. Maxwell and B. McFarlane (eds), *China's Changed Road to Development* (pp. 9–20). Oxford: Pergamon Press.

Kellas, J. G. (1998). *The Politics of Nationalism and Ethnicity* (2nd edn). Basingstoke: Macmillan Press.

Law, W.-W. (2006). Citizenship, Citizenship Education and the State in China in a Global Age. *Cambridge Journal of Education*, 36(4), 597–628.

Law, W.-W. (2010). The State, Citizenship Education, and International Events in a Global Age: The 2008 Beijing Olympic Games. *Comparative Education Review*, 54(3), 343–67.

Law, W.-W. (2011). *Citizenship and Citizenship Education in a Global Age: Politics, Policies, and Practices in China*. New York: Peter Lang Publishing.

Law, W.-W. (2013a). Globalization, Citizenship Education, and International Events: 2010 Shanghai World Exposition Education in China. In K. J. Kennedy, G. P. Fairbrother and Z. Zhao (eds), *Citizenship Education in China: Preparing Citizens for 'The Chinese Century'* (pp. 100–27). New York and London: Routledge.

Law, W.-W. (2013b). Globalization, National Identity, and Citizenship Education: China's Search for Modernization and a Modern Chinese Citizenry. *Frontiers of Education in China*, 8(4), 596–627.

Law, W.-W. (2014). Understanding China's Curriculum Reform for the 21st Century. *Journal of Curriculum Studies*, 46(3), 332–60.

Law, W.-W., and Ng, H.-M. (2009). Globalization and Multileveled Citizenship Education: A Tale of Two Chinese Cities, Hong Kong and Shanghai. *Teachers College Record*, 111(4), 851–92.

Law, W.-W., and Xu, S. (2013). Education, Work, Citizenship of Youth in China: Its Strategies, Achievements, and Challenges. *Sisyphus – Journal of Education*, 1(2), 128–60.

Levenson, J. R. (1968). *Confucian China and Its Modern Fate: A Trilogy* (Vol. 1). Berkeley: University of California Press.

Lovell, J. (2011). *The Opium War: Drugs, Dreams and the Making of China*. London: Picador.

Lu, X. (1973). 公民科歌 [Song for the Civics Education Subject]. 鲁迅全集 *[Complete Collection of Lu Xun's Writings]* (Vol. 7, p. 807). 北京：人民文学出版社 [Beijing: People's Literature Publishing House].

Lu, X. (1982). 狂人日記 *[The Journal of a Crazy Man]*. 香港：雅苑出版社 [Hong Kong: Yayuan Publishing House].

McCowan, T. (2009). *Rethinking Citizenship Education: A Curriculum for Participatory Democracy*. London: Continuum.

Mao, Z. (1977). 关于正确处理人民内部矛盾的问题 [On the Correct Handling of Contradictions Among the People]. 毛泽东文集 *[Selected Writings of Mao Zedong]* (Vol. 7, pp. 204–44). 北京：人民出版社 [Beijing: People's Press].

Marginson, S. (1999). After Globalization: Emerging Politics of Education. *Journal of Education Policy*, 14(1), 19–31.

Meissner, W. (2006). China's Search for Cultural and National Identity from the Nineteenth Century to the Present. *China Perspectives*, 68, 41–54.

Mencius (2003). *Mencius* (D. C. Lau, trans. bilingual ed.). Hong Kong: Chinese University Press.

Ministry of Education (2001). 基础教育课程改革纲要（试行） *[Guidelines on the Curriculum Reform of Basic Education, Pilot]*. 北京：教育部 [Beijing: Ministry of Education].

Ministry of Education (2002). 品德与社会课程标准（实验稿） *[Curriculum Standard for Moral Character and Society: Pilot Version]*. 北京：北京师范大学出版社 [Beijing: Beijing Normal University Press].

Ministry of Education (2004). 关于发布《中小学生守则》、《小学生日常行为规范（修订）》和《中学生日常行为规范（修订）》的通知 *[Regulations for Primary Students and Secondary Students, Revised Code of Conduct for Primary Students' Daily Behaviors, and Revised Code of Conduct for Secondary Students' Daily Behaviors]*. 北京：教育部 [Beijing: Ministry of Education].

Ministry of Education (2011a). 义务教育品德与社会课程标准 *[Curriculum Standards for Primary Education and Junior Secondary Education: Moral Character and Society]*. 北京：北京师范大学出版社 [Beijing: Beijing Normal University Press].

Ministry of Education (2011b). 义务教育品德与生活课程标准 *[Curriculum Standards for Primary Education and Junior Secondary Education: Moral Character and Life]*. 北京：北京师范大学出版社 [Beijing: Beijing Normal University Press].

Ministry of Education (2011c). 义务教育思想品德课程标准 *[Curriculum Standards for Primary Education and Junior Secondary Education: Thought and Moral Character]*. 北京：北京师范大学出版社 [Beijing: Beijing Normal University Press].

Ministry of Education (2011d). 义务教育英语课程标准 *[Curriculum Standards for Primary Education and Junior Secondary Education: English Language]*. 北京：北京师范大学出版社 [Beijing: Beijing Normal University Press].

Ministry of Education (2013). 孔子学院发展规划（2012–2020年）*[Development Plan for Confucius Institutes, 2012–2020]*. 北京：教育部 [Beijing: Ministry of Education].

Ministry of Education (2014). 中小学生守则（征求意见稿）*[Regulations for Primary Students and Secondary Students (Draft for Consultation)]*. 北京：教育部 [Beijing: Ministry of Education].

Ministry of Education, Republic of China (1991a). 小学校教则及课程表 [Regulations and Curriculum of Primary Schools]. In X. Qu and L. Tang (eds), 中国近代教育史资料汇编:学制演变 *[Documents on History of China's Education: Change of Academic Structure]* (pp. 690–7). 上海：上海教育出版社 [Shanghai: Shanghai Education Press].

Ministry of Education, Republic of China (1991b). 中学校令施行规则 [Regulations on the Implementation of Secondary School Policy]. In X. Qu and L. Tang (eds), 中国近代教育史资料汇编:学制演变 *[Documents on History of China's Education: Change of Academic Structure]* (pp. 669–76). 上海：上海教育出版社 [Shanghai: Shanghai Education Press].

Miu, W. (1912). 中华中学生修身教科书 *[Textbook on Self-Cultivation for Secondary Students of China]*. 上海：中华书局 [Shanghai: Zhong Hua Book Company].

Pan, S.-Y. (2009). *University Autonomy, the State, and Social Change in China*. Hong Kong: Hong Kong University Press.

Pan, S.-Y. (2013). Confucius Institute Project: China's Cultural Diplomacy and Soft Power Projection. *Asian Education and Development Studies*, 2(1), 22–33.

Schulz, W., Ainley, J., Fraillon, J., Kerr, D., and Losito, B. (2010). *ICCS 2009 International Report: Civic Knowledge, Attitudes, and Engagement Among Lower-secondary School Students in 38 Countries*. Amsterdam: International Association for the Evaluation of Educational Achievement.

Sedikides, C. and Brewer, M. B. (2001). Individual Self, Relational Self, and Collective Self: Partners, Opponents, or Strangers? In C. Sedikides and M. B. Brewer (eds), *Individual Self, Relational Self, and Collective Self* (pp. 1–4). Philadelphia, PA: Psychology Press.

Smith, A. D. (1991). *National Identity*. London: Penguin.

Sun, B. Z. (1974). 六十年来中国教育 *[Chinese Education since the 1910s]*. 台北：正中书局 [Taipei: Cheng Chung].

Sun, Y.-S. (1984). 孙中山全集 *[Complete Collection of Sun Yat-sen's Writings]*. 北京：中华书局 [Beijing: Zhong Hua Book Company].

Tan, S. (1981). 谭嗣同全集 *[Complete Collection of Tan Sitong's Writings]* (Enlarged edn). 北京：中华书局 [Beijing: Zhong Hua Book Company].

Wang, G. W. (1977). *China and the World since 1949: The Impact of Independence, Modernity and Revolution*. London: Macmillan.

Wu, Y. (1985). 吴虞集 *[Collection of Wu Yu's Writings]*. 成都：四川人民出版社 [Chengdu: Sichuan People's Press].

Wu, Z. (2011). Interpretation, Autonomy, and Transformation: Chinese Pedagogic Discourse in a Cross-cultural Perspective. *Journal of Curriculum Studies*, 43(5), 569–90.

Wu, Z. (2014). 'Speak in the Place of the Sages': Rethinking the Sources of Pedagogic Meanings. *Journal of Curriculum Studies*, 46(3), 320–31.

Yin, H. (2002). 中國文化的展望 *[Reappraisal of Cultural Change in Modern China]*. 上海：上海三联书店 [Shanghai: San Lian Publishing House].

Yu, Y.-S. (2004). 中國近世宗教倫理與商人精神 *[Chinese Religious Ethics and the Spirit of Capitalism]*. 台北：联经出版事业公司 [Taipei: Linking Publishing].

Yuan, Z. (2001). The Status of Confucianism in Modern Chinese Education 1901–49: A Curricular Study. In G. Peterson, R. Hayhoe and Y. Lu (eds), *Education, Culture, and Identity in Twentieth-century China* (pp. 193–216). Hong Kong: Hong Kong University Press.

Zeng, Z., Zhang, J.-Z., and Li, Q. (eds). (1986). 中国教育史简编 *[History of Chinese Education]*. 江苏：江苏教育出版社 [Jiangsu: Jiangsu Education Press].

Zhang, Z. (1901). 劝学篇 *[China's Only Hope: An Appeal by Her Greatest Viceroy]* (S. I. Woodbridge, trans.). Edinburgh and London: Oliphant, Anderson & Ferrier.

Zhuge, Y. (2001). 宋代士大夫的境遇与士大夫精神 *[Position and Spirit of Scholar Bureaucrats in Song Dynasty]*. 中国人民大学学报 [Journal of Renmin University of China], 1, 107–12.

4 *Gewu Zhizhi* and curriculum building

Limin Bai

Introduction

Originated in Confucius' *Great Learning* (Daxue), the term *gewu zhizhi* 格物致知 (investigating things and extending knowledge) embodies the Neo-Confucian vision of person-making. Person-making, *shuren* 树人 in Chinese, lay at the core of Confucian educational tradition. The term came from *Guanzi* 管子, a Chinese classic recording the wisdom and deeds of the School of Guan Zhong during the Spring and Autumn period (770–476 BC):

> Within a year there is nothing more important than growing grains; for a ten-year term one should plant trees; for a lifelong consideration nothing would be better than nurturing people.
>
> (Guanzi, 3)

This analogy between growing grains, planting trees and nurturing people evolved into a phrase *bainian shuren* 百年树人, suggesting that education is a long-term task. A similar expression *bainian daji* 百年大计 emphasizes the connection between education and future.

What is the Neo-Confucian vision of person-making? How did Neo-Confucian educators design their education programme to achieve their goal of fostering and shaping a person modelled on a Confucian image of *junzi* 君子, a gentleman? And how did later generations of educators and thinkers balance the person-making and practical learning in their educational practice? In seeking answers to the above questions, this chapter examines how the definition and interpretation of the term *gewu zhizhi* evolved along with Chinese intellectual efforts to construct the framework for Chinese learning which, in turn, had a profound impact on the development of educational curricula or curriculum building in different historical periods. The discussion points to the shared humanistic values in the Confucian approach to education and in the Renaissance ideal of a liberal education, and argues for the significance of the search for a common humanity in our rethinking of the content and aim of a modern Chinese education.

'Gewu Zhizhi': from the Neo-Confucian vision of person-making to practical learning

The term *gewu zhizhi* in the *Great Learning* contained a clear instruction that those who wished to appease the world and to govern the state well should first establish harmony in their households. In order to reach such harmony they had to achieve their own moral cultivation first. In this program of moral cultivation, self-cultivation is the foundation and pre-requisite for the betterment of others; the achievement of self-cultivation relies on one's efforts to extend knowledge, and the extension of knowledge lies in the investigation of things (Gardner, 2007, pp. 4–5). Confucian scholars before Zhu Xi 朱熹 (1130–1200), and Cheng Yi 程颐 (1033–1107), had long debated the meaning of the 'investigation of things'.[1] But it was Zhu Xi who interpreted it by embracing knowledge in the moral, natural and political realms as one unity, and giving the concept individual, social and cosmic dimensions. Within these dimensions, the meaning of the term is presented as being concerned with individual morality, social interaction and political activity (Cheng, 1979, p. 37).

Zhu Xi's interpretation reflected the Song Neo-Confucian concept of man on the basis of a new metaphysics. In this metaphysical system, man, *tian* 天 (heaven), and *di* 地 (earth), were regarded as one body. Zhang Zai 张载 (1020–1077), also an influential philosopher of the Song dynasty, claimed:

> Heaven is my father and Earth is my mother, and even such a small creature as I finds an intimate place in their midst. Therefore that which fills the universe I regard as my body and that which directs the universe I consider as my nature.[2]

In this definition, a man was not just a son of his parents but also a son of Heaven and Earth.

How did a human being become one with Heaven and Earth? A general principle in Song Neo-Confucianism was to bring one's moral nature into practice in accordance with *li* 礼 (ritual). Philosophically, they considered that the natural activities such as 'seeing, hearing, thinking, reflection and movement' (de Bary, 1966, p. 58) should be regulated by the Principle of Nature (*ziran zhi li* 自然之理). According to Mencius, the Principle of Nature was the harmony and order of things, and this was also the work of sagehood (Mencius, 5B: 1). Song Neo-Confucians expounded this idea using the terms in the *Book of Changes*: 'the character of the sage is "identical with that of Heaven and Earth; his brilliancy is identical with that of the sun and moon; his order is identical with that of the four seasons; and his good and evil fortunes are identical with those of spiritual beings"' (Chan, 1967, p. 6). In modern anthropology, ritualized behaviour is related to the harmony and order of a society. In Song Neo-Confucianism, the harmony and order of a society and of the universe were integrated. The harmony and order of a society was based on the harmony and order of the universe.

The practicality in their discussion was also clearly defined. They called metaphysics 'the idea.' For example, Zhu Xi said that people should not 'just hold on to the idea of filial piety'; instead, they had to 'know the way to practice it,' such as how to 'serve their parents and to take care of their comfort in both winter and summer' (Chan, 1967, p. 66). The way to practice in the theory of the Cheng Zhu school was by focusing on *xiaoxue* 小学 (elementary learning), where the *gewu* 格物, was 'the direct understanding of such-and-such an affair'; while *daxue* 大学 (higher learning), was the search for *suoyiran* 所以然, that is, 'the investigation of such-and-such a principle – the reason why an affair is as it is' (Gardner, 1990, p. 90).

The Song Neo-Confucian concept of man and the metaphysical perception of the universe allowed later scholars to seek *li* 理 (the Principle), in the diversity of things, including natural phenomena.[3] As Benjamin Elman (2007) shows in his study of *Ming Dynasty Compendia and Encyclopedias (Leishu)*, the approach of Yuan-Ming scholars to the investigation of things shifted to an emphasis on pursuing the wide variety of scholarship which covers both natural things/phenomena and human affairs, and *wu* 物 thus contained a broader scope referring to things, phenomena, events and affairs. Their incorporation of more practical elements into the framework of knowledge provided a common ground for the Chinese reception of 'natural history' introduced into China by early Jesuits. Elman (2007) points out:

> When the Jesuits presented an alternative genealogy for 'natural history' in an Aristotelian conceptual language (= *scientia*), Chinese collaborators such as Li Zhizao (1565–1630) translated their description of the structure of the visible world in the language of the late Ming theory of knowledge, namely *gewu qiongli* (investigation of things and exhaustively mastering principles).
>
> (p. 149)

This then laid a significant foundation for the mutual accommodation between Christianity and Confucianism, and between natural studies and moral/spiritual cultivation.

As is known to the students of Chinese history, the early Jesuits were fully aware of the power of knowledge in China and East Asian societies. Ricci's cultural accommodation policy was largely characterized by the concept of *xueshu chuanjiao* 学术传教 (evangelism via knowledge/scholarship). As mentioned above, in the framework of traditional Chinese learning, the study of natural phenomena, technology, ethics and philosophical teachings formed an organic whole. Ricci understood this and used the word *tianxue* 天学 (learning from heaven),[4] to integrate Western learning into the Chinese system, and Christianity blended together with scientific knowledge as Western learning (Sebes, 1988, p. 40). In Ricci's journal, the term *questa scientia* contained the meaning of both 'scientific' knowledge and 'learning from heaven,' as the term is translated as 'this knowledge.' This ambiguity is perhaps attributed to the original meaning of *scientia* which, as Elman (2006, pp. 3, 15) noted, was an *Aristotelian concept* referring to any kind of organized knowledge in Ricci's time, and thus included theology. It was not surprising that in 1626 Li Zhizao published *Tianxue Chuhan* 天学初函 (Learning from Heaven), which included natural studies as well as religious writings (Peterson, 1988, pp. 141–2). Both Ricci and Li Zhizao saw the relationship between the study of the natural world and God, its creator, and the term *tianxue* enabled them to embrace metaphysics as well as physics.

During the Kangxi reign (1661–1722), under imperial patronage, the *literati* grew increasingly interested in the knowledge of Western astronomy and mathematics introduced by the Jesuits (Bai, 1995). Later, *kaozheng* 考证 (evidential research) scholars such as Dai Zhen 戴震 (1724–1777), Qian Daxin 钱大昕 (1728–1804) and Ruan Yuan 阮元 (1764–1849), 'successfully incorporated technical aspects of Western astronomy and mathematics into the literati framework for classical learning' (Elman, 2010, p. 390). The principle of evidential research was embodied in two phrases: *shishi qiushi* 实事求是 (to search for the truth through concrete facts) and *wuzheng bu xin* 无证不信 (no belief without evidence). Eighteenth-century evidential scholars placed emphasis on 'exacting research, rigorous analysis, and the collection of impartial evidence drawn from ancient artifacts and historical documents and texts' (Elman, 2010, p. 388), aiming to recover original Confucianism via *hanxue* 汉学 (Han learning).

Although it was not until the nineteenth century that evidential scholars' 'search for the truth through concrete facts' was consolidated with *gewu zhizhi* in Song learning, investigation of things and the extension of knowledge (Elman, 2010, p. 389), a defining line between *gezhi* 格致 (an abridged term of *gewu zhizhi*) approaches in Song learning and evidential scholarship had actually been drawn in the eighteenth century when Chen Yuanlong 陈元龙 (1652–1736), published his *Gezhi Jingyuan* 格致镜原 (Mirror Origins of Investigating Things and Extending Knowledge), in 1735. The book 'represented a post-Jesuit collection of practical knowledge' including astrology/astronomy, geology, human affairs, plants and trees, and insects (Elman, 2010, p. 391).

The eighteenth century evidential scholarship laid a solid foundation for later generations of Chinese scholars to embrace Western learning with the blessing of their own ancient authority. Meanwhile, the combination of natural studies and religious doctrines enabled not only the early Jesuits but also the Christian missionaries that followed to package secular knowledge and Christianity together. These two knowledge systems developed in a seemingly separate way, but were interlocked and mutually interacted with one another. This is evidently embodied in the nineteenth-century missionary writings, the curriculum of missionary schools in China and the native Chinese pursuit of statesmanship for practical use (*jingshi* 经世, learning).

In late nineteenth-century China, Christian teaching, Confucian classics and science subjects comprised three components in the curriculum of the major mission schools. By and large, missionary educators of the time established and operated the schools by modelling the Western learning component of the above model on the liberal education they had received in their home countries.[5] In 1872, Calvin Wilson Mateer (1836–1908) developed a three-point formula for the success of Tengchou Presbyterian College: the Chinese language was used as the teaching medium, traditional Chinese education was supplemented by Western learning and Christian character was emphasized (Hyatt, 1976, pp. 166–7; Wang, 2000, p. 27). In 1881 under the leadership of Mateer, the Tengchow College developed a regular course of study, which, in the view of Mrs. Mateer, 'was a program equivalent to the ordinary college curriculum in America' (Hyatt, 1976, p. 183). Mateer was very proud of his college that offered such broad knowledge. In his view, Christian schools had to educate men in Christianity and Western science which would enable them to outshine men equipped with a traditional Confucian education (Mateer, 1890, pp. 459–60).

Such views were shared by other missionary educators, such as Junius H. Judson (1852–1930), the principal (1880–1911) of Hangchow High School, which later became the Presbyterian College in Hangchow. In Table 4.1, the first column lists the weaknesses in the Chinese education system as perceived by Judson, and the second column lists topics included in Judson's curriculum that were aimed at addressing these weaknesses.

Benjamin Elman argues that Protestant activities and achievements in translation, publication and education contributed significantly to the introduction of modern science in late Qing China. He further points out that it was the joint efforts between native Chinese scholars and Christian missionaries that created an intellectual common ground on which they 'compromised' the Chinese concept of *gezhi* and 'a notion of modern science informed by Christian natural theology for missionaries.' Moreover, 'such compromises reproduced

Table 4.1 Judson's comparison of the curriculum in Chinese education and missionary schools

Weakness in Chinese Education System	Judson's Curriculum Included
• Lacked knowledge of other nations and held overweening regard for their own	• Geography and history
• Failed to provide students with a basic knowledge of nature	• Natural philosophy, chemistry, astronomy and anatomy
• Ignored most of the arts and sciences	• Arts and sciences
• An inability for close and patient logical thought and investigation	• Geometry, trigonometry and algebra
• Lack of taste, imagination and insensibility to beauty and the principles of order and harmony.	• Music and sports.

Source: Adapted from Catalogue of Hangchow High School (1894), 上海, 中国: 杭州育英义塾 [Shanghai, China: American Presbyterian Mission Press], pp. 1–2.

the Sino-Jesuit term for natural studies (*scientia*), but it now referred to modern science (*gezhi xue*), not early modern science (*gezhi*)' (Elman, 2005, p. 319). Reflected in curriculum building, this suggests a conceptual evolution of *gezhi* learning developed from a moral cultivation programme to a search for the Principle in the diversity of things, to the inclusion of the natural studies of the early Jesuits, and then to modern science subjects in the missionary school curriculum. We may contend that this development of the concept of *gezhi* learning helped missionary educators to transfer Western liberal education onto Chinese soil and enabled the Chinese to perceive it 'on their own terms.'[6]

Meanwhile, the sociopolitical situation in China after the Opium War in the 1840s took away the ease with which late Ming scholars had encounters with the Jesuits during the seventeenth century. The study of Western knowledge in evidential research in the eighteenth century could not continue to be a pure scholarly search for the truth from Confucian classics; rather it became an urgent matter relating to the survival of China. Under such circumstances, the *jingshi zhiyong* 经世致用 (statesmanship for practical use) thus emerged as a new knowledge system emphasizing the use of Western technology to combat the intrusion of Western powers. In this *jingshi* framework *gezhi* learning was then extended to include scientific knowledge from the West.

Practicality was at the core of this *jingshi* learning structure, and its specific purpose was to make China as strong and prosperous as Western powers. Christian missionaries, Chinese converts, scholar- or official-reformers and their sympathizers appeared to have all agreed that China needed practical learning which incorporated Western science and technology, in order to secure the future of China.

Under these circumstances, the concepts of *gezhi* and *shixue* 实学 (practical learning) were redefined, and Western learning became a significant component of the original Chinese knowledge system. This in turn influenced educational reforms and curriculum building. Of course, tensions and struggles between the old and the new were inevitable, and consequently many scholars had to justify why China had to modify its time-honoured scholarship and learn from the West. The foreword (by a Qing scholar named Wu Qingyuan 吴磬远) to Yuan Junde's collectaneas, for example, discussed the relationship between *renyi zhi dao* 仁义之道 (Confucian learning) and *fuqiang zhi shu* 富强之术 (Western science and technology, lit., methods of becoming prosperous and strong). In his view, the two should not be separated as two conflicting things. His logic behind this point was that if one talks about *ren* 仁 (humanity) and *yi* 义 (righteousness) without touching upon any knowledge relevant to how one should make his country prosperous and strong, this is then not truly the Confucian learning (Wu's foreword to Yuan 1901, pp. 1a–3a). Wu's argument shows the Chinese mentality formed after the Opium War in the 1840s and which has profoundly influenced Chinese culture and society ever since. Moreover, the glory of China's civilization in the past had also become a core component in this mentality. This mentality turned into a powerful pressure that contributed to the campaign for China's *jiuwang* 救亡 (survival), and the *jiuwang* topic was prevalent in late Qing textbooks in such subjects as Chinese language, history, geography and *xiushen* 修身 (moral cultivation).

Meanwhile, Zhang Zhidong 张之洞 (1837–1909) proposed a new balance between moral cultivation and practicality which was concerned with *jingshi* knowledge and mainly related to economy and technology. Zhang's *zhongti xiyong* 中体西用 formula intended to synthesize Western technology as the *yong* 用 (means) for strengthening China and Confucian moral practicality as *ti* 体 (substance). This approach to East–West integration can be exemplified by the 1903 draft policy for the modern school system, which included a new curricular programme from preschool to higher education. Zhang Zhidong was responsible for the final version of this design, which reflected his attempt to integrate the moral universal in Confucianism and the material world equipped with Western science and technology. To this effort, Zhang Zhidong's notion of the investigation of myriad things included not only Western science and technology but also Confucian moral principles (Lin, 2005, pp. 5–24). This is also what Wu Qingyuan argued in saying that the metaphysics of Confucianism should be unified with knowledge that would bring prosperity to a country, as mentioned above.

From the perspective of a linear development of Chinese scholarship, the empirical road travelled by Qing evidential research scholars brought Chinese and Western learning together into a new synthesis that prioritized 'ancient learning' for a new age (Sela, 2011). Hu Shi 胡适 (1891–1962), in the early twentieth century illustrated this synthesis with his scientific experimentation with ancient Chinese philosophy. In his view, the methods used by Qing evidential research in philology and phonology were 'effective in practice and scientific in kind'; and their work 'bore obvious resemblance of that of the antiquarians in seventeenth-century Europe' (Wang, 2001, pp. 58, 18). Through the scholarly pursuit of Hu Shi and his followers at Peking University, such as Gu Jiegang 顾颉刚 (1893–1980), we see the legacy and development of 'searching for the truth through concrete facts,' and how traditional Chinese learning was studied for scientific comparison.

Rethinking the mission of education: search for a common humanity

The historical journey presented in the above section urges Chinese scholars and educators to rethink the mission of Chinese education in a global age. From the brief outline of this journey we see that the *gezhi* learning in its original sense brought about a unity of knowledge concerning individual moral cultivation, social order and natural phenomena. A sense of common humanity was at the core of the Neo-Confucian education programme. Meanwhile, the diversity of Yuan-Ming scholars' approaches to knowledge extended the scholarly space which existed in the Song Confucian *gezhi* scheme, and which provided a ground for the Chinese perception of the *scientia* knowledge of the Jesuits in the seventeenth century. Later, evidential research and the nineteenth-century pursuit of practical learning developed this approach further to embrace modern science. On the other hand, however, a traditional balance between the moral universe and the material world was lost in the face of Western powers. Generations of Qing scholar and government reformers worked hard to seek the best way to create a new educational programme by synthesizing Chinese–Western learning. Apart from Zhang Zhidong's *ti-yong* formula, Liang Qichao 梁启超 (1873–1929), a leading reformer in late Qing and the most influential thinker from the 1890s through the second decade of the twentieth century, put forward an idealized new mode of learning which would be neither Chinese nor Western but in fact both Chinese and Western (Liang, 1920/1972, p. 161; Hsu, 1959, p. 113). Liang never realized his dream and twentieth century China witnessed the gradual separation of the spiritual universe and the material world within the education system. The collective memory of China's humiliation appeared to have taught the Chinese a crucial lesson that 'being *luohou* 落后 (backwards) would lead China to be bullied by powerful nations' (*luohou jiuyao ai da* 落后就要挨打). This memory, working together with China's glorious past, prompted the Chinese eagerness to learn modern science from the West. This mentality has dominated the modern Chinese school curriculum, and modern science and technology, as illustrated in the well-known Chinese expressions *kexue jiuguo* 科学救国 (using science to save China) and *kexue xingguo* 科学兴国 (science for China's prosperity), have since become the key to China's nation building and the renewal of its glory.[7]

From this perspective we may see that under the pressure of Western intrusions the ideal of education for person-making in curriculum building since late Qing appeared to have gradually become insignificant, and modern education has placed much more emphasis on the power of modern science and technology. However, many thinkers and educators soon found deficiencies in modern education. This first started with the scholar reformers and educators in the early republican era. Most of them in late-Qing reform movements actively promoted their reform programmes which were based on models from Western civilizations; but they later discovered the ugly side of the imperialist West. Reflected in the content of textbooks, we can notice how they lost their admiration for the mighty power of the West. Instead, many scholars and educators began to criticize colonialism and the law of the jungle. For example, a 1913 geography textbook of Commercial Press characterized the British victory over Transvaal South Africa in 1902 as *bu wu* 不武 – not a morally justified military accomplishment – because it was like the fights between tigers and rabbits (Zhuang and Tan, 1913, pp. 6a–6b; Bai, 2008).

Soon the world witnessed the disasters of the Great War of 1914–1918. Chinese intellectuals such as Liang Qichao had to rethink their previous perception of the West, of modernity and of China's future.[8] Liang travelled to Paris for the Peace Conference at the Palace of Versailles (along with other influential scholars of the time), and recorded his impressions of Europe after the Great War, which were a stark contrast to the image of the modern and superior civilization he previously conceived and hoped for China. In his re-evaluation of the West and China's future, Liang particularly pondered on science, materialism, religion and cultural values. He said that the nineteenth-century scientific revolution and industrialization destroyed three foundations of the old European civilization, that is, the feudal system, Greek Philosophy and Christianity. The rise of modern science and materialism had replaced the Christian God with the law of the jungle, the *ruo rou qiang shi* 弱肉强食 (lit. the weak ones would be the food/meat of the strong ones). The outcome of such rules, said Liang, was exemplified by the disasters of the Great War. He witnessed such crises during his travels around Europe and used the phrase *qiang mianbao* 抢面包 (fighting for bread) to describe the cruel reality that Europe faced in the aftermath of the War (Liang, 1936/2003, p. 12).

Regarding educational programmes and curriculum building, more scholars in the 1920s and 1930s began to re-consider the concept of education, its aim and content and its links to China's future. According to their assessment, China should not accept and follow Western models blindly. For example in 1936, Pan Guangdan 潘光旦 (1899–1967), as the most distinguished sociologist and eugenicist in China, criticized Chinese 'new education' stating that it 'did not teach those being educated how to become human beings (*zuoren* 做人), and how to become *shi* 士 (gentlemen)' (Pan and Pan, 1999, Vol. 3, p. 358). In his view, education in literacy, skills and professional training cannot be regarded as the education of *shi*. What he meant here is that various types of education in a modern school system can only be viewed as schooling, providing vocational and professional training after basic literacy education. Schooling teaches skills which should not be mistaken as nurturing students to be *shi* or gentlemen.[9] Although the term *shi* Pan used here is a concept from the Confucian classics, his definition of it is rather modern. In his definition, the virtues of *zhong* 忠 and *duxin* 笃信 are the essence of the quality that a *shi* should possess. The concept *zhong* in Confucian teaching refers to loyalty, indicating that a loyal person would have the virtue of sincerity and honesty (*duxin*). In Pan Guangdan's view, 'loyalty' is equivalent to 'conviction' in English. Another feature of the quality that a *shi* should possess is *shu* 恕, which Pan says is 'tolerance' in English. In his opinion, a *shi* should have a broad mind that could understand and tolerate other people's views, especially those different from his own. This *shu* then means *bo* 博, indicating a broad and liberal mind that can embrace all aspects of knowledge and views of the world; meanwhile *zhong*, or loyalty, refers to the firm faith and stance a *shi* should hold. With such quality, Pan then used the term *hongyi* 弘毅 to characterize the attributes of a *shi*'s character (Pan and Pan, 1999, Vol. 3, pp. 359–60), which coincides with the humanistic virtues advocated by the ancient Greek philosophers.

Pan's article was written in 1936, at a time when China faced a series of new crises: military threats from Japan and conflicts between various political forces. He realized that the so-called new education system focused on the training of skilled workers and professionals but neglected the nourishing of one's quality as a human being, and he felt this would not help the development of China or resolve issues in society.

The same view is also expressed by Czesław Miłosz (1911–2004), the 1980 Nobel Laureate for literature, though from a different perspective. Miłosz was truly 'a veteran of European turmoil',[10] bearing witness to bloodshed and terror such as the Soviet invasion of his beloved Lithuania, the Holocaust and the Warsaw Ghetto. With his rich and unique experience in life, he pondered upon the relationship between religion, science, and human society, pointing out that in modern society, 'what young people are taught in high school and the university is a naïve picture of the world':

> In this naïve view, we live in a universe that is composed of eternal space and eternal time. Time extends without limits, moving in a linear way from the past to the future, infinitely. Functionally speaking, mankind is not that different from a virus or a bacteria. He is a speck in the vast universe.
>
> Such a view corresponds to the kind of mass killing we've seen in the past century. To kill a million or two million, or ten, what does it matter? Hitler, after all, was brought up on the vulgarized brochures of nineteenth-century science.
>
> (Haven, 2006, p. 71)

He then called for restoring 'in some way the anthropocentric vision of the universe' where 'man was of central importance' (Haven, 2006, p. 72).

Miłosz's call takes us to the roots of humanistic education in the culture of classical Athens in the fifth and fourth centuries BC. The humanistic and anthropocentric spirit 'characterized the religious dimension of Greek life: The world of nature and the divine world were, for them, a single unity' (Aloni, 2003, p. 13). From this point of view we can easily see the similarity between the metaphysical universe in Neo-Confucianism and ancient Greek faith, which laid the foundation for classical humanistic education in which the notions of *arête* and *paideia* were at the core. The term *arête* 'means skill, excellence or virtue, and is usually related to the activity or function in which you can be expected to demonstrate your essence or vocation.' *Paideia* refers to 'the ideal assemblage of human virtues – of the body, spirit and character – which should be regarded as a model of excellence for a good and full human life' (Aloni, 2003, p. 14). These two aspects in humanistic education are actually what Pan Guangdan identified as skill training and education of *shi*. Ancient Greek philosophers, from Socrates and Plato to Aristotle, all claimed 'that wisdom or knowledge is the supreme human virtue', and Aristotle believed that knowledge did not 'guarantee the development of a moral and happy human being,' as knowledge can be acquired, but one's moral attributes (such as courage, generosity, honesty, decency, self-restraint and moderation) cannot be produced through this kind of knowledge (Aloni, 2003, p. 21). Aristotle further warned us that 'when human beings are at their best, and knowledge and moral character serve one another, they reach the height of perfection, but when they reject law and justice, their reason can serve evil purposes, and then they deteriorate and become more savage and cruel than all animals' (Aloni, 2003,

p. 24). This is what Milosz witnessed during the Second World War and what Liang Qichao observed when he toured Europe in the aftermath of the First World War.

Although there were a variety of views in Renaissance thought, and what we can discuss in this chapter is a brief and simplistic version, we all agree that European Renaissance thought placed much emphasis on man and his dignity. It was in the fourteenth century and during the fifteenth century, 'Renaissance scholars began to use the term "humanities" (*studia humanitatis*) for the disciplines they studied, taught, and liked. The term, borrowed from Cicero and other ancient writers . . . came to signify . . . grammar, rhetoric, poetry, history, and moral philosophy.' By the use of the term 'humanities,' Renaissance scholars expressed their 'professional concerns for man and his dignity,' and the study of these subjects was regarded as being 'especially suitable for the education of a decent man' (Kristeller, 1972, p. 7). Such a humanistic approach to man and his place in the world 'was not entirely new' and similar ideas 'can be found in ancient and medieval writers' (p. 2).

Similarly, the same journey to humanity through education can be found in China. The Song Neo-Confucian scholars called for 'learning for the sake of the self', and this Self had to be realized via a process of 'obtaining or extending knowledge through the investigation of things.' As mentioned earlier, both *wu* 物 or things, and *zhi* 知 or knowledge in this maxim, embraced metaphysics as well as physics. From a metaphysical perspective, one's mind and the world would meet through self-cultivation. Meanwhile, the aspects of physics in the term *gewu*, as Elman (2005) observes, linked 'a more native trope for investigating things among literati' with 'a notion of modern science informed by Christian natural theology for missionaries' (p. 319). What is equally important is that the *scientia* of the Jesuits in the seventeenth century was bearing the fruit of the reconciliation of the Christian doctrine and Greek philosophy during the Renaissance period; and Christian natural theology was also reconciled with scientific knowledge of the time. As suggested in earlier discussion, this characteristic of early Jesuits' *tianxue* or 'learning from heaven' enabled the Chinese to find a common ground between the *gezhi* learning and the Jesuit *scientia*. Such a scholarly development and continuation also shows a process of fusion between Confucianism and Christianity, religious and secular learning and East and West, from which we may understand how Western liberal education and modern science were transferred onto Chinese soil.

Of course, this was a long and complex adaption and evolution of the concept of *gezhi* learning, but the most important and unquestionable result of this journey is that it provided the Chinese with a broad theoretical framework within which to build a knowledge system and curriculum. This broad framework made it possible for Chinese scholars and educators to synthesize modern scholarship and traditional Chinese learning, and to blend self-cultivation in a moral sense and the study of the natural world as an integrated learning process. Meanwhile, Christian missionaries adopted the same approach in their education practice in China, and Western science and technology in the curriculum of their higher education institutions coexisted with humanistic content in the Confucian tradition (Lutz, 1971; Hayhoe, 1996). This illustrates the fusion of Western and Chinese learning of the late Qing period, an intellectual effort made by both Chinese and missionary educators. More importantly, this may also allow us to find a shared point between the Confucian concept *ren* 仁 and the Renaissance concept of humanity (Bai, 2010).

Education in both Renaissance and Song Neo-Confucianism periods was seen as a significant instrument for creating a new type of human being. The Christian idea reflected in the English humanist approach that everyone is equal before God was the call for civility in place of nobility, and the aim of education was to shape the complete citizen. This core value in English humanist thought regarding education was reflected in a liberal curriculum. The missionary school education in the nineteenth century introduced its basic features and content into China along with Christianity. In Chinese, Confucius' maxim that *you jiao wu lei* 有教无类 (in education there should be no distinction in classes) shares the same egalitarian spirit as those humanist educators, and education is the means to realize this equality. This equality can be understood as humanity, because the word *ren* 人 (person or people) in traditional Chinese philosophy and educational thought was often combined with a core concept in Confucianism: *ren* 仁 (benevolence or humaneness; Bai, 2010, pp. 104–29). What Pan Guangdan called the education of *shi* 士 is actually a humanistic education designed to foster people's humanity. This was the essential principal of the Song Neo-Confucian educational programme.

Conclusion: education for humane talent

Unfortunately, the balance between practicality in moral cultivation and practicality in economy and technology was lost in the face of Western powers and in China's move to modernization. The problems in contemporary Chinese education have their roots in traditional Chinese education, but are also associated with China's perception of the nature of education. As the evolution of the Chinese concept *gezhi* shows, Mr. Science was introduced and welcomed into China at a time when China was in crisis and under threat from Western powers. Such socio-political conditions were also related to the rise of nineteenth-century science which, according to the Chinese perception, defeated religion, especially the creation theory. Meanwhile, Confucianism and traditional Chinese values also faced challenges, and China called for its own Renaissance, aiming to adopt Mr. Science and Mr. Democracy for the renewal of Chinese supremacy. Reflected in the purpose of education, China has found difficulties in balancing the two competing goals: training for human capital and education for humane talent.

Of course, this is not only a 'China problem.' In the West there have been ongoing discussions about the dimension of liberal education (Mulcahy, 2008). In light of the problems in today's education system, we need to rethink the essence of liberal education and its dynamics in a global age. In China many people have now started to 'reflect on the lack of imagination, creativity, and even good health on [the] part of the Chinese students' (Yang, Chai and Huang, 2013, p. 23), and a wave of educational reform has emerged to search for New Education. This bottom-up initiative saw a wide range of experiments in curriculum reforms that lead to the emergence of various forms of education, such as home-schooling and Waldorf schools,[11] aiming to address the issues in current Chinese education. For example, the curriculum of a Xuetang in Beijing, designed for home schooling, contains a broad range of courses spanning the fields from humanity to science subjects, physical education and life experience. In the areas of humanistic education, it includes classics, children's literature, reading and writing, communication skills, civic education, life education and English. As for the science subjects, children are taught mathematics, natural sciences, ecology and the history of science. Artistic education is also part of the curriculum, including poetry and music, calligraphy, dancing and even 'Go' game (*weiqi* 围棋). Perhaps the most innovative part of this curriculum is referred to as 'comprehensive practice,' ranging from handcraft to labour work, and to travelling and sightseeing (Yang, Chai and Huang, 2013, p. 149).

This home-schooling curriculum reminds us of the essence of liberal education that the missionary educators introduced into China. From Judson's comparison between the curriculum in Chinese education and missionary schools, we can see that Judson's curriculum directly addressed the weakness in the traditional Chinese education system, namely the failure to provide students with knowledge of other nations and a basic knowledge of nature, and which ignored most of the arts and science subjects. In Judson's view, such education then produced a group of so-called 'talents' who were unable to think logically and independently, and who lacked taste, imagination and creativity. Judson's comments were a reflection of the opinion of missionary educators and Westerners who lived in China at that time. Many Chinese people might find such comments insulting, especially since they came from a missionary educator! However, the above home-schooling curriculum appears to have addressed exactly the same issues in current formal education practice in China.

It is undeniable that in the current Chinese education system 'the development of human beings has come across the unprecedented crisis' (Yang, Chai and Huang, 2014, p. 249). This was the acknowledgement from the International Forum on New Education held in Ningbo in 2012. One of the most important achievements of this forum is that it calls for the return of 'the divine soul of education' which is to 'serve for social progress and people's spiritual development,' and help people become 'aspiring and noble' (Yang, Chai and Huang 2014, p. 249). This person-making focus coincides with what I have proposed in this study: education for humane talent rather than capital talent.

However, what should we do in order to separate humane talent from capital talent? And most importantly, how would people's humanity be nurtured through education? These are critical issues that China's current education reform would have to address. Waldorf education, both its concept and practice, may shed some light on it. It states:

> Education in our materialistic, Western society focuses on the intellectual aspect of the human being and has chosen largely to ignore the several other parts that are essential to our well-being. These include our life of feeling (emotions, aesthetics, and social sensitivity), our willpower (the ability to get things done), and our moral nature (being clear about right and wrong). Without having these developed, we are incomplete – a fact that may become obvious in our later years, when a feeling of emptiness begins to set in. That is why in a Waldorf school, the practical and artistic subjects play as important a role as the full spectrum of traditional academic subjects that the school offers. The practical and artistic are essential in achieving a preparation for life in the 'real' world.[12]

In other words, Waldorf education aims to 'educate the whole child, integrating rigorous academics with emotional and spiritual growth and physical skills' (Cape Ann Waldorf School, 1999, p. 1; cited in Stehlik, 2008, p. 232). Here is a Waldorf school's curriculum description:

> Waldorf Education recognizes and honors the full range of human potentialities. It addresses the whole child by striving to awaken and ennoble all the latent capacities. The children learn to read, write, and do math; they study history, geography, and the sciences. In addition, all children learn to sing, play a musical instrument, draw, paint, model clay, carve and work with wood, speak clearly and act in a play, think independently, and work harmoniously and respectfully with others. The development of these various capacities is interrelated. For example, both boys and girls learn to knit in grade one. Acquiring this basic and enjoyable human skill helps them develop a manual dexterity, which after puberty will be transformed into an ability to think clearly and to 'knit' their thoughts into a coherent whole.
>
> (Cape Ann Waldorf School, 1999)

Clearly, the curriculum of Waldorf education is 'within the humanistic/holistic tradition' (Stehlik, 2008, p. 232). Its pedagogical approach is firmly rooted in anthroposophy, a term originated from the Greek, 'anthropos – human' and 'sophia – wisdom.' Training capital talent through schooling is to focus on the intellectual aspect of the human being while ignoring their well-being and all-round development. This materialistic focus in education has dominated the mainstream of education in the West as well as in contemporary China. Waldorf education, in contrast, aims to educate the whole child, fostering humanity and humane talent.

Both Miłosz's call for the restoration of 'the anthropocentric vision of the universe', and the anthroposophical approach in Waldorf education, emphasize the central position of human beings in the universe. In Greek tradition the world of nature and the divine world were a single unity where man was of central importance. Anthroposophy cares about the spiritual development of the individual and human society. In the Neo-Confucian metaphysical system, human beings, *tian* (heaven), and *di* 地 (earth), were regarded as one body. Reflected in the Neo-Confucian vision of person-making, as discussed in the beginning of this chapter, it requires a person to 'put his moral nature into practice and bring his physical existence into complete fulfillment' in order to match Heaven and Earth. In English humanist terms this is to foster 'the decent man' through liberal education. Regardless of its different traditions these ideas point to a common approach to humanity. And the pluralistic nature of this common approach allows us to bridge the gap between past and present, and renew the essences of various traditions for education at a global age.

The International Forum on New Education in Ningbo claims that education is 'essentially a conscious culture transmission' (Yang, Chai and Huang 2014, p. 249). This is so true, but a common humanity must emphasize plurality in the transmission of cultural traditions. This can be exemplified in the concept and practice of Waldorf education. It was first established in a Western country with Christian culture as its foundation, but it draws from all traditions which are infused throughout the curriculum, and thus represent a broader understanding of education and its relationship with cultures and cultural values. The growing popularity of Waldorf schools in the world, including in China, has proven that its nurture for pluralistic-cultural values allows its adaption to different cultural settings.

Within a more specific Chinese context, a common humanity should be understood as what Pan Guangdan referred to as the virtue *shu* 恕 or tolerance, and from *shu* to reach the unity of human dignity, which is a new dimension of *zhong* 忠 or loyalty. This new dimension of the traditional Chinese values in education should not be interpreted as a simplistic revival of Confucianism. Instead, it is a proposal about what an educated person should be; namely, an educated person should be able to traverse spiritual and material boundaries, cross cultural boundaries and embrace different scholarly traditions with a broader knowledge and universal outlook, as well as with professional skill.

In conclusion, the notion of 'educating the whole child/person' is a philosophical principle, which should be used to guide educational theory and practice in a global context. The current 'New Education' (with its innovative curricula) advocated by educators in China, as well as the Waldorf schools across the world, are both illustrative and inspiring. It demonstrates the awareness of the ideal of a new modern education: to foster a young generation equipped with both a humanistic spirit and scientific knowledge. For this ideal, we need to continuously search for a well-rounded curriculum with a new balance between *arête* and *paideia*. This is the mission of every educator in this world.

Notes

1 For a discussion of *The Great Learning* and its interpretation before Zhu Xi, see Gardner 1986, pp. 17–26.
2 Zhang Zai, 'Western Inscription' as cited in de Bary (1966, p. 497).
3 For a study of Zhu Xi's natural philosophy, see Kim (2000).
4 There are various translations of the term *tianxue*. Willard Peterson translates it as 'learning from heaven' (see Peterson, 1998). But Dr. Paul Rule thinks the term should be translated as 'heavenly learning', since 'heaven' in the term is the object but not the source of study (see Paul Rule's unpublished manuscript on Chinese Rites, chapter 4). I am grateful to Dr. Paul Rule for providing me with his argument and this information.
5 For the influence of American Protestant educators and their school curriculum on China's educational reforms from the late Qing to the 1930s, see Buck (1980).
6 'On their own terms' is a point borrowed from Benjamin Elman's expression in his work (2005) to describe how the content of liberal education was transmitted and built into the curriculum of a modern Chinese school system.
7 For a detailed discussion of this Chinese mentality, see Cohen (2002, pp. 1–39).
8 For a discussion of the intellectual milieu during this period, see Sachsenmaier (2007, pp. 109–31).
9 For a discussion of the traditional Chinese concept *shi*, see Bol (1992, pp. 15–16, 32–75); for a brief discussion of the similarities and differences between the Chinese *shi* and the English gentry, see Bai (2005, pp. 226–227).
10 S. Heaney (2011), Seamus Heaney on Czesław Miłosz's centenary. Available online at: http://guardian.co.uk/books/2011/apr/07/seamus-heaney-czeslaw-milosz-centenary (accessed 23 August 2013).
11 The Waldorf Schools are alternative teaching establishments which operate on the educational beliefs of the Austrian philosopher Rudolf Steiner (1861-1925). The first Waldorf School opened in 1919 in Germany and there are now over one thousand Waldorf schools in the world. The emergence and development of the Waldorf schools in China provides an alternative to the highly disciplined mainstream approach to education
12 Why Waldorf Works. Available online at: http://whywaldorfworks.org/02_W_Education/faq_about.asp (accessed 20 August 2014).

References

Aloni, N. (2003). *Enhancing Humanity: The Philosophical Foundations of Humanistic Education*. Dordrecht, The Netherlands: Springer.
Bai, L. M. (1995). Mathematical Study and Intellectual Transition in the Early and Mid-Qing. *Late Imperial China*, 16(2), 36–73.
Bai, L. M. (2005). *Shaping the Ideal Child: Children and Their Primers in Late Imperial China*. Hong Kong, China: The Chinese University Press.
Bai, L. M. (2008). Children as the Youthful Hope of an Old Empire: Race, Nationalism, and Elementary Education in China, 1895–1915. *Journal of the History of Childhood and Youth*, 1(2), 210–31.

Bai, L. M. (2010). Human Capital or Humane Talent? Rethinking the Nature of Education in China from a Comparative Historical Perspective. *Frontiers of Education in China*, 5(1), 104–29.

Bol, P. K. (1992). *'The Culture of Ours': Intellectual Transitions in T'ang and Sung China*. Stanford, CA: Stanford University Press.

Buck, P. (1980). *American Science and Modern China, 1876–1936*. Cambridge, MA: Cambridge University Press.

Cape Ann Waldorf School (1999). *Frequently Asked Questions About Waldorf education*. Available online at: http://capeannwaldorf.org/about/faq (accessed 20 August 2014).

Catalogue of Hangchow High School (1894). Shanghai, China: American Presbyterian Mission Press.

Chan, W. T. (trans.) (1967). *Reflections on things at hand: The neo-Confucian anthology*. New York, NY: Columbia University Press.

Cheng, C. Y. (1979). Practical Learning in Yen Yuan, Chu His and Wang Yang-ming. In W. T. de Bary and I. Bloom (eds), *Principal and Practicality: Essays in Neo-Confucianism and Practical Learning* (pp. 37–67). New York, NY: Colombia University Press.

Cohen, P. (2002). Remembering and Forgetting: National Humiliation in Twentieth-Century China. *Twentieth-Century China*, 27(2), pp. 1–39.

de Bary, W. T. (ed.) (1966). *Sources of Chinese Tradition*. New York, NY: Columbia University Press.

Elman, B. A. (2005). *On their own terms: Science in China, 1550–1900*. Cambridge, MA: Harvard University Press.

Elman, B. A. (2006). *A Cultural History of Modern Science in China*. Cambridge, MA: Harvard University Press.

Elman, B. A. (2007). Collecting and Classifying: Ming Dynasty Compendia and Encyclopedias (leishu). *Extrême-Orient, Extrême-Occident*, 1, 131–57.

Elman, B. A. (2010). The Investigation of Things (gewu 格物), Natural Studies (gezhixue 格致学), and evidential studies (kaozhengxue 考证学) in Late Imperial China, 1600–1800. In H. U. Vogel and G. Dux (eds), *Concepts of Nature: A Chinese-European Cross-Cultural Perspective* (pp. 368–99). Leiden, The Netherlands: Brill.

Gardner, D. K. (1986). *Chu Hsi and the Ta-hsueh, Neo-Confucian Reflection on the Confucian Canon*. Cambridge, MA: Council on East Asian Studies, Harvard University.

Gardner, D. K. (trans.) (1990). *Learning to be a Sage: Selections from the Conversations of Master Chu. Arranged topically*. Berkeley, CA: University of California Press.

Gardner, D. K. (2007). *The Four Books: The Basic Teachings of the Later Confucian Tradition*. Indianapolis, IN: Hackett Publishing.

Haven, C. L. (ed.) (2006). *Czesław Miłosz: Conversations*. Jackson, MS: University Press of Mississippi.

Hayhoe, R. (1996). *China's Universities, 1895–1995: A Century of Cultural Conflict*. New York, NY: Garland Publishing.

Heaney, S. (2011), *Seamus Heaney on Czesław Miłosz's centenary*. Available online at: http://guardian.co.uk/books/2011/apr/07/seamus-heaney-czeslaw-milosz-centenary (accessed 23 August 2013).

Hsu, I. C. Y. (trans.) (1959). *Intellectual Trends in the Ch'ing Period*. Cambridge, MA: Harvard University Press.

Hyatt, I. T., Jr. (1976). *Our Ordered Lives Confess: Three Nineteenth-Century American Missionaries in East Shantung*. Cambridge, MA: Harvard University Press.

Kim, Y. S. (2000). *The Natural Philosophy of Chu Hsi (1130–1200)*. Philadelphia, PA: American Philosophical Society.

Kristeller, P. O. (1972). *Renaissance Concepts of Man, and Other Essays*. New York, NY: Harper & Row.

Liang, Q. C. (1920/1972). 清代学术概论 [*Intellectual Trends in the Qing Period*]. 台北, 中国: 启业书局 [Taipei, China: Qiye Press].

Liang, Q. C. (1936/2003). 欧游心影录 [Impressions of (my) Travels in Europe]. In 饮冰室合集 [*Collected Works and Essays from the Ice-Drinker's Studio*] (Vol. 7, pp. 1–162). 北京, 中国: 中华书局 [Beijing, China: Zhonghua Book Company].

Lin, X. Q. D. (2005). *Peking University: Chinese Scholarship and Intellectuals, 1898–1937*. Albany, NY: State University of New York Press.

Lutz, J. G. (1971). *China and the Christian Colleges, 1850–1950*. Ithaca, NY: Cornell University Press.

Mateer, C. W. (1890). How May Educational Work Be Made Most To Advance the Cause of Christianity in China? In *Records of the General Conference of the Protestant Missionaries of China, held at Shanghai, May 7–20, 1890* (pp. 456–67). Shanghai, China: American Presbyterian Mission Press.

Mulcahy, D. G. (2008). *The Educated Person: Toward a New Paradigm for Liberal Education*. Lanham, MD: Rowman & Littlefield Publishers.

Pan, N. G. and Pan, N. H. (1999). 潘光旦选集 [*Selected Works of Pan Guangdan*] (Vol. 3). 北京, 中国: 光明日报出版社 [Beijing, China: Guangming Daily Press].

Peterson, W. J. (1988). Why Did They Become Christians? Yáng T'ing-yun, Li Chih-tsao and Hsu Kuang-ch'i. In C. E. Ronan and B. B. C. Oh (eds), *East Meets West: The Jesuits in China, 1582–1773* (pp. 129–52). Chicago, IL: Loyola University Press.

Peterson, W. J. (1998). Learning from Heaven: The Introduction of Christianity and Other Western Ideas into Late Imperial China. In D. Twitchett and F. W. Mote (eds), *The Cambridge History of China*, 8(2), 789–839. Cambridge, MA: Cambridge University Press.

Sachsenmaier, D. (2007). Chinese Debates on Modernization and the West after the Great War. In J. C. E. Gienow-Hecht (ed.), *Decentering America* (pp. 109–31). New York, NY: Berghahn Books.

Sebes, J. (1988). The Precursors of Ricci. In C. E. Ronan and B. B. C. Oh (eds), *East Meets West: The Jesuits in China, 1582–1773* (pp. 19–61). Chicago, IL: Loyola University Press.

Sela, O. (2011). Qian Daxin (1728–1804): *Knowledge, Identity, and Reception History in China, 1750–1930* (Unpublished doctoral dissertation). Princeton University, Princeton, NJ.

Stehlik, T. (2008). Thinking, Feeling, and Willing: How Waldorf Schools Provide a Creative Pedagogy That Nurtures and Develops Imagination. In T. Leonard and P. Willis (eds), *Pedagogies of the Imagination: Mythopoetic Curriculum in Educational Practice* (pp. 231–44). New York: Springer.

Wang, Q. E. (2001). *Inventing China Through History: The May Fourth Approach to Historiography*. Albany, NY: State University of New York Press.

Wang, Z. X. (2000). 基督教与中国近现代教育 [*Christianity and Education in Modern and Contemporary China*]. 武汉, 中国: 湖北教育出版社 [Wuhan, China: Hubei Education Publishing House].

Yang, D. P., Chai, C. Q. and Huang, S. L. (eds) (2013). *Chinese Research Perspectives on Educational Development.* Leiden: Brill.

Yang, D. P., Chai, C. Q. and Huang, S. L. (eds). (2014). *Chinese Research Perspectives on Educational Development.* Leiden: Brill.

Yuan, J. D. (1901). 富强斋丛书 *[Collected Works from the Prosperous and Strong Studio].* 上海, 中国: 小仓山房 [Shanghai, China: Xiaocang Shanfang].

Zhuang, Y. and Tan, L. (1913). 共和国教科书: 新地理 *[Republican Series: Chinese Geography]* (Vol. 6). 上海, 中国: 商务印书馆 [Shanghai, China: Commercial Press].

5 A vision for one's own life

Lessons from Hu Shi and Liang Shuming on education in China

Huajun Zhang

The problem: the crisis of Chinese education

With the top scores of the PISA test being achieved in Shanghai in recent years, Chinese basic education receives increasing attention and even admiration internationally. However, the debate on 'test-oriented education' (*yingshi jiaoyou* 应试教育) as opposed to 'quality education' (*suzhi jiaoyu* 素质教育) continues. In the past decade, 'super high schools' (*chaoji zhongxue* 超级中学) emerged in many provinces. Different from the traditional key schools, these 'super high schools' are often huge – more than ten thousand students – and are highly desired by students and parents for the high rates of entry into top universities. A common characteristic of the super high schools is that they execute a very strict and highly efficient time schedule on a day-by-day basis. The schooling at these schools is comparable to military training, as students have to count their time by the minute in order to follow the school's rigid schedule. These 'super high schools' are often located in areas where the competition to university entrance is very fierce. In these areas, population levels are high and income is relatively low. Though very popular and desired by students, parents and local governments, these 'super high schools' are often criticized by the public for their test-oriented training. Students and teachers in this type of school are often called test machines.

In contrast to the 'super high schools', there is another type of high school emerging in big cities like Beijing and Shanghai. These schools often promote developing students' individuality and thus have a very flexible and diverse curriculum to meet students' varying needs. Students in this type of school are often from high SES (socio-economic status) families and have good academic performance records before they enter high school. Most of the students have some expertise or special skills that their parents helped them to cultivate from a young age, such as the ability to play musical instruments or playing a sport at a professional level. Many of the students at this type of high school will not take the standardized college entrance exam and will go to universities abroad when they graduate from high school. These schools are often considered as the flags or pioneers for quality education.

Many people propose that the latter type of school will become the trend and future of China's basic education reform. However, I would suggest that these two types of schools are not so different but are actually similar in many ways. Both types of schools are tailored to moulding particular types of people. 'Super high schools' aim to mould students into people who can effectively score high test results. As for the quality education schools, they aim to produce students who can equip themselves for many diverse specialities. In this scenario, the ability to take tests effectively may be one aspect, but certainly not all.

In both types of schools some skills or specialities are emphasized and taken as the standard for students' academic performance. If we take education as a process of person-making, both types of schooling only make a particular type of student with some particular sets of skills. These types of schools exclude other possibilities for human development. In other words, this process of education is not creating individual and unique people, but creating set career paths for students to follow. I propose that this is the key problem of China's education system. We lose the vision of educating through cultivating the diverse individuality of students based on their 'vision for life'. In the current practice of education, the goal for education is fixed and highly homogeneous. The characteristics of flexibility, diversity and openness in education are largely ignored.

When education does not help a student to build his or her own vision for life, it is not surprising that instrumentalism permeates the process of education. No matter whether it is in test-oriented schools or the so-called quality education schools, students are the objects of educational practice. That is to say, the individual student is only the embodied instrument or tool to meet some particular goals, which may not be relevant to his or her personal interests. Some purposes and goals of education have been fixed in advance, and individual students only need to tailor themselves to meet these goals, which may be far from their 'visions for life'. The fixed goal can be an offer from a domestic or international prestigious university or an opportunity to start along a career-path they have long dreamed of. This kind of goal is not a problem in itself but may be problematic if it becomes the sole vision for education, and excludes other alternative paths. Students as immature individuals may be influenced by this fixed goal of education and will not be given the space or opportunity to imagine other possibilities for his or her life. In this process of education, students' diverse interests and unique characteristics are tailored into prescribed categories. Students develop their sense of self in the prescribed categories and often lose their individualism and 'vision for life' when they find they cannot fit into the prescribed categories, or are excluded from the categories for success.

In instrumentally-oriented education, students do not learn to cultivate their own desires but are encouraged to seek particular standards of success. On top of that, the sense of self is largely ignored in the experience of schooling. Without cultivating the diverse and creative individualities, education reform will reach a deadlock.

The structure of the chapter

What is the problem with instrumentally-oriented education and students not learning to cultivate their own aspirations through their education? Instrumentalism indicates that the individual takes others and the self as the tool or instrument to meet prescribed goals. This instrumental focus is so dominant that the individual often loses his or her 'vision for life', and instead follows a predetermined path.

To reflect on this situation of instrumentally-oriented education, I will first present a brief historical perspective on the view of the modern individual at the turn of the twentieth century, when China experienced a dramatic transformation and modernization throughout the entire country, including the education sector. Next, I will make a comparative analysis of Hu Shi (胡适) and Liang Shuming's (梁漱溟) idea on the self. Then, I will propose a concept of individuality that emphasizes the possibility of cultivating individuality as a never-ending process of self-transformation through inner experience. This chapter suggests that self-transformation through inner experience is the way for the individual to build their own 'vision for life' and thus build connections with others.

If we compare the educational systems during different periods of modern China over the twentieth century, it is becomes clear that the idea of self-cultivation is embedded in the Confucian tradition as well as the Daoist and Baddish tradition, but that this is lost in the process of modern China's education transition (Tu, 1999). Self-cultivation has not been a part of the education process, as education has become an external tool for testing and regurgitating authorized knowledge rather than for developing self-understanding and creating new knowledge.

A brief examination of China's modern history reveals that either the society dominates the self (for example, in Mao's time) or the self turns exclusive and hostile to others (for example, in today's highly competitive and market-ized society) (Zhang, 2013). As I explore this issue in the history of China's modern transition, I find that a dichotomy between 'the small self' and 'the big self' (*xiaowo dawo* 小我大我) has existed in each distinctive period of China's modern history and may relate to the negligence of self-cultivation and thus education's failure to meet the subjectification in China's continuing modern transformation.

In order to do this, I define subjectification by applying the theory of educational theorist Gert Biesta (2012) on three functions of education: *social-ization*, *qualification* and *subjectification*. Biesta argues that becoming qualified is mostly about the acquisition of knowledge and skills. Socialization mainly refers to the individual merging into society and becoming part of existing traditions and practices. Subjectification refers to the formation of a person's 'qualities' as individual in the process of education.

In this chapter, I argue that instrumentally-oriented education in today's practice is related to the dichotomy between 'the small self' and 'the big self' in the different periods of China's modern transformation. The loss of focus on self-transformation makes the connection between 'the small self' and 'the big self' impossible, or only superficially possible. The 'vision for life' thus becomes difficult without the sense of self-transformation, a concept I will explain in the following section.

This failure to achieve subjectification has in turn led to an instrumentalist approach that has prevailed in educational theories and practices throughout the country. Therefore, it is the purpose of this chapter to explore a new understanding of individuality that will move beyond the dichotomy between 'the small self' and 'the big self'. I suggest that learning to cultivate the self, and realizing self-transformation as the practice of subjectification, may help the individual to develop one's own mind, and thus to deconstruct the mechanical instrumentalist mode of thinking.

The comparison of the concepts of individuality outlined by Hu Shi and Liang Shuming was not pursued by accident. Hu Shi (1891–1962), a disciple of John Dewey at Columbia University, returned to China in 1917 after finishing his PhD in philosophy, took a teaching position at Beijing University and became an enthusiastic contributor and later chief editor of the journal *New Youth* (新青年). Supported by this journal, which was the most influential journal among young people during that period, Hu gained fame and influence among the youth as he became a leading figure during the May Fourth Movement. His view on individuality promoted the acceptance of the dichotomy between 'the small self' and 'the big self'. His views established the model for the ideal modern Chinese citizen: 'the small self' is important but not ideal, and 'the small self' should be prepared to serve 'the big self', also known as society.

Liang Shuming (1893–1988), on the other hand, was considered to be conservative and his theories are often criticized as being influenced by old culture, which had long been regarded as dead and irrelevant in the eyes of radical liberals and the progressive youth of the time. However, Liang's view on individuality was embedded in his thinking on China's modern transformation and reflected a different understanding of being a modern person in modern China. Although he considered himself a lifelong Buddhist, Liang was also called 'the last Confucian' by his American biographer Guy Alitto (1986) as his academic contribution was his re-interpretation of Confucian thought in the context of modern China. In particular, his concept of '*lixing*' (ethical rationality, 理性) is a creative re-interpretation of Confucianism and provides a critical resource for developing a new individuality that transcends the dichotomy between the 'small self' and 'big self'.[1]

The intention of this comparative study of Hu Shi and Liang Shuming is not to praise one and dismiss the other, nor is it a critique of Hu's or Liang's thoughts. There is no doubt that both Hu Shi and Liang Shuming are significant figures in China's modern history. The comparison of Hu and Liang focuses solely on their views of individuality and not on their overall philosophical ideas. The purpose of the comparison is to understand the dichotomy between 'the small self' and 'the big self', its limitations, and the means of overcoming it and developing a new view on individuality. The development of this new concept of individuality is intended to contribute to a revival of the tradition of self-cultivation through, and in, education.

The dichotomy of the small self and the big self: a historical perspective

As Tu Wei-ming (1985) suggested, the self in Confucianism has been an open and ongoing entity. Unlike the closed and unchangeable nature of the ego (*si* 私), the self has the potential for endless transformation towards perfection. It may embrace the family, the state, nature and even the cosmos as part of this self. Tu's explanation of the self suggests the potential of individual growth by means of breaking the closed system of the ego, and embracing an open system that allows for an ongoing process of self-cultivation and for a broader vision of the self.

Unfortunately, the significance of self-cultivation has been criticized, misinterpreted and seriously undermined in the history of China's modernization. When Confucianism became the target of critics of China's backwardness, a dichotomy between 'the small self' and 'the big self' replaced the rich tradition of self-cultivation of Confucianism and dominated public discourse. In contrast to the ongoing process of self-cultivation as described above, the dichotomy between 'the small self' and 'the big self' separates the individual and society by labelling 'the small self' as the individual, and 'the big self' as the nation or society. In this dichotomy, 'the small self,' or the 'I', is associated with the closed system of the ego and thus requires change in order to benefit the nation or society –that is, 'the big self'. 'The small self' and 'the big self' thus become two separate domains, and the individual loses the possibility of self-transformation towards a broader vision of the self. The individual as a 'small self' is the subject of change for the benefit of society, 'the big self'. A boundary is firmly established between 'the small self' and 'the big self', between the individual and society. In this dichotomy, the self becomes a closed and exclusive entity, and society easily dominates the individual. The potential for the individual to cultivate the self and to foster a broader vision of the self is suppressed. Here, the instrumentally-oriented approach is embedded in 'the small self' (the individual) as the tool for 'the big self' (nation or society) (Xu, 2009).

Liang Qichao (梁启超, see Bai, Chapter 4; Zhao, Chapter 2) is the first scholar in modern Chinese history to propose the dichotomy between 'the small self' and 'the big self'. In his article 'The Origin of China's Backwardness', written in 1980, Liang wrote 'There is a difference between the small self and the big self. The so-called "big self" is the self in groups; the so-called "small self" is the self in the individual body' (Xu, 2009). Liang interprets the concept of 'the small self' and 'the big self' in the framework of the relationship between the individual and the state in the context of the national crisis at the turn of the twentieth century. Drawing on the theory of evolution, Liang contrasts the mortality of 'the small self' with the immortality of 'the big self'. Therefore in this situation 'the big self', represented as the state or society, was favoured, and 'the small self' was equated with the ego and became the target of change for the sake of the society or the state (Xu, 2009).

Liang Qichao's concept of the dichotomy of the small self and the big self became popular in May Fourth liberal intellectuals' discourse, especially Hu Shi. During the years before and after the May Fourth Movement (1915–1922)[2] Confucianism was blamed for the country's backwardness and weakness. It was also during this time that the value of self-cultivation favoured by Confucian scholars was rejected. Instead, Western individualism was advocated and as a result the individual in the name of 'the small self' was praised.

Therefore, the result of radical Westernization in terms of modernization during that period was the rejection of Confucian self-cultivation on one hand, and the promotion of Western individualism on the other. The result of this being that the independence and autonomy of the self in the Western view of individualism was advocated but the ethical responsibility of the individual and others was ignored. In the Western cultural tradition of individualism, the ethical responsibility of the individual to others was largely realized through religious belief: the individual as the servant of God. However, Chinese society did not have the same religious tradition. Instead, the ethical relationship between the individual and others was realized through the practice of self-cultivation, and the broadening of one's ethical relationship to others through self-cultivation. In Confucian tradition, an ideal man is one who realizes self-cultivation (*xiushen* 修身) and is thus able to regulate the family (*qijia* 齐家), govern the state (*zhiguo* 治国) and bring peace to the country (*ping tianxia* 平天下) (Tu, 1985).

In the process of the radical Westernization that took place during the May Fourth Movement, liberal intellectuals advocating Western culture only embraced part of the ideal of individualism, and ignored the ethical relations between the individual and others (through God). At the same time, they also rejected the Confucian tradition of self-transformation with regards to others (from self-cultivation to bringing harmony to the universe). Without the desire of the self to build connections with others – either through God or through self-cultivation – the individual easily becomes an instrument for external purposes. In the context of the national crisis the aforementioned historical period, 'the small self' (the individual) becomes the tool for 'the big self' (society or state). Although some intellectuals such as Liang Shuming questioned this idea of 'the small self' being educated for the betterment of 'the big self', it was largely accepted at the time and had a strong impact on the minds of young people (Xu, 2009).

In a historical study titled 'Panxiao Discussion' (潘晓讨论) which happened in the 1980s, He Zhaotian (2010) argued that this continuous acceptance of the dichotomy between the small self and the big self later led to the spread of an exclusive and competitive self in the marketization of society from the 1990s up to the present day. Without an expanding vision of the self-transformation with regards to others, the individual is easily influenced by the logic of marketization, the exclusive logic of competition for one's own success.

In other words, the individual does not have the power to develop his or her own mind and instead is only able to follow social trends for success. Without one's own 'vision for life', it is not surprising that the instrumentalist mode of thinking, which focuses on the external purposes of life, is prominent in education and in social life.

I have outlined the history of the debate on the dichotomy between 'the small self' and 'the big self'. To propose a new concept of individuality that goes beyond the dichotomy of the small self and the big self, I now turn to a comparative analysis of Hu Shi's and Liang Shuming's views of individuality and review their respective conceptions on individuality.

Hu Shi's view on individuality: the small self *for* the big self

Hu Shi's description of the 'small self and big self'

As a leading figure in the May Fourth movement, Hu Shi was a very influential intellectual, both through his actions and his words. In the article 'On Ipsenism' Hu considers the ideal concept of 'the small self' as an Ipsen ego. In Hu Shi's view, the small self is not necessarily 'bad'. Instead, it is desirable, and it is necessary in order to develop 'the big self'. Hu quotes Ipsen: '*If you want to do good for the society, the best way to do so is to construct yourself into a well-functioning machine first. . . . if you encounter a shipwreck, you should save yourself first*' (Hu, 2006, p. 5).[3] This passage explains Hu's concept of individuality, he suggests that full development of individual potential is the primary condition of a well-functioning society. However, his affirmation of individual development is impeded by the immediate purpose of serving the social good. It is interesting but not surprising that he used the metaphor of 'a well-functioning machine' to indicate the concept of the self. This metaphor emphasizes the individual only in a functionary capacity. The inner value of individual development, which may not turn out to be any particular clear functionary use, was ignored in Hu's concept of individuality. He does not comment on how the individual addresses the conflicting interests of the individual and society. In addition, he makes the hasty conclusion that every well-functioning individual will automatically contribute to a progressive and advanced society.

Hu further describes his notion of 'the big self' in the article 'On Immortality'. He argues that 'the small self' is mortal but 'the big self' – society – is immortal: 'All kinds of small selves in the past, present and future combine together into a big self. The small self will die but the big self is immortal. . . . the immortality of the big self determines that *the small self has to be responsible for the big self*' (Hu, 2006, p. 30–31).[4] In this passage, Hu Shi confirms his earlier view that 'the small self' should serve the good of 'the big self'. This direction of individual development towards the social good is a personal responsibility, and this responsibility legitimizes the existence of the small self.

However, we also clearly observe that the individuality referred to by Hu does not concern the inner experience of the individual but rather emphasizes the responsibility of the individual to society. The inner landscape of the individual mind is ignored as the mind is directed towards an external purpose: the social good.

Hu fails to realize that his view on the relationship between the individual and society will not necessarily lead to positive social development. Later on, he even adjusts the tone of the relationship between the individual and society to further emphasize social development as a priority. In the article 'On New Life of Non-Individualism,' Hu wrote: 'I do not agree with the view that to improve the society we need to improve the individual self first. . . . Instead, we need to improve the system, habits, thoughts and education. . . . By improving society, we improve the individual as a consequence' (Hu, 2006, p. 243). Being fearful that the emphasis on individual development would lead to a selfish society, Hu departed from his earlier individualist position and emphasized the necessity of social progress as the foundation of individual development.

Problems with Hu's conception of individuality

As indicated in the above discussion, Hu did not hold a constant view of individuality. He highlighted the significance of an independent self to distinguish himself from the traditional view of the self, embedded in various relationships. However, his Ipsenist self was, to some extent, a dynamic one. He suggested that scientific critical questioning was a means of constructing this independent and small self (Hu, 2006). Ipsen did not only influence his views, but Hu also claimed that his thoughts were largely influenced by Thomas Henry Huxley (1825–1895) and John Dewey (1859–1952). Huxley's motto 'Give me evidence!' was very well received in the minds of the liberal leaders of the May Fourth Movement, and Dewey was Hu's teacher who much respected and proposed the use of the scientific method for the development of intelligence as an approach to constructing a democratic community. However, although Hu claimed to be a faithful disciple of Dewey and it appeared that Hu's concept of the self echoed Dewey's elaboration of the self and society in his philosophy of experience (Dewey, 1916/1944), Hu's understanding of the self lacked a sense of the inner resources that Dewey valued in terms of religious attitudes or aesthetic experience (Dewey, 1960, 2005). As a result, Hu fails to develop any insight into the inner landscape of the individual and thus constructs a boundary between the small self and the big self without the resources to bridge the two, while only emphasizing social responsibility. However, where does this social responsibility come from? Can we have a sense of social responsibility by following the speech of our leaders?

Given this absence of concern for the inner resources of the self, it is not surprising to find an inconsistency in Hu's views on the relationship between the individual and society. He could not construct a continuous connection between 'the small self' and 'the big self'. Due to the lack of this connection, either the small self would withdraw from society, an approach that Hu despised, or the small self would be regarded only as a subject responsible to serve the good of society, an approach that Hu embraced. Hu believed that the scientific method could play that role of connecting 'the small self' to 'the big self,' guiding the individual to become a responsible citizen serving the social good. Tan (2004) noted that Hu exaggerated the importance of the scientific method in his interpretation of Dewey's thought. Moreover, his application of the scientific method did not embrace the faith in the individual's inner strength, which was a part of Dewey's philosophy (Dewey, 1991).

The historian Yu Yingshi (1995) commented that a trend of the May Fourth intellectual leaders was the combination of politics with the life of the individual. That is, the understanding of individuality was highly motivated by the political purpose of educating 'new people' who could make a contribution to strengthening the nation-state. This comment may also apply to Hu's changing attitudes on the relationship between the individual and society, demonstrated in the earlier paragraphs. These attitudes were in turn closely related to the changing political climate at the time. In such a heavily political context, the small self was sadly submerged in the public discourse for the social good. Yu (1995) lamented that the tradition of cultivating the inner strength of the self through daily experience, a tradition that had thrived since the Ming (1368–1644) and Qing (1644–1912) periods, was suspended in radical discourse around promoting science and democracy during the May Fourth Movement. Meanwhile, religious resources inherited in the Western discourse of science and democracy were almost completely ignored by such Chinese adherents as Hu Shi.

In sum, I suggest that Hu's negligence of the need to nurture the inner resources of the individual led to his inconsistent arguments regarding the relationship between 'the small self' and 'the big self.' He attempted to address this inconsistency by contrasting the two concepts and favouring the latter concept. He then proposed an anti-individualist approach. His deliberate abandonment of the Chinese tradition of cultivating the inner self through reflection on daily experience resulted in the lack of any connection between the self and society, and thereby lost the aspiration to transform towards a broader self. The separation between the self and society resulted in the individual being directed to focus solely on the external purposes of life. For the May Fourth Movement, this instrumentalist mode of thinking dominated the mentality of intellectuals. When the individual focuses only on external purposes, the self is easily lost.

Liang Shuming's view on individuality: inner self with *lixing*

As a contemporary of Hu Shi, Liang Shuming faced the same social conditions as Hu. Responding to the social crisis he lived through, Liang experienced a serious personal crisis in his early years. In contrast to his May Fourth rivals who had received a traditional Chinese education, Liang was a follower of Western utilitarianism and had studied Western theorists in his childhood, the consequence of his father's strong influence, Liang Ji (梁济, 1858–1918), who later committed suicide. Liang was soon disappointed in utilitarian theories and converted to Buddhism. Despite claiming himself to be a lifelong Buddhist, he regained his faith in Chinese society through a re-interpretation of Confucianism (Liang, 2000). Liang made efforts to integrate his thinking on personhood and national development into a consistent question that became his lifelong exploration.

A key concept I have identified in Liang's thought is the 'inner self'. In Chinese, Liang calls this concept '*shen xin da yuan*' (深心大愿) (Liang, 2012). The direct translation is 'a deep and big heart'. I use the term 'inner self' to refer to Liang's notion of *shen xin da yuan* because it reflects Liang's view on the self, a view that only when the individual embraces this 'deep and big heart' does he or she achieve the stable sense of self, the self not easily impacted and dominated by a changing environment. This sense of self is the inner resource for the individual to cope with his or her relationship to society and to develop an organic and evolving relationship with others. The self may then be developed into a broader vision that embraces others as part of the self. By reaching the inner self, Liang realized the integrity of his self in his dedication to intellectual and political life (Liang, 2012).

Liang's view on individuality: building continuous connection with others through the inner self

Liang criticized Hu Shi's theory on the 'small self for the big self' on several occasions. In the responses to the 'Li Chao Event' (李超事件),[5] Hu Shi and other May Fourth liberal intellectuals criticized the vices of the traditional family system that they believed prevented women's liberation (Liu, 1994). However, Liang Shuming adopted a different perspective and commented that cultivating the inner self is the best approach to supporting the independence of the individual (Liu, 1994). Liang also opposed Hu's idea of 'the immortality of the big self' (Hu, 2006), arguing that the idea of sacrificing the self in order to serve society was misleading for the individual, especially for youth, despite sounding like a noble and meaningful act. Liang argued that this attitude was irrelevant to the solution of real problems that many youth faced during the radically changing society of the time: vanity, uncertainty about the future, purposelessness, and a loss of significance in living. Amid this rapid social change, the attitude of committing the self to serving society was actually irrelevant to the individual's pursuit of the meaning of life. This pursuit of the meaning of life was an artificial goal created by the leaders of society, rather than a goal naturally evolving from the inner experience of the individual, originating in the desire of the heart (Liang, 1991).

Diverging from Hu Shi, Liang made the following claim:

> The meaning and value of life cannot be found. If you find one, it must
> be a fake one. 'Where is the meaning and value of life' is not a valid question
> because life itself has no meaning or value . . . A real and whole life does
> not need meaning or value . . . Leave behind your attitude of 'looking for.'
> . . . The so-called responsibility is only to yourself, not to anybody else or
> to the 'everlasting immortal big self'. My responsibility is only to the self,
> here and now.
>
> (Liang, 1991, p. 763–764)

However, Liang did not advocate attitudes of extreme individualism or nihilism.
Instead, he emphasized exploring the possibility of facing real needs from the
body and the heart rather than surrendering oneself to any external and artificial
goals before gaining a clear sense of self-identity. In this way, his words 'don't
look for' do not mean passively doing nothing and leaving the self to whatever
he or she is. He continued:

> Everybody has some energy in their body. Only when the energy can be
> released through activities, can life be vivid and happy as well as appropriate.
> In my opinion, everybody should follow their unique talent and then release
> the energy inside of their body . . . In all, find a way to make full use of
> their energy. This is the happiness of life; this is the meaning of life. Life,
> then, can be interesting.
>
> (Liang, 1991, p. 766)

In Liang's view, only when releasing energy from our body are we as individuals
able to gain power as active and independent agents to do what is necessary,
no matter the level of difficulty. We also gain moral insight to direct our actions.

Liang took this confidence in the energy inside of oneself as the foundation
of Confucian thought, making the following claim: 'In the Confucian view, *the
meaning of life lies in continuously and actively practicing the meaning or
significance of life (li, 理) which the individual realizes*' (Liang, 2011, p.119).[6]
This claim suggests Liang's faith in the individual as an active and independent
agent for solving life's problems. Life flourishes by practicing the meaning of
life developed by the individual, and not through systemic arrangements outside
of the individual's life. Furthermore, the meaning and significance of life (*li*)
lies in an ethical relationship between the self and others (Liang, 2011). This
li requires the individual to continuously make efforts to build meaningful connections with others. The effort of this involves the integration of understanding
and practice in the ongoing situations the individual is in.

As indicated in the discussion, Liang had discarded the dichotomy between
'the small self' and 'the big self' and considered that this distinction constructed
boundaries between the individual and others. Such a distinction thus prevents
the individual from making meaningful connections with others, and as a result
life becomes mechanical and rigid. Alternatively, Liang (2011) suggested that

the individual may gain power as an active and independent agent by releasing the energy within the self. The meaning of one's own life is thus connected with the life of others. Liang considered this process of releasing the energy within and connecting the self with others as the development of the inner self, or building a deep and big heart.

Inner self with 'Lixing'

It appears that this capacity of following one's unique talent and releasing one's energy as stored inside is mysterious. In Liang's (2011) view, although it is difficult to interpret, this condition of humanity is critical to understanding Confucianism as a potential approach for China's modern transformation. This notion of individual development may correct the misleading dichotomy wherein 'the small self' merges into 'the big self' and avoids leading the individual into a mechanical or instrumentalist way of life.

In Liang's earlier works, such as *Eastern and Western Cultures and Their Philosophies*, Liang (2000) used the concept of intuition to describe this capacity of the individual. Liang considered keen intuition to be 'humaneness' (*ren* 仁), as translated from a key Confucian term. This creative explanation of Confucianism is key to understanding Liang's thoughts. Liang suggests that intuition is an ability that all individuals originally possess, that is very profound by nature but that various social habits tend to diminish the strength of this intuition (Yan, 2004). Therefore, the individual must constantly cultivate the self to maintain his or her intuitive faculty. It is only at that point that the individual is able to follow his or her own needs, and to release the energy inside his or her body: to continuously and actively practice the significance or meaning of life as it is experienced without worrying about dogmas imposed by society. In this way, the individual is practicing 'goodness' or 'humaneness' in his or her own unique way, without constructing barriers to meaningful connections with others.

To use keen intuition and realize 'goodness', Liang suggests that we must avoid the deliberate calculation of gains and loss, and reach 'perseverance' (*gang* 刚), another Confucian term. In Confucianism, *gang* is an important aspect for self-cultivation. It implies the willingness to suffer difficulties and struggles following the decision to be fully engaged in an act, to gather the required passion, and finally to release energy from inside. *Gang* is the inner strength the individual builds up through difficulties and struggles. It is also an inner decision the individual must make as well to not fall into habits or existing conventions, but to focus on the present and be open to any new possibilities to create a new self and to escape the restrictions constructed by one's environment (Zhang, 2013).

In Liang's later works, he uses the conception of *lixing* (ethical rationality 理性) to replace the conception of intuition. However, during this time his key understanding of Confucianism and his basic belief in the individual as an active and independent agent did not change. The change in concepts used did not only reflect an ideological and political response to different social contexts

(Allito, 1986) but also indicated Liang's continuous engagement with Western thought, which had an important influence on China's modern transformation (An, 1997; Yan, 2004).

In a modern time deeply moulded by science and technology in various social aspects, including human thinking, the concept of intuition was relatively mysterious and vague. Furthermore, this concept suggested an anti-intellectual trend, one with which Liang did not want to be associated. Consequently, he used the concept of *lixing* to replace *zhijue* (intuition 直觉), a concept that appears contradictory with *zhijue*. The word '*li*' contains the meaning of intelligence (*lizhi* 理智) as well as ethical feeling (*lunli* 伦理) (Liang, 2011, p. 81). *Lixing* is the subtle use of the mind (*renxin zhi miaoyong* 人心之妙用) and suggests an intelligent method of thinking that does not rely solely on strict reasoning based on pre-defined principles. This approach counts on all types of human feelings as the foundation of ethical relationships between the self and others. In Liang's words, *lixing* includes 'seeking perfection of the self' and 'intensively communicating with affection to others' (*xiangshang zhixin qiang, xiangyu zhixin hou* 向上之心强, 相与之心厚) (Liang, 2012, p. 193). It includes personal feelings based on the individual's evolving understanding of relations with others and his or her effort to reach meaningful connections with others. Here, 'others' also includes with nature and the cosmos. Meanwhile, Liang suggests that although everybody possesses *lixing*, it is easy to lose this sense. Therefore, the individual must continuously cultivate the self to sharpen one's *lixing*, thereby cultivating the inner self.

Liang used the concept of *lixing* to oppose the dichotomy between knowledge and the mind, the dichotomy between object and subject, and the dichotomy between intelligence and feeling. Instead, *lixing* is a peaceful reality of feeling and intelligence, knowledge and action, self and others. It is the ethical practice of connecting the life of the self with others, and making it into a complete life.

An Yanming (1997) explained that Liang's later concept of *lixing* better meets the spirit of a modern man, and that the concept is Liang's creative re-interpretation of Confucianism:

> *Lixing* becomes the cornerstone of Chinese ethical society for two reasons. In the first place, *lixing* bestows a precious inner discipline and ethical consciousness and is therefore able to partially fulfil the task of religion to unite the entire nation. This is primarily due to the efforts of Confucius himself, who always encourages people to examine themselves, to ponder everything, dependent on their own minds, and to cultivate their own capabilities of differentiation . . . Confucius offers people no doctrine except the idea of self-reflection. He teaches people to believe in nothing but their own *lixing*.
>
> (p. 353)

In summary, Liang's concept of *lixing* contains the different aspects of intelligence (*lizhi*), ethical understanding (*lunli* 伦理) and affective feeling (*qinggan* 情感), but does not deviate from any aspect of these constituent concepts. *Lixing* is an effort to reach a harmonious understanding of the self as a whole person and to thus gain the inner strength to creatively build meaningful connections with others. It is a modern interpretation of Confucius' idea of 'humaneness'. Facing complicated and contradictory life situations, the individual remains an active and independent agent, creatively building connections with others.

Indeed, this status of *lixing* is not a static entity that one may gain once and never lose; it is a never-ending process that the individual is engaged in. It is the subtle use of the mind (*miaoyong* 妙用) that the individual employs as an active and independent agent while engaging in meaningful connections with the world. Engaging the inner experience to reach *lixing* is a practice of self-cultivation in itself.

Self-transformation: caring for one's own vision for life

Through the discussion of Hu Shi's and Liang Shuming's idea on the relationship between the self and others, we can see that the difference between the two is critical. Hu suggests that the realization of 'the big self' is the ideal of self-realization and that 'the big self' needs to be responsible to the world other than the self. However, Liang opposed this idea of the self that turns to the responsibility to others. Instead, Liang suggests that the individual only needs to be responsible to the self. Being true to the calling of the self, the individual is able to build a connection with others and be responsible to others. Thus, Liang's ethical ideal on *lixing* is the ethics towards others. We realize the ethics towards others by releasing energy from inside our selves. Concerning ourselves with the sense of the self is the foundation of the moral inspiration of caring about others. Therefore, Liang suggests that the effort of the individual is not to take moral lessons and learn to be a moral person. Instead, the individual needs to focus on every minute of his or her life and experience the meaning of his or her ongoing daily life. Through his or her own experience, he or she learns to release the energy on his or her own, and learns to practice the meaning of life that he or she understands. As individual beings, we are always in this process of trying to build meaningful connections with others in creative ways. It is also the process of self-transformation in which the individual creates one's own 'vision for life'.

Responsibility is an ethical feeling that emerges in the above-mentioned process of self-transformation. When the individual creatively builds meaningful connection with others, the self and others are related so that the self gains the voice from inside to respond to the call from others. As Levinas suggested, rather than the ego and consciousness being central to our experiences, our primordial condition is that we live in a world among others and the world surrounding us affects us in a fundamental way (Zhao, 2015). Therefore, when Liang suggests the focus on the ongoing experience of the individual, and placing caring onto the experience, he has already considered a world which is not ego-centred, but a world where every individual connects with each other. This world is not strange or foreign to the individual, but can be intimate because of the meaningful connection of the individual with others that are built creatively in his or her life. For the individual, this world is open to the unknown others and the individual realizes ongoing self-transformation when his or her life is opened up to others. In Levinas's words, this pre-ego experience also means building equal relationships between the self and others (Zhao, 2015).

When the individual lives in the world among others, the individual has a natural need to build connections with others and to also respond to others' need to build these connections. This need for responding to others is a sense of responsibility. Therefore, responsibility is not a duty of the individual but a *need* of the individual. This is the difference between Hu Shi and Liang Shuming's view. Hu takes responsibility to others as one's duty to turn 'the small self' into 'the big self', but he does not explain where the duty of the responsibility to others comes from. Liang suggests that this responsibility is not a duty but instead is a need of the individual when the individual can release his or her energy from inside and develops his or her own 'vision for life'. This is the self-enlightenment (*zijue* 自觉) of the individual. Within the context of this self-enlightenment, self-realization and responsibility to others combine to form one concept, not two. The dichotomy between 'the small self' and 'the big self' also disappears.

Through the exploration of a concept of individuality, which is beyond the dichotomy between 'the small self' and 'the big self,' what I would like to highlight is that we must fully understand the limitation of the dichotomy between 'the small self' and 'the big self', which remains an influential concept in contemporary Chinese education. This dichotomy prevents the emergence of an active and independent individual as an agent in social life and thus leads to mechanical and instrumentalist approaches towards educational practice. The alternative conception of individuality that I propose here focuses on the possibilities of building meaningful connections with others by cultivating one's inner self: releasing one's unique talents and energy from within, and thus enlarging the sense of self through a never-ending process of self-cultivation.

Turning back to the problem on Chinese education addressed at the beginning of the chapter, China's contemporary education is deeply caught up in instrumentalism-oriented practices. This idea of instrumentalism produces abnormal forms of schooling such as the 'super high schools'. It also produces the elitist schools in big cities that gather the best social, economic and cultural resources available, all in the name of exploring the approach of 'quality education'. The deadlock of the so-called 'quality education' (*suzhi* education) will not be resolved if we do not cultivate a new concept of individuality which is deeply embedded in the Chinese cultural heritage and has origins mainly in Confucianism and Taoism, but is also open to Western discourse in the context of modernization and globalization. This chapter is an attempt to explore the idea of individuality, which emphasizes the significance of the inner experience of the self and self-transformation by building meaningful connection with others. According to Liang (2011), a democratic society is based on the meaningful connection of individuals who are able to share their affectionate feelings. This ideal urges us to practice a new understanding of individuality by emphasizing the passion to one's own 'vision for life' that is not only unique but also inclusive.

Notes

1 Ip (1991) translated *lixing* as ethical rationality.
2 I distinguish the May Fourth Movement from the May Fourth Incident, which occurred on 4 May 1919. With the May Fourth Movement, I am referring to the period from 1915 to 1922. Zhou Cezong (1960) has a detailed description on the distinguishing features of this time period.
3 The italic emphasis was by Ipsen and repeated by Hu Shi.
4 The italic emphasis was added by the author of this chapter.
5 'Li Chao Event': Li Chao was a female student at the Beijing National Female Normal School. Her family did not support her studies, and she died as a result of illness in August 1919 and her family did not care about her death. The attitude of her family aroused public anger, launching substantial debate on the liberation of Chinese women.
6 The italic was added by the author of this chapter to highlight the key discovery of Liang in Confucianism.

References

Alitto, G. (1986). *The Last Confucian: Liang Shuming and the Chinese Dilemma of Modernity*. Berkeley: University of California Press.

An, Y. (1997). Liang Shuming and Henri Bergson on Intuition: Cultural Context and the Evolution of Terms. *Philosophy East and West*, 47(3), 337–62.

Biesta, G. (2012). Philosophy of Education for the Public Good: Challenges and an Agenda. *Educational Philosophy and Theory*, 44(6), 581–93.

Dewey, J. (1916/1944). *Democracy and Education*. New York: The Free Press.

Dewey, J. (1960). *The Quest for Certainty: A Study of the Relation of Knowledge and Action*. New York: Capricorn.

Dewey, J. (1991). *A Common Faith*. New Haven, CT: Yale University Press.

Dewey, J. (2005). *Art as Experience*. New York: Perigee.

He, Z. (2010). 从'潘晓讨论'看当代中国大陆虚无主义的历史与与观念成因 [The Historical and Conceptual Origins of Nihilism in Contemporary Mainland China as Observed in the 'Pan Xiao Discussion']. 开放时代 *[Open Times]*, 7, 5–44.

Hu, S. (2006). 胡适论人生 *[Hu Shi on Life]*. 合肥：安徽教育出版社 [Hefei: Anhui Education Press].

Ip, H. (1991). Liang Shuming and the Idea of Democracy in Modern China. *Modern China*, 17(4), 469–508.

Liang, S. (1991). 梁漱溟全集第4卷 *[The Complete Work of Liang Shuming] Volume 4*. 济南：山东人民出版社 [Jinan: Shangdong People's Press].

Liang, S. (2000). 东西文化及其哲学 *[Eastern and Western Cultures and Their Philosophies]*. 北京：商务印书馆 [Beijing: Commercial Press].

Liang, S. (2011). 中国文化要义 *[Essence of Chinese Culture]*. 上海：上海人民出版社第2版 [Shanghai: Shanghai People Press, 2nd edn].

Liang, S. (2012). 精神陶炼要旨 [The Key Points of Self-Cultivation], in S. Liang (ed.), 教育与人生：梁漱溟教育文集 *[Education and Life: Collection of Liang Shuming's Essays on Education]*. 北京：当代中国出版社 [Beijing: Contemporary China Press].

Liu, C. (1994). 五.四思想家关于人的解放道路的思考 – 胡适、陈独秀、梁漱溟论李超事件的比较分析 [May Fourth Thinkers' Views on the Approach for Individual Liberation: A Comparative Study of Hu Shi, Chen Duxiu and Liang Shuming on 'Lichao Event']. 安徽史学 *[Anhui Historiography]*. 2, 50–3.

Tan, S. (2004). China's Pragmatist Experiment in Democracy: Hu Shih's Pragmatism and Dewey's Influence in China. *Metaphilosophy*, 35 (1/2), 44–64.

Tu, W. (1985). *Confucian Thought: Selfhood as Creative Transformation*. Albany, NY: State University of New York Press.

Tu, W. (1999). *Humanity and Self-cultivation: Essays in Confucian Thought*. Boston, MA: Cheng & Tsui.

Xu, J. (2009). 大我的消解 – 现代中国个人主义思潮的变迁 [The Disappearance of Big Self: The Change of the Idea of Individualism in Modern China]. 中国社会科学辑刊 *[Chinese Social Sciences Quarterly]*, pp. 1–21.

Yan, B. (2004). 仁直觉生活态度：梁漱溟对孔子哲学的创造性诠释 [Humanity, Intuition and Life Attitude: Liang Shuming's Creative Interpretation to Confucius' Philosophy]. 东岳论丛 *[Dongyue Forum]*, 25(5), 86–90.

Yu, Y. (1995). 中国近代个人观的改变 [The Changing Views on Individuality in Modern China]. 中国文化与现代变迁 *[Chinese Culture and Modern Transformation]*. 台北：三民书局 [Taibei: Sanmin Books].

Zhang, H. (2013). *John Dewey, Liang Shuming and China's Education Reform: Cultivating Individuality*. Lanham, MD: Lexington Books.

Zhao, G. (2015). Transcendence, Freedom, and Ethics in Levinas' Subjectivity and Zhuangzi's Non-Being Self. *Philosophy East & West*, 65(1), 65–80.

Zhou, C. (1960). *The May Fourth Movement: Intellectual Revolution in Modern China*. Cambridge, MA: Harvard University Press.

Part II

Rediscovering China's cultural roots of education

6   Person-making through Confucian exegesis

Zongjie Wu

For over two thousand years, the Chinese pedagogy has been moulded by Confucian classics. Texts of antiquity occupied a central place in person-making as well as in transforming society. Today's historical past is differentiated from the present, reorganized into national heritage (整理國故) and locked into museums and archives for preservation and gaze. Classical text is offered for learners merely to acquire a qualification of 'cultural literacy' in Biesta's (2009) terms. 'The past is appreciated because it is over' (Lowenthal, 1985, p. 62). But for pre-modern Chinese scholars, the past is a past of word, a meaning reservoir that could continuously illuminate the present. Pedagogy opens it up to us for personal growth. It is believed that words from the remote antiquity as transmitted through verifiable texts were sacred and always active. Each Chinese character in the Classical scripture must be carefully examined for its vitality to the present. Jennings (1891), in his study of the Classic of Poetry, claims that

> there are many things in the book which are antiquated and out of date and fashion to the Chinese themselves; but the language, and the mode of thought, and many usages are substantially the same as those we see today.
>
> (p. 8)

For Confucian scholars, reading Classics is not only the privileged approach to humanistic education, but also has the possibility of transforming culture and people. Cultural regeneration depended on the reinterpretation of Confucian Classics.

Pedagogy is essentially a process of meaning-making. I argue that this is not only a question of synchrony inside a linguistic system, but also of diachrony, the tracing of meanings back to what was said in the past (Wu, 2013). I understand that today's Chinese pedagogic discourse has been profoundly reshaped by 'modern' conceptions of rationality – a form of thinking owing much to the European Enlightenment. By stating this, I was mainly referring to the mode of signification – the way of relating language to the source of meanings. Ferdinand de Saussure (1960) explains such a mode of signification as meaning that is determined by its synchronical relation to others. New knowledge is created in the mind by recombining the signs in a closed linguistic system. Such a way of using language has dominated the production of knowledge in education. Foucault (1972) provides a critique by naming it as 'discontinuous atemporal combination',

> Whether as a synchrony of positivities, or as an instantaneity of substitutions, time is avoided, and with it the possibility of a historical description disappears. Discourse is snatched from the law of development and established in a discontinuous atemporality. It is immobilized in fragments: precarious splinters of eternity.
>
> (p. 166)

In the 'synchrony of discursive formations' (Foucault, 1972), various objects of new knowledge obey the same rules of formation, the same way of thinking, the same order in which a discourse is identified, named, explained and elaborated into concepts for knowledge.

In pre-modern China, new knowledge was made only by referring to what was said in the past by sages, which hit at the very heart of the learners, and penetrated the brain into the body. At each moment of historical transformation, Confucian scholars would first examine the meanings in question by means of tracing their change back to the ancient source. Important documents compiled for the governance of the empire were mostly written with a temporal structure. Transmitting without creation (述而不作) or creation by transmitting had been the principle believed and respected by almost all Confucian scholars. Such a tradition is different from that of reading religious scripture, for instance, the Buddhist and Christian scriptures, which were mostly translated from the languages, lost at some historical point. In the perspective of cultural continuity, translation is merely an imagination, a reinvention of otherness, a losing of primordial roots for tracing and interpreting. Much of the exegesis, therefore, has been limited to the indoctrination of value and faith surrounding the religious ideas. This comes at the expense of an examination of deeper curricular issues rooted in language. Contrary to this, the exegesis of Confucian classics was primarily based upon the investigation of meaning transmission. The sense of sacredness is not derived from a divine wellspring, but the genealogy of Dao (道統), the unbroken tradition where meanings have been passed down from the ancient.

The chapter contains four main sections. Firstly, I will present the Confucian vision of person-making, the steps from the mind being aroused to the accomplishment of the freedom of virtue. I will then examine the criteria in the assessment of 'person' by looking at the traditional examination composition in the late-nineteenth century. The main focus of the chapter is on the texture of Confucian classics, which laid down the foundation of Confucian pedagogy. I will reveal, through detailed analysis of the scripture, the origin of meanings in its first instance as shown in the transmitted ancient text, and how the ancient meanings continuously flow over for thousands of years. Finally, I will address the primordial foundation of signification by exploring a Chinese concept of meaning – *wen* (文; texture, pattern, fabric), which was seen as the very genesis of meaning in the remote past. One of the major contributions I wish to make is to bring the concern with the notion of person-making into the interpretation of pedagogic text – the analysis of the mode of interpretation towards *junzi*. To me a language of person-making should be sought in scriptural exemplars by restoring the traditional mode of reading the Classics. I have no doubt that the same effort should be made in the West to rethink its tradition of exegesis, which was primordially rooted in the ancient tradition of Hebrew scriptural interpretation, and was uprooted when the scripture was translated from Hebrew to Greek, to Latin, to modern European languages, and eventually became a broken tradition in the modern rise of historical consciousness (Briggs, 2011; Frei, 1974; Gadamer, 1986).

Junzi as the vision for person-making

Recently there has been discussion about the reorientation of educational function that goes beyond the acquisition of knowledge and skills, and the socialization into particular norms and values (Biesta, 2009; Zhao, 2014; also see Zhao and Deng, Chapter 1). Apart from qualification and socialization, Biesta raises a more fundamental question in terms of subjectification: what kind of person or subject should be made for the way we approach knowledge and socialization. He argues that 'any education worthy of its name should always contribute to processes of subjectification that allow those being educated to become more autonomous and independent in their thinking and acting' (Biesta, 2009, p. 41).

But the problem of Biesta's point arises from the concept of autonomy and independence which only represents the value of a particular culture which cannot be applied to those who do not share this tradition. Perhaps we may not be able to find any term or statement that could universally specify what the child, or student must become. To be more precise, the question of person-making is beyond rational discussion. It is entirely rooted in the interpretation of persons situated in a particular cultural and historical context, and revealed in the discursive traces of a good person's mode of acting and speaking. For Confucius, to be a good person is to engage in the interpretation of these traces as recorded in the text. The curriculum text that helps Confucius to achieve this goal is 'Six Classics',[1] which recorded the traces of sages' and worthies' acting over the course of some two millennia before Christ. A diachronic approach to the exegesis of the text, accompanied by an examination of one's own personal experience, serves for making a *junzi* (君子 good person, man of real talent and virtue) in the admiration and imitation of ancient sages and worthies (聖賢). So the purpose of subjectification is articulated in the exemplars instead of prescription or indoctrination. The essential characteristics of Confucian pedagogy is, on the one hand, the great capacity of meaning-making buried in the texture of scripture, and on the other, the incessant modification of self by daily examination of one's behaviour against what has been interpreted from the text. In one of Confucius' disciples, Zengzi's words, 'I daily examine myself on three points: whether, in transacting business for others, I may have been not faithful; whether, in intercourse with friends, I may have been not sincere; whether I may have not practiced what is passed down' (*The Analects*, 1. 4). It is plausible to argue that Six Classics are not primarily provided for students to acquire intellectual cultivation, though they have had the function, but to offer meaning resource for interpreting self towards *junzi*, a Chinese indigenous term, embracing Confucian vision of a good person.

Throughout *The Analects*, *junzi* is one of the words most frequently mentioned, for all together 107 times. Confucius says 'A sage it is not mine to see; could I see a *junzi*, that would satisfy me.' But it seems that Confucius gives no consistent answer to the meaning of becoming *Junzi*. When his faithful disciple, Zilu asked about *junzi*, Confucius answered, 'The cultivation of himself in reverential carefulness.' Zilu was noted for his valour, sense of justice and good governance. He asked further 'And is this all?' 'He cultivates himself so as to give rest to others,' was the reply. 'And is this all?' again asked Zilu. The Master said, 'He cultivates himself so as to give rest to all the people. He cultivates himself so as to give rest to all the people – even Yao and Shun were still solicitous about this' (*The Analects*, 14.42). Here we see how Confucius elaborates upon the meanings, according to Zilu's personal weakness and his ideal of becoming a good statesman. Instead, when his disciple, Zigong, who was best known for his speech and diplomacy, asked about *junzi*, Confucius said, 'He acts before he speaks, and afterwards speaks according to his actions' (*The Analects*, 2.13). Sima Niu is described as 'talkative and restless' (多言而躁), being anxious for losing a brother. He asked Confucius about *junzi*, the Master said, '*Junzi* has neither anxiety nor fear.' Niu said, 'Being without anxiety or fear! Does this constitute what we call the superior man?' The Master said, 'When internal examination discovers nothing wrong, what is there to be anxious about, what is there to fear?' (*The Analects*, 12.4). From the three cases, we may get a sense of how Confucius approached the question of subjectification. He cultivated each student according to his unique context and personality, but without losing the direction both he and each student attempted to accomplish. It could be argued that the fundamental purpose of education is embodied in the teacher as a person instead of sets of rules and standards. To give teachers the autonomy to act as a person towards 'uniqueness' (Biesta, 2009, p. 41) and infinity (see Zhao, 2014) is perhaps the right way to bring fundamental purpose back into education. This kind of teacher would act in a amanner as described by a Confucious disciple below:

> Yan Yuan, in admiration of his Master, sighed and said, 'I looked up to them, and they seemed to become more high; I tried to penetrate them, and they seemed to become more firm; I looked at them before me, and suddenly they seemed to be behind. The Master, by orderly method,

skillfully leads men on. He enlarged my mind with learning, and taught me the restraints of propriety. When I wish to give over the study, I cannot do so, and having exerted all my ability, there seems something to stand right up before me; but though I wish to follow and lay hold of it, I really find no way to do so.'

(*The Analects*, 9.10)

Becoming a person is an interpretive process in nature either at the level of textual exegesis or daily cultivation towards *junzi*. Confucius identifies three aspects of pedagogy in terms of person-making. That is, poetry as language instruction, rites as the daily practice, and music as the accomplishment of freedom of virtue.

The Master said, 'It is by the Odes that the mind is aroused. It is by the Rules of Propriety that the character is established. It is from Music that the finish is received (興於詩，立於禮，成於樂).'

(*The Analects*, 8.8)

Reading Poetry is the interpretation of exemplars for making sense of the purpose of becoming a person. In the performance of rites, the body of self is interpreted according to the social propriety, and in music, a person learns to act spontaneously, joyfully and harmoniously with others without feelings of constraint, just like playing a piece of beautiful music in an orchestra. So an ancient scholar, Chen (1999) comments on the three aspects:

Learning [to become a person] begins from language, thus arising from the Poetry. Action is in the middle stage, thus established in [the performance of] rites. The end is virtue, therefore accomplished in music. (學始於言，故興於詩。中於行故立於禮。終於德故成於樂.)

This brings into view the 'lost sight of questions about values, purpose and the goodness of education' (Biesta, 2009, p. 36). I have elsewhere explored the function of rites and music in person-making education (Wu, 2014). This chapter will focus on the beginning of education – to provoke a vision (purpose) of goodness of education through interpreting classical scripture – the Book of Poetry.

Zhiyi – the assessment of person-making

Today's question about the nature of Chinese traditional pedagogy mostly centres on the Imperial Civil Examination (*keju*), a system of recruitment for civil officials based on their competence in making meanings out of the Confucian classics. Cheng (2011), referring to the examination, argues that millions of young people turned themselves into scholars who knew nothing but memorizing the classics by heart: 'There was little beyond the Civil Examination that could be counted as "education"' (p. 594). Elman (2000), a distinguished scholar who has devoted his scholarship to the study of the examination system, considers such accusations as *a priori* judgements tied to the European modernity discourse. He points out that they have successfully exposed the failure of the examinational/educational systems *only* against an ahistorical standard of knowledge specialization in science, a study 'deemed essential for nation-states to progress beyond their indigenous traditions' (pp. xxi–xxiii).

I am fully aware that, for more than 1000 years, there were periodic debates addressing the unintended consequence of the examination system. But my interest in the Civil Examination is not in the system but in the *language*, specifically the way of meaning-making implied in the interplay of interpretation, memorization and writing/speaking that gives students a form of pedagogic consciousness. The Civil Examination was officially and formerly named *zhiyi* (制義; to make meaning out of the classics). It was claimed that the purpose of person-making was primarily to establish a language instead of knowledge so that learners could speak/act in the place of the sages.[2] This linguistic perspective, hardly explored today, may offer an alternative way of thinking, an intellectual tool to reconstruct visions of person-making pedagogy that resonate with the Western and Eastern pasts.

China has accumulated the largest and longest-enduring of humankind's documentation of the past. Chinese literate elites constantly scrutinized that past as recorded in words, and caused it to function in the life of an ever-changing present (Ryckmans, 2008). This source of meanings came from several ancient Classics that were widely believed to be collected/compiled and handed down by Confucius. The Classics were generally acknowledged as the reservoir of meanings for all indigenous schools of Chinese thought, including Taoism. In the early-twentieth century, such a pre-modern tradition was detached from the classics, that is, from 'the ideology of its past and by revealing this past as ideological' and useless (Foucault, 1972, p. 5). The abolition of the examination system made a radical break and shift in the mode of signification, which suspended the continuous flow of meanings from the past to privilege a 'synchrony of discursive formations' (p. 184). As a result, Chinese pre-modern ways of knowing and thinking were perceived as unintelligible and/or backward.

What was the mode of signification operating in the interpretation of the Classics? Chinese literate elites developed a way of thinking about constructing new thoughts, which was merged with the various forms of commentary around a classical text. Innovative ideas were created and developed only by referring to classical texts and expressing them as a commentary.[3] Even those identified as the greatest thinkers in Chinese history, such as Zhu Xi (朱熹) in the Song Dynasty (960–1279 CE), Dong Zhongshu (董仲舒) in the Han Dynasty (206 BCE –220 CE) as well as Confucius himself, framed their cogitations in the form of commentaries on some of the most ancient texts, later canonized as the 'Six Classics'. It was believed that important thoughts emerged in interpretation, by signifying the meanings from the past rather than in the creative construct of 'the statements that precede and follow it' in a logical order inside a system (Foucault 1972, p. 31).

This style of knowledge production implicates a critical mode of signification, challenging a linguistic consciousness that is taken for granted. What is said is thus not only a question of synchrony with all the other signs inside a structure, but meanwhile of diachrony by registering meanings to what was said by sages. For candidates in the Imperial Examination, a well-made thesis must be planted with layers of meaning that could be empirically traced in the layers of classical and historical texts until the sensory contour of a living word reached the textual profoundness of the ancient. The flame of passion of how one should act was activated in the dialogue between existential self and ancient sages, referring to people, actions and things that had happened.

Such a mode of pedagogy was still pursued and was discernible even in the eight-legged essay[4] in the late-nineteenth century, just before the system was discontinued. I quote the official comment on the quality of Yu Biyun's (1868–1950 CE) examination exposition – ranked third at the highest Imperial Civil Examination in 1898:

> First, the essay was planted with meanings from the classics, just like a string of rosary beads, each character penetrated with Dao and every single word returning to the source of origin. Second, the author has an unyielding conviction in his mind; therefore, he is not hesitant in choosing the words. He writes at one go, just like the style of Yan's calligraphy, strong and abundant. Third, its articulation is pervasive and firm that it is able to penetrate one's heart. It could be noted as 'to establish the meanings of classics in an unshakable manner'. The wording and phrasing all originate in classics or their commentaries, resulting in an elegant style of writing.
>
> (Gu, 1992, p.244)

What is immediately striking about the evaluative comments is its stress on the textual manifestations of classical profundity, or simply the mastery of a language closest to the style of the classics. Here the emphasis is not on what idea has been formulated or retrieved from the classics, but on the linguistic competence required to plant rich meanings from the past into each word of the composition. Knowledge was primarily exegetical in character and expression, rather than something that can be created in a 'system of reason' (Popkewitz, 2008). The interplay of the commented and commenting built a bridge between the ancient and the now, to foster a deep sense of understanding, as Gadamer (1986) explains, 'They both flow together into one owned and shared world that encompasses past and present and that receives its linguistic articulation in the speaking of man with man' (p. 283). The commentarial form of knowledge construction is considered the most prestigious and critical, and is understood as a creative form of intellectual practice through which not only scholarship is approached, but also a *junzi* is cultivated (Henderson, 1991, p. 3). A literal sense of reading (listening to) the sages' words turns into conviction, hope and engagement of the writing self.

From the critical perspective, by dissolving the ancient sense of words into present articulation, the candidate's linguistic consciousness was called into close and minute re-examination. The language we are familiar with is disturbed by the same words but fused with layers of different meanings generated at different historical moments. To return to Yu Biyun's 800-character exposition: How does a single utterance pack in dense layers of interpretations and meanings against a context wherein China faced enormous domestic and international challenges by the end of the nineteenth century? Following the eight-legged composition structure, Yu Binyun starts the middle leg (main part) by quoting seven characters from Mengzi, one of the Confucian classics: 'Since the Zhou Court moved to the East' (自周室東遷而後), signifying a historical period (771 BCE) that Confucius feared for so greatly that he committed himself to edit *The Spring and Autumn Annals*, a classical book, in order to restore the ritual order of the society. In another classical book (*Book of Change*), the moment was interpreted by the divination of Hexagram Kui, 'Two daughters may live together, but their aspirations do not pursue the same path' (二女同居而其志不同), implicitly signifying the situation of 'Ti-Yong dichotomy' ('Chinese learning for fundamental principles and Western learning for practical application'), attempting to bring together Chinese and Western cultures into a whole (Wu, 2011, p. 581; also see Bai, Chapter 4; Zhao, Chapter 2). 'This is a bizarre movement with internal rebellion attacked by outside forces' (內叛外抗，動相乖戾) (Yang, 1999). The implanted insight derived from the hexagram appears exotic, charming, but unintelligible and 'superstitious' within the limitation of modern episteme. The Hexagram signifies ineffably the modern fate of China, which turned out to be unavoidable and irresistible.

After a word-by-word trace of Yu Biyun's textual origins in the corpus of Chinese classics, I found that there are also numerous commentaries on each character with cross-reference to other canonical texts. Each word was planted with such an abundance of ancient meanings that only those who had a good knowledge of the classics and a situated understanding of 'contemporary' China could comprehend the profound implication for the time. Here, not only historically different layers of meanings, but also different modes of thinking – history and divination – interpenetrate each other in a single utterance. It is understandable why the 800-character essay could be enough to give the Emperor a window to detect the candidate's inner talent and virtue that he could decide whether the examinee be endowed with the responsibility of the Imperial governance. Hence the commentary on Yu Biyun's exposition says,

> It scrutinizes the traces of governance in turbulence from the ancient to the present, whereby we see his aspiration to rescue the time. He commits his studies to the source of governance. The power of his writing is so strong and deep that the essay manifests itself only as the tip of an iceberg. He is indeed the rare talent for the country.

> (Gu, 1992, p. 244)

In Yu Biyun's essay no contemporary issue is mentioned, but readers can identify clearly how the text embraces a concern with the present. What the examination detected is not merely the candidate's master of knowledge, or the overall qualification of political and cultural literacy, but also the kind of person, his value, aspiration, determination, propriety of acting, all being manifested in his mastery of sages' language. It is difficult to think that a present short examination essay, constituted usually by only synchronically organized propositions and argument, could reveal a candidate's talents and character so profoundly.

Such a mode of enunciation is also reflected in the style of the examination question that Yu Biyun responded to. It was supposedly asked directly by the Emperor or on his behalf. However, its composition simply juxtaposed two passages from Confucius' *Analects* without any exploration, or even linking phrases. The question text runs as follows:

> The Master said, 'If in your affairs you abandon yourself to the pursuit of profit, you will arouse much resentment' (*The Analects*, 4.12). The Master said, 'If a person is able to govern the state by means of ritual propriety and deference, what difficulties will he encounter? If, on the other hand, a person is not able to govern the state through ritual propriety and deference, of what use are the rites to him?'
>
> (*The Analects*, 4.13, see also Slingerland, 2003)

If we consider that Yu Biyun's examination was situated in a social and political turmoil when China and its Confucian ritual-based society was about to collapse, and the Chinese people were shocked by the power of Western 'profits' (*li* 利), both the question and its response reveal this deep concern – a profound anxiety about China's future. It is surely not a mechanical repetition of the canonical text, retreating from the memory as many modern people envisage. The subtle rephrasing of classics is to make the past speak again in order to throw light on the present. The generic structure of the eight-legged essay engages candidates in a comparative epistemology by detecting the ancient meaning of sages to make sense of the critical moment that China was forced to pursue material strength and economic profits.

Liu Dahan (1698–1780 CE), a scholar of the Qing Dynasty, thinks of this way of speaking as a heart-to-heart dialogue between the candidates and the sages in a context that any 'contemporary' linguistic consciousness was put under scrutiny. He comments on the hidden level of interpretation, arguing that:

> this is not a composition by yourself, nor a simple commentary of your interpretation on the classics, rather you have to first of all clean up your mind to engage into deep meditation, and to make your heart conform to the sages and then speak out, which is naturally similar to the style of Classical language.
>
> (Huang, 2007, p. 105)

Zhuxi (1130–1200 CE), whose interpretations of the Classics were the orthodoxy dominating the Civil Examination, makes a similar point: 'You write as if you are talking with the ancients. During the interaction, no word is not mutually responding to each other' (see Huang, 2007, p. 107). Every act of writing/speaking keeps to itself in listening to the sages' words. Heidegger (1971) once said, 'Language speaks. Man speaks in that he responds to language. This responding is a hearing' (p. 210). I want to argue that, ideally, when candidates were writing within the eight-legged structure, they were pedagogically locked into the sages' linguistic consciousness in the discussion of contemporary issues so that 'the words are flowing out of Dao/Saying 註疏者，八股之先河 ' (Zhuxi, see Huang, 2007, p. 107).[5] Such a style of peda- gogic discourse served as the core of a Confucian education that received meanings from the past and affirmed its vitality for the present.

Elman (1997) sums up the essence of Chinese intellectual tradition by quoting an ancient slogan, 'I comment on the Six classics and the Six classics comment on me' (六經注我，我注六經) (p. 77). It is in the interpenetration of sages' words and mine, and the past and the now, that the literal sense of the scripture is transformed into a person speaking and acting with sages. According to Zhang Taiyan (1869–1936 CE) this reciprocal mode of commentarial thinking piloted the eight-legged essay as the examination discourse (注疏者，八股之先河) (see Huang, 2007).

Textual manifestation of interpretation towards *junzi*

To understand how meanings are creatively made out of the texture of Chinese Classics, we may ask: what kind of genre Confucian classics look like? Where is the source of inspiration which could continuously nourish personal growth and social transformation? What kind of mode of interpretation can provoke a vision that inspires readers to pursue goodness? I now demonstrate with a stanza of poetry extracted from a piece of a five stanza (four lines each) poem called 'Guan Ju' (關雎), which has been read in modern Chinese education for cultural dispositions, but in pre-modern age for person-making.

The poem is included in The Classic of Odes also translated as the Books of Poetry, or The Book of Odes. Sima Qian, the first historian living in between 145 BCE and 87 BCE, records: The old poems amounted to more than 3,000. Confucius removed those which were only repetitions of others, and selected those which could be servable for the inculcation of propriety and righteousness (Sima, 1959, p. 1936).

Confucius' interest in the Poetry is its function for person-making. By reading the poetry, he said to his disciples that 'In the home, they teach you about how to serve your father, and in public life they teach you about how to serve your lord.' (*The Analects*, 17.9; see Slingerland, 2003). It is obvious that learning Poetry is positioned far beyond the ordinary sense of literacy education. The poem analyzed here is placed in the first of The Book of Odes, being regarded as the most important text for transforming the moral behaviour of the society. It is classified under the title of 'Wind from the States', translated sometimes as lessons or manners of the states. It is said that the poems were collected from the people under the order of King Wen (1152 BCE–1056 BCE) so that he might examine from them the good or bad in the manner of people, and thus ascertain his own moral status of governance.

> Kwan kwan go the ospreys.
> On the islet in the river,
> The modest, retiring, virtuous, young lady:
> For our prince a good mate she.
> 關關雎鳩 在河之洲; 窈窕淑女 君子好逑。

(Legge, 1871: 1)

The stanza with four Chinese characters each line appears to be so simple and straightforward. Granet (1932, p. 27) reads the poem as a record of a rural festival involving boys and girls beginning to court each other. The opening image of birds calling to each other is taken by Granet as a metaphor for the young couples, hiding away to seduce each other in private. Such an interpretation is widely shared by many modern scholars who want to challenge the authority of Confucian value. If the poem is read as such, how could it conduce to propriety and righteousness? Why could such a poem make Confucius declare that 'now in its relation to human being, the Guan Ju above is like Heaven; below it is like Earth. Mysterious and dark is the virtue it hides (夫 《關雎》 之人, 仰則天, 俯則地, 幽幽冥冥, 德之所藏)'? We therefore need to examine the mode of signification, specifically, the way of interpreting poetic language. It is the language itself that really speaks in the poem. In Confucius' term, 'if you do not learn the Odes, you will be without words' (不學 《詩》, 無以言).

Confucius first founded the interpretive orientation, which guides later generations to make pedagogic meaning out of the scripture. He comments: 'The Guan Ju [fishhawks] is expressive of enjoyment without being licentious, and of grief without being hurtfully excessive (關雎樂而不淫, 哀而不傷) (*The Analects*, 8.8, trans. Legge).' After Confucius, three different schools of interpretation (i.e., the Qi, Lu and Han schools) had developed, all pointing to the virtue of wife, a purpose to regulate moral relation. By 150 BCE during Han Dynasty, the Mao school of Odes (毛詩) emerged and dominated the imperial academy. The mode of pedagogical meaning-making could be revealed as the layers of interpretations in the textural evidences of Mao Odes (see Figure 6.1).

In Mao's book, in addition to the poem that was printed in big font, layers of historical fragments generated at different epochs of time were recorded and woven together to secure the connection of ongoing interpretations. These fragments were mostly authentically recorded by editors of different generations by means of noting historical events, supplying the names and details of time and place to which it believes each word of the poem alludes. Generally, most of the inserted notes are traceable for its external historical texts of reference. The text shown in Figure 6.1 was organized in four strands: canonical text (*jing* 经) first selected by Confucius, *zhuan* (毛傳 Mao's commentaries) by Mao Heng in Han dynasty (206 BCE–220 CE), *jian* (箋 notes) noted by Zheng Xuan (127–200 CE), and *shu* (疏 further commentaries) noted and compiled by Kong Yingda in 642 CE. Apart from this, numerous books of commentaries had been produced for various political purposes till Confucian tradition of scholarships was completely disconnected in modern time.

Each strand of notes represents a particular interpretation, a 'contemporary' reaction to what had been interpreted before. Though the original lines mentioned neither virtue nor king or queen, in the Little Preface of the poem, Mao's commentary first established association of the poem with the virtue of queen, and its educational vision in terms of WIND:

> The Kwan ts'eu celebrates the virtue of the queen.
> This is the first of the Lessons of manners. By means of it the manners of all under heaven were intended to be formed, and the relation of husband

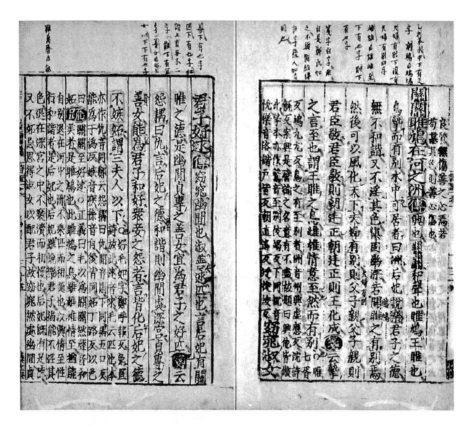

Figure 6.1 Pages extracted from *Maoshi Zhushu*

and wife to be regulated; and therefore it was used at meeting in village, and at the assemblies of princes.

(Legge, 1871, p. 36)

Education transforms the people just as the wind moves things. The Little Preface further explains that the educational power in the poem exhibits the wind (education) of King Zhou, whose royal land sat in the north surrounded by its Feudal States, showing that his pedagogic influence went from the north to the south. Therefore in the poem, we have joy in obtaining virtuous ladies to be mates to her lord. The poem exhibits the virtue of the chaste, modest and retiring young lady whose name is Taizi (太姒). We may now look at the interpretation of the textual detail itself.

The first two characters of the poem, *kwan kwan* (the cry of the birds), was defined by Mao to be 'the harmonious notes of the male and female answering each other'. Six hundred years later, Kong Yingda in his *shu* (see Figure 6.1), elaborated the meaning of 'harmonious' by saying,

> 'Harmonious' means peace and happiness in the heart, agreement and appropriateness in the will and intention. Such a mode [of harmony] prevails when doing anything. That is why it says that there is no place that is not harmonious.

Mao defined the second two characters 雎鳩 in the first line, 'a bird of prey' (王雎也) adding a commentary 'The birds love each other to the extreme, but keep at a distance from each other!' (鳥摯而有別); 'islet' (洲) is read as 'habitable ground, surrounded by water.' Kong Yinda further explains the kind of bird by quoting definitions from many sources, for instance, from Guo Pu in *Erya*, it is described as 'a kind of eagle, now, east of River Jiang called it e (鶚), preferring staying on islet of river, hunting fish'; from Lu Ji, the bird's size is described as big as a *chi* (鴟), with eyes deep set. Such a style of commentaries shows its treatment of meaning with great cautiousness and care. Zheng in his sub-commentary explains that Mao's word *zhi* 摯 (it has two connotations of either violence in hunting prey or extremely sincere) means *zhi* 至 (extremely, same pronunciation with 摯). This small difference in choosing a meaning indicates he discarded the 'violent "bird of prey" in favour of "a bird of most affectionate, and yet most undemonstrative of desire"' (Legge, 1871, p. 3). It thus enhances the interpretation of 'righteousness', which Confucius and his followers intended. Such a word-by-word denotation takes the form of incessant interrogation into the tiny and subtle meaning of each character, which modern people may simply take for granted. This tiny meaning could be understood as Heidegger's (1962) 'primordial signification',[6] grounded in transcendental awareness of Being in the world (p. 62). All the characters of the poem are still used as common words today in China, but detached from the tradition of exegesis, the characters have been gradually synchronized into a system of signs, no longer rooted in the soil of antiquity. The interrogation meanwhile pushes readers into a deep inquiry into the genesis of meanings when language emerged first as Way (dao 道). Thus meaning-making is oriented, first of all, towards the opening of transcendental awareness about the birds. In Heidegger (1971), now,

> [P]oetry is the saying of the unconcealedness of what is . . . It is the Open that pervades and guides them. But for this very reason they remain their own ways and modes in which truth orders itself into work.
>
> (p. 74).

Interpretation thus reveals thing as thing, world as world. In the primordial signification, moral consciousness arises by the way of being personally inspired on the path to self-cultivation. In Mao's commentary, what is opened as shown above, is read in the elaboration leading to its moral, ritual and educational cultivation:

> The virtue of the queen [is revealed] in her manner of having pleasure with her lord. She is in harmony in every aspect, without being excessive in sex. She remains resolutely retired in secluded [quarters], just as the ospreys maintain the proper distance from each other. In this way it was then possible to transform the empire. When husband and wife keep in proper distance, there will be love between father and son. The love leads to the respect between ruler and ministers, which eventually make the government behave in a correct way, and only then, the transformative power of the kingly virtue is accomplished.

Throughout Chinese history, Confucian literati often developed their political pursuits through reinterpreting the poetry. In the May Fourth Movement, awakened by Western literary criticism, many revolutionary scholars, like Hu Shi (胡適) and Gu Jiegang (顧頡剛), attempted to get rid of Confucian ideological domination. They questioned the authorship and credibility of Mao's commentary in order to shed the layer of moralistic interpretation in favour of the artistic expression of love and desire. Gu adopts the perspective of New Historiography (新史學) to claim that the Odes form the beginning of Chinese literature history, and should be read for their literary merits in a Western perspective. The accumulated interpretations over thousands of years are merely the layers of dust and rubble covering the people's poetry. He argues that, 'The correct interpretation of the poetry can only be obtained under the enlightenment of Maxims-Leninism' (Gu, see Yao, 1958, p. 4). The debates seem to mean that the variation in the mode of exegesis is not a matter for obtaining true meanings, but rather a shift in the mode of thinking which implicates a political agenda. Many scholars who sit in the area of modern literature criticism pursue a reading of aesthetic, stylistic or symbolic favour from the poem. They usually reject the traditional association to ethnics. For instance, Wang (1974) in his study of the Classics as oral poetry regards the traditional interpretation as a distortion both of its generic character and of the original definition of shih [poetry] in general. Indeed there are countless interpretations to the meaning of poem. Here the question is not which interpretation is correct or not, but which mode of interpretation is pursued, associated with different educational purposes. The traditional mode of interpretation reveals an essential principle of person-making, while the modern commitment to truth seeking is to reduce the interpretation to merely cultural literacy.

To sum up, from what has been shown in the Mao's school of commentary, three levels of interpretation could be notified. Firstly, the exegesis of each character which names and describes the bird (osprey, fish-hawk, mallard or another species of duck) and its manner (such as crying to each other, keeping in pairs but at a distance from each other) makes the 'primordial signification' by observing the traces of natural beings. This includes the 'observation' of sexual allure that is not contaminated by any value-laden interpretation, only at the *transparent* and *primordial* level of meaning (in Heidegger's term), '[M]ysterious and dark is the virtue it hides'. A slight variation in the reading of each character could mean a big difference in value formation. This level of meanings was primarily laid down in the remote time by sage kings or under their virtuous influence, which thereafter was handed down by Confucius. Secondly, a transition was made from transcendental signification to value-making through further interpretation. This transition is named by Mao as *xing* (興 stimulation, inspiration, incitement, allusive). In *xing*, the primordial meaning of bird, plant, water, islet is transformed into moral inspiration. Readers are aroused to pursuing virtue, laying down the possibility of person-making. At the third level, various exegetical schools associate the value with historic figures, affairs or political and educational pursuits in order to establish exemplars of behaviour. For instance Mao's commentaries associate the lady with virtuous Taizi whom King Wen married. And The Lu and Han schools read the poem as a satirical response to the improper behaviour of King Kang and his wife. By registering concrete historical sources and references, the poem moulds moral standards for readers to take action. Though different schools assume different purposes in composing the poem, encouraging (美 praise) versus criticizing (刺 satire), they all follow Confucius' intention: 'It is by the Odes that the mind is aroused' to virtue. It was until the rise of modern hermeneutics that the Poetry was reduced to cultural literacy.

In comparing with modern commentaries, Mao's interpretation is primarily oriented on person-making intention, either to rulers or common people. Reading poetry is not regarded as literacy cultivation, or learning historical truth, but aimed at transforming people acting as a person. Confucius said,

> 'When you enter any state you can know what subjects (its people) have been taught. If they show themselves men who are mild and gentle, sincere and good, they have been taught from the Book of Poetry' (入其 國，其教可知也。其為人也，温柔敦厚，《詩》教也).

'If they show themselves men who are mild and gentle, sincere and good, and yet free from that simple stupidity, their comprehension of the Book of Poetry is deep' (其為人也，温柔敦厚，而不愚，則深于《詩》教也).

(Legge, 1885, p. 255)

The Poetry has such a profound function all because its language is deeply rooted in soil of 'primordial signification'. To know the significance of primordially reliving the past, I would like to elaborate upon a Chinese concept *wen*, the primordial level of meaning aforementioned as genealogic practice in its textual mode.

Wen: the soil of meanings

During the Tang Dynasty (618–907 CE), China was obsessed with the intrusion of translated Buddhist discourse, somehow similar to the situation of contemporary China that has been deeply transformed by Western discourse. In response, Confucian literati launched a reform of writing/rhetoric in order to maintain its roots of tradition. This is called the *Ancient Prose Movement*, defined as a way of writing and speaking linguistically grounded on the consciousness of Classical texts, which greatly influenced the formation of the Civil Examination and Chinese pedagogy.

Han Yu (768–824 CE) was the major advocate of *Ancient Prose*. He explained his pursuit by listing a genealogy of classical kings who, in his mind, were wise and benevolent, and transmitted the Way of Antiquity. Today many people think that it was Confucius who laid down the foundation of Chinese civilization. However, Confucius saw himself only as the 'transmitter rather than creator' (述而不作, *The Analects*, 7.1) of the classical kings he called the '*Three Dynasties*' (三代, 2070 BCE–771 BCE) (*The Analects*, 15.25). Both Confucius and Laozi, the founder of Taoism, respected and admired them greatly. Han Yu explained how the meanings of Antiquity had flowed from ancient times, through Confucius' effort of transmission, and finally reached the contemporary in the form of Classical text:

> If someone asks, 'What Dao (Tao) is this Dao?' I will reply, 'This Dao, what I call the Dao, is not what Laozi and the Buddha meant by Dao. This is what Emperor Yao transmitted to Emperor Shun. Emperor Shun transmitted it to Emperor Yu. Emperor Yu transmitted it to Emperor Tang. Emperor Tang transmitted it to King Wen, King Wu and the Duke of Zhou. King Wen, King Wu and the Duke of Zhou transmitted it to Confucius. And Confucius transmitted it to Mengzi. When Mengzi died, it was not transmitted further.

(Han Yu, 1985, p. 18)

Here we see a genealogical line drawn to connect the names of sage kings and worthies who transmitted the Dao, which was manifested in the texture of Mao's

Poetry as analyzed above. Confucius is depicted here as someone who only played a role in securing the continuous flow of classical meanings. He committed himself to the task of gathering together the available records of previous dynasties, on divination, poetry, ritual, music, official documents and chronicles, and edited them into *Six Classics.* The authority of the Classics is believed to derive from the genealogy of sages who transmitted the Dao. It could be argued that Chinese pre-modern pedagogy, before it was discontinued, reflected and embodied the ancient vision of transmitting meanings of antiquity. How, and why, could the classical texts continuously function as the source of meanings for China?

Each utterance in the classics is featured with a 'subtle phrasing' (微言 *weiyan*; hidden meaning, subtle connotation, esoteric meaning) which is oriented to the essence of silence, the nameless Dao. This subtle phrasing can be understood as non-representational in the sense that the language resists any possibility of reducing it to a stagnant concept, a truth, a mirror of facts, which has been illustrated by my analysis of the poem. What is the hidden meaning we may think of? It should not be conceived of as some mysterious and secret message that the ancients hid, waiting for later generations to discover. This is what Confucius constantly mentioned in terms of *wen* (文) (texture, pattern, fabric), a linguistic as well as a cultural term only available in Chinese philology. *Wen*, standing for the textual/visual/poetic awareness of language, refers to the deepest sense of intelligibility and clarity felt in the heart. Kern (2001) explains that the depth and significance of the word *wen* can only be matched by a few others such as *Dao* and *Qi*. A Chinese philologist of the Han Dynasty, Xu Shen (c.58–147 CE), in his book *Shuowen Jiezi* (Talking the Patterns to Explain Characters; 說文解字) explained,

> When Cang Jie first invented writing systems, he imitated the forms of things according to their resemblances. Therefore, the created graphs were called *wen* or patterns. Later, the scope of writing was expanded by combining the form (pictographs) and phonetics and the results were called *zi* or 'compound graphs'.
>
> (Xu Shen, 1981, p. 15A)

Xu Shen (1981) further illustrates that 'on looking at the tracks of birds and animals, [it was aware] that certain patterns and forms were distinguishable' (p. 15A). The bird flying by has left its footprints; likewise the speech and actions of kings were recorded as they acted. Hence the manner of the ospreys on the islet in the river was observed and recorded down as *wen* in the poem of Guan Ju to illuminate the ethical relationship between husband and wife. The *Six Classics* is not supposed to be read as ideas, theories, thoughts that were purposely written by ancient kings. They were simply records of the authentic footprints of natural beings and kings' 'living and doing'. Zhang Xuecheng (1738–1801 CE), a Qing Dynasty historian, argues with regard to the Classics that 'ancient people did not write books; they only recorded what they had done' (Zhang, 2004). The records manifested as *wen* do not attempt to represent and conceptualize the world, but play the role of 'World-Disclosure', 'openness', and 'unconcealment' in Heideggerian terms (Heidegger, 1962). Xu Shen concludes that *wen* is the soil of words, 'the root of the images of things, and characters [words] were born and grew up in its milk' (文者物象之本，字者孳乳而生).

In modern linguistics *wen* is often misinterpreted as the pictographic representation of an idea, analogous to a sign in European language, defined by Saussure in his structural linguistics. Derrida rejects this presupposition that a Chinese character has an arbitrary relation of the signifier and the signified, arguing that 'a signifier is from the very beginning the possibility of its own repetition, of its own image or resemblance' (Derrida, 1997, p. 91). *Wen* is thought to be the pattern of heaven, earth and human, laden with cosmological unawareness such that *wen* unveils itself primordially as Being (Heidegger, 1962) instead of telling. It is the soil of meaning for signs, oriented towards 'seeing', and 'listening' as a way of access to intelligibility. Words, including modern Chinese characters whose function was Westernized as signs, function for communication and representation; *wen* is in essence to illuminate Dao and is grounded primarily in the natural virtue of revealing. Xu Shen (1981) explains the role of *wen* in education, 'He who talked of *wen* promoted education, and illuminated the transformation at the king's court' (p. 15A). Confucius, regarding himself as the Heaven-appointed transmitter of *wen*, said when his life was threatened in Kuang,

> Now that King Wen is gone, is not culture (*wen*) now invested here in me? If Heaven intended this culture to perish, it would not have given it to those of us who live after King. Since Heaven did not intend that this culture (*wen*) should perish, what can the people of Kuang do to me?
>
> (*The Analects*, 9.5; see Slingerland, 2003).

The Analects itself is a book recording Confucius' footprints, his Being-in-the-World, embodied with *wen* handed down from the Three Dynasties. The book therefore is short, fragmentary and poetic without the coherence and logic that modern people can reason with.

Person-making is an act of interpretation in the primordial signification of *wen*. Reading Classics for their *wen* is always interpretive, elusive and creative, and can never be exhausted. Michael Nylan (2001) comments, 'new meaning can in theory be generated endlessly from the same classic . . . "within the four seas" interpretive lines explicating the classics would "grow as numerous as trees in the forest"' (pp. 14–15). Many readers of Confucian classics have tended to believe that there is only one 'true meaning' to be uncovered through normative reading. Obtaining normative meanings is not the right way of interpreting *wen*. Classical texts merely disclose *wen*. Its interpretation entirely depends on the readers themselves. *Wen* holds the source of meaning, calling for different interpretations for different people over the course of histories. Chinese classics are the most remote ancient texts that are still intelligible today, owing to the continuing efforts of interpretation over thousands of years. I tend to accept what Heidegger claims that '[L]anguage, by naming beings for the first time, first brings beings to word and to appearance. Only this naming nominates beings *to* their beings *from out of* their being' (1971, p. 73). *Wen* conveyed in the classics, is beings that have been brought to language. *Wen* possesses a hiddenness that its interpretation is never closed. *Wen* does not hand out ideas. It does not apply knowledge, but it calls for interpretation.

The meaning of Antiquity in terms of *wen* has acted and will act just like milk to nourish the Chinese pedagogic discourse of any time. They offer to us a disclosure of virtue, a heart for learning, and a care for all knowledges. This is not a truth asserted with numerous concepts and ideas, but an authentic language showing us how to learn and why. Pedagogic discourse planted with meanings of Antiquity not only secures the attainment of a deep understanding of the world, and of the moral virtue to act properly in society, but also yields all the possibilities for learners to achieve practical competence and skills that modern education desires (see Wu, 2013). Today, a silent but forceful movement, called 'the Classic-Reading Education Movement' is emerging in China, mostly driven by non-government forces. 'What is the role of the tradition's classics, and how should the classics be studied in today's school?' (Deng, 2011, p. 562). In what way could the mainstream of the Chinese education react understandably to the movement? This all depends on the recovery of the traditional authentic mode of interpreting classical scripture. Person-making is a process of increasing self-understanding in the world. We do not understand ourselves unless it be brought into *wen*. For instance, an understanding of the husband and wife should be first of all a listening to the ospreys calling each other on the islet in the river. Every determination of man-made value, either freedom, autonomy, uniqueness defined in the West, or propriety, righteousness, benevolence pursued in ancient China, grows in the concrete visualization of wen, the mystery of Dao in word.

Conclusion

> I think of ancient men,
> And find my true heart.
> 我思古人，實獲我心

This is an extract from another poem included in the *Classics of Odes*. It depicts a virtuous lady who found herself strengthened to endure her painful experience by her study of the ritual meanings of the green colour of cloth in antiquity (Wu, 2013). The poem meanwhile describes a Chinese tradition continuously lived and relived for thousands of years, that is, using the ancient to inspire the present (與古為新). Confucius teaches his disciples to think how best 'to make the ancient new'. The Ancient Prose Movement during the late Tang Dynasty and the Song Dynasty was an innovative response to the influence of Buddhism on the emperors. Since the early part of the twentieth century, Chinese nationalism has believed that it was the Confucian Classics, and their commentary traditions, that were responsible for bringing China, defenceless and moribund, to the brink of destruction (Laurence, 1971, p. 1). They demanded the abandonment of this tradition by blocking the source of meanings, removing the Classics from an active role in society, and thereby sending them to the museum.

> We want to have the men of antiquity only be men of antiquity and not be leaders of today. We want to have ancient history only be ancient history and not be the ethical teachings of today. We want ancient books only to be ancient books and not be today's resplendent repositories of the lay. . . . In sum, we are sending them to the museum.
>
> (Gu, quoted from Laurence, 1971, pp. 60–1)

Tan (2011) argues that the Confucian classics 'should not be approached as if they were museum pieces, records of a lost world and civilization.' 'One would need to discover or reconstruct the continuity' (p. 628) that, following Foucault's genealogy, was interrupted by the rational search of a single idea of continuities (Foucault, 1972). It is not constructive to think of Confucian pedagogy as a 'thing' fixed in the past that should be restored. It is all a matter of how to make the past come alive by means of 'finding my true heart'.

It is important to understand that 'language is neither an expression nor an activity of humankind. Language speaks.' 'Its speaking speaks for us in what has been spoken' in the past (Heidegger, 1971, pp. 197, 210). I cannot think of such a language only available in the Chinese classics. Smith (2012) is trying to excavate in his work 'the Western tradition for those lost languages which once spoke in the same spirit and intent of Confucius', which, according to Smith holds the possibility of breaking the East/West binary for a mutual enrichment (p. 6). Nor is classicism kept in the library. It also lives with us unconsciously as a way of life. Ruth Hayhoe (2014) presents eleven life stories of influential Chinese educators, showing how they adapted effectually the European ideas of education to the Chinese indigenous contexts that owed much to the Confucian pedagogic tradition. Perhaps in those forgotten, ignored, marginalized, and muted spheres of common life, we may find more of a living Confucian legacy that could also serve as a source for creating a new pedagogy.

In my previous work (Wu, 2005, 2011), I proposed a historical task, a search for a pedagogic language appropriated/or appropriate for modernization and globalization. In this chapter, I explore the meanings of person-making in the scripture of Confucian Classics. I believe that the language and the mode of interpreting that have travelled through many millennia of speech/speaking and only one century of silence may serve as a compass to fulfil the mission.

Notes

1 As Confucius explains the role of Six Classics in education: 'All Six Arts help to govern. *The Book of Rites* helps to regulate men, *The Book of Music* brings about harmony, *The Book of Documents* guides activities, *The Book of Poems* passes on meanings, *The Book of Change* reveals supernatural transformation, and *The Spring and Autumn Annals* shows what is right' (see Sima, 1959, p. 3197).

2 Liang Zhanggu (1775–1849), who wrote 24 volumes of *Zhiyi Chonghua*, a book about the eight-legged essay, explained, 'I called *zhiyi* 'speaking in the place of sages', which requires comprehensive demonstration of talent, knowledge and understanding' (余謂制義 '代聖賢立言', 亦須才, 學, 識兼到) (Liang, 1976, p. 529).

3 The commentary way of knowledge construction could be traced to Confucius. According to Henderson (1991), Confucius was regarded by scholars since the Han Dynasty as the first commentator in Chinese history (p. 30). After a comparative study of Confucian and Western exegesis, Henderson claims that in the West commentaries occupy a similar place (p. 3).

4 The eight-legged essay is a composition genre comprised of eight sections. The genre was developed to secure that the candidates can respond to examination questions, linguistically in the place of the sage, or a commentary style of writing, based on the Confucian classics. Passing the essay was necessary in order to pass the Imperial Civil Examination.

5 I follow Heidegger in translating '*Dao*' into 'Saying'. Heidegger assimilates the Chinese concept to argue that 'In language as Saying there holds sway something like a Way.' 'Within this Way, which belongs to the essence of language, is concealed the distinctive feature of language' (see May, 1996, p. 38).

6 Heidegger's concept of 'primordial signification' could be understood as the reading of the phenomenological world without referring to the system of signs. He argues that [T]he phenomenology of Dasein is a hermeneutic in the primordial signification of the word, where it designates this business of interpreting (Heidegger, 1962, p. 62).

References

Briggs, R. S. (2011). Scripture in Christian Formation: Pedagogy, Reading Practice and Scriptural Exemplars. *Theology*, 114(2), 83–90.

Chen, X. D. (1999). *Lunyu Quanjie* 論語全解 *[Comprehensive Annotations on The Analects]*, Vol. 4. Available Online as the Electronic Version of Siku Quanshu. Shanghai/Hong Kong: Shanghai People's Press/Chinese University Press.

Cheng, K. M. (2011). Pedagogy: East and West, Then and Now. *Journal of Curriculum Studies*, 43(5), 591–9.

Deng, Z. (2011). Confucianism, Modernization and Chinese Pedagogy: An Introduction. *Journal of Curriculum Studies*, 43(5), 561–8.

Derrida, J. (1997). *Of Grammatology*, trans. G. C. Spivak. Baltimore, MD: The Johns Hopkins University Press.

Elman, B. A. (1997). Zaisuo Kaojuxuan 再说考据学 [Re-Comment On Textual Research]. *Dushu* 读书, 2, 72–80.

Elman, B. A. (2000). *A Cultural History of Civil Examinations in Late Imperial China*. London: University of California Press.

Foucault, M. (1972). *The Archaeology of Knowledge*, trans. A. M. Sheridan Smith. London: Tavistock.

Frei, H. (1974). *The Eclipse of Biblical Narrative: A Study in Eighteenth and Nineteenth Century Hermeneutics*. New Haven and London: Yale University Press.

Gadamer, H. G. (1986). On the Scope and Function of Hermeneutical Reflection. In B. R. Wachterhauser (ed.), *Hermeneutics and Modern Philosophy* (pp. 277–99). Albany: State University of New York.

Granet, M. (1932). *Festivals and Songs of Ancient China*, trans. E. D. Edwards. London: George Routledge.

Gu, T. (ed.) (1992). Qingdai Zhujuan Jicheng. 清代朱卷集成 *[Collection of Imperial Examination Papers in the Qing Dynasty]*, Vol. 86. Taipei: Chengwen Publication Press.

Han, Y. (1985). Han Changli Wenji Jiaozhu. 韩昌黎文集校注 *[Annotated Complete Works of Han Changli (Han Yu)]*, Ma Qichang (ed.). Shanghai: Shanghai Guji Publication.

Hayhoe, H. (2014). Hopes for Confucian Pedagogy in China? *Journal of Curriculum Studies*, 46(3), 313–19.

Heidegger, M. (1962). *Being and Time*, trans. J. Macquarrie and E. Robinson. London: SCM Press.

Heidegger, M. (1971). *Poetry, Language, Thought*, trans. A. Hofstadter. New York: Harper & Row.

Henderson, J. B. (1991) *Scripture, Canon, and Commentary: A Comparison of Confucian and Western Exegesis*. Princeton, NJ: Princeton University Press.

Huang, Q. (2007). Zhuxi: 'Dai Shenxianliyan' De Qimengzhe [Zhuxi: The Enlightening Man For 'Speak in the Place of the Sages']. *Journal of Southeast University (Philosophy and Social Science)*, 9(3), 104–8.

Jennings, W. (1891). *The Shi King, the Old 'Poetry Classic' of the Chinese: A Close Metrical Translation With Annotations*. London: George Routledge and Sons.

Kern, M. (2001). Ritual, Text, and the Formation of the Canon: Historical Transitions of Wen in Early China. *Toung Pao*, 87(1), 43–91.

Laurence, A. (1971). *Ku Chieh-Kang and China's New History: Nationalism and the Quest for Alternative Traditions*. Berkeley: University of California Press.

Legge, J. (1871). *The Chinese Classics, with a Translation, Critical and Exegetical Notes, Prolegomena, and Copious Indexes. Vol. 4, Part 1. The She-King*. London: Frowde Henry.

Legge, J. (1885). *The Sacred Books of China, the Texts of Confucianism, Part IV, The Li Ki, XI XLVI*. Oxford: The Clarendon Press.

Liang, Z. (1976). Zhiyi Conghua. 制义丛话 *[Collected Comments on the Crafting of Eight-Legged Civil Examination Essays]*, Reprint of 1859 Edition. Taipei: Guangwen Bookstore.

Lowenthal, D. (1985). *The Past is a Foreign Country*. Cambridge: Cambridge University Press.

May, R. (1996). *Heidegger's Hidden Sources: East Asian Influences on His Work*, trans. G. Parkes. London: Routledge.

Nylan, M. (2001). *The Five 'Confucian' Classics*. New Haven CT: Yale University Press.

Popkewitz, T. S. (2008). *Cosmopolitanism and the Age of School Reform: Science, Education and Making Society by Making the Child*. New York: Routledge.

Ryckmans, P. (2008) The Chinese Attitude Towards the Past. *China Heritage Quarterly*, No. 14. Available online at: http://Chinaheritagequarterly.Org/Articles.Php?Search term=014_Chineseattitude.Inc&Issue=014 (accessed 28 June 2014).

Saussure, Ferdinand De (1960). *Course in General Linguistics*, trans. Wade Baskin. London: Peter Owen.

Sima, Q. (1959). *Shiji [Records of the Great Historian]*. Beijing: Zhonghu Shuju.

Slingerland, E. (2003). *Confucius Analects: With Selections From Traditional Commentaries*. Indianapolis, IN: Hackett.

Smith, D. G. (2012). On Studying Confucius: Pitfalls and Possibilities in Global Times. *CTE Newsletter 2012* (pp.3–5). CTE SIG, American Educational Research Association.

Tan, S. H. (2011). Why Study Chinese Classics and How To Go About It. *Journal Of Curriculum Studies*, 43(5), 623–30.

Wang, C. H. (1974). *The Bell and the Drum: Shih Ching as Formulaic Poetry in an Oral Tradition*. Berkeley and Los Angeles: University of California Press.

Wu, Z. (2011). Interpretation, Autonomy, and Transformation: Chinese Pedagogic Discourse in a Cross-Cultural Perspective. *Journal of Curriculum Studies*, 43(5), 569–90.

Wu, Z. (2013). The Chinese Mode of Historical Thinking and its Transformation in Pedagogical Discourse. In T. Popkewitz (ed.), *Rethinking the History of Education: Transnational Perspectives on its Questions, Methods, and Knowledge* (pp. 51–74). New York: Palgrave Macmillan.

Wu, Z. and Han, C. (2014). Pedagogy Towards Diversity: A Cross-Cultural Approach to Historicizing the Present. In M. Pereyra and B. Franklin (eds) *Systems of Reason and the Politics of Schooling: School Reform and Sciences of Education in the Tradition of Thomas S. Popkewitz* (pp. 180–206). New York: Routledge.

Wu, Z. J. (2005). *Teachers' Knowing in Curriculum Change: A Critical Discourse Study of Language Teaching*. Beijing: Foreign Language Teaching and Research Press.

Xu, S. (1981). Shuowen Jiezi Zhu. 说文解字注 *[Explaining and Analyzing Characters]: Annotated by Duanyucai (1735–1815)*. Shanghai: Shanghai Guji Press.

Yang, J. (1999). *Zhouyi Bianlu* 周易辨录 *[Records of Commentaries on the Book of Change]*, Vol. 4(1545). Available Online as The Electronic Version of Siku Quanshu. Shanghai/Hong Kong: Shanghai People's Press/Chinese University Press.

Yao, C.-H. (1958). Shijing Tonglun. 诗经通论 *[Wok on the Shijing. Edited by Gu Jiegang]*. Beijing: China Publishing House.

Zhang, X. C. (2004). Wenshi Tongyi. 文史通义 *[General Meaning of Historiography]*. Beijing: Zhonghua Shuju.

Zhao, G. (2014). Freedom Reconsidered: Heteronomy, Open Subjectivity, and the 'Gift of Teaching'. *Studies in Philosophy and Education*, 33(5), 513–25.

7 Person-making and citizen-making in Confucianism and their implications on contemporary moral education in China[1]

Xiaoling Ke

Introduction

Ever since China adopted the opening up and reform policy in 1978, the world has witnessed a sustained, miraculous economic boom in China. In the meanwhile, as a result of the overemphasis on economical development and negligence of moral cultivation, China also suffers from a serious moral decline. Traditional Chinese values are shredded by the lure of money-worship. Immoral behaviours are prevalent, such as academic cheating, bribery and corruption, the killing of accident victims, land taken illegally, and toxins purposefully added to food, with a sole purpose of making or saving money. How to reverse the moral decline becomes a common concern among Chinese people. Also, Chinese leaders call for both cultural inheritance and innovation (*chuancheng wenming, kaituo chuangxin* 传承文明，开拓创新) as important means to establishing and bulwarking the socialist core value system (*shehui zhuyi hexin jiazhiguan* 社会主义核心价值观) and fulfilling 'China's dream', signalling a promising step forward from announcing socialism as the sole foundation of moral culture to embracing Confucianism and incorporating Confucianism into the school moral education system. Against such social backdrops an examination of the current moral education and way of properly incorporating Confucianism into the moral education curriculum is relevant and urgent since a well-established morality is crucial to the welfare of a society.

In the meanwhile, we cannot overlook the fact that Confucianism has been used as an instrument for ideological education, which caused detrimental effects on Chinese society and was accused of cultivating obedient and passive Chinese people (Tran, 2002; Yuan, 2001; Zhao, 2013; also see Law, Chapter 3). Because of this there was a strong anti-Confucianism sentiment during the New Cultural Movement in the 1920s. Nearly one century later, when China encounters a serious moral crisis, it is time to ask whether the revival of Confucianism is necessary and if it is necessary, in what ways we can revive Confucianism in order to address current moral degeneration, overcome it and re-establish the moral culture in China.

To answer these questions, in this chapter I aim to discuss how Confucian understanding of person-making and citizen-making can illuminate contemporary moral education in China, especially in this ever-changing world that is characterized by globalization that blurs the national boundary. In the first part, I scrutinize the current endeavours to revive Confucianism. Then moral education in recent decades in China is reviewed with an aim of diagnosing the problems within moral education. Next, I explore the meaning of person-making and citizen-making, the major functions of Confucian moral education. I argue that China needs to embrace the original understanding of person-making (inner sagehood) and citizen-making (outer kingliness) in Confucian moral education, and guard against the appropriation of Confucianism to serve ideological purposes. I further suggest that China should emphasize developing students' self-cultivation, their independent and critical thinking, and most importantly, their praxis of authentic Confucianism.

The revival of Confucianism

Historically, Confucianism has experienced upheavals and even crises for significant periods, especially during the New Culture Movement in the 1920s and the Cultural Revolution (1966–1976). Despite the vicissitudes of Confucianism in Chinese history, having governed Chinese society and regulated various aspects of Chinese people's lives for more than 2000 years, Confucianism remains an important cultural heritage for Chinese people, shapes the mentality and cultural tradition of Chinese people, and has become the 'mother morality' (Yang, 2013) for Chinese people. The reasons behind the enduring status of Confucianism lie not only in the fact that it is declared as state orthodoxy and supported by the government and scholars, but also that the general public have been practicing Confucian rituals and observing Confucian moral teachings (Yu, 2010). Contemporary China is at a time of dramatic changes in every aspect of social life. Chinese people are eager to reestablish moral culture entangled in tradition/modernity, globalization/localization and materialism/spiritualism. The current revival of Confucianism reflects and responds to Chinese people's strong inner aspiration for the restoration of Confucian values and morality. It is both imperative and urgent to contemplate the true value of Confucianism for the contemporary moral education in China so as to facilitate the reestablishment of moral culture and combat the severe crisis of moral degeneration in China. This accounts for the loud cry for, and practice of, the revival of Confucianism in contemporary China at the governmental level, in the academic world and among the general public.

At the governmental level, the first indication of governmental support for the revival of Confucianism was the establishment of institutions authorized by the Chinese government (Peng, 2011). In 1984, the Chinese Communist Party Central Committee secretariat resolved to establish a government-funded China Confucian Foundation (CCF, *zhongguo kongzi jijinhui* 中国孔子基金会). In October 1994, the International Confucius Federation was established.

This marked a major shift in the attitude of the Communist Party of China (CPC) government towards Confucianism. A public signal of official embracement of Confucianism is apparent when the 2008 Olympics in Beijing opened with the quoting of *The Analects* of Confucius. Following that, President Xi Jinping reiterated his resolution to revive Confucianism within the framework of preserving cultural diversity, respecting different civilizations, learning from other cultures, and inheriting and developing traditional Chinese culture (维护多样性、尊重不同文明、正确学习借鉴，及发展与传承的相互结合) when he visited the Confucian Mansion, Confucian Research Institute in Qufu, Shandong in November 2013, when he talked to the students in Beijing University in May 2014, and when he addressed an international seminar to mark the 2,565th anniversary of the birth of Confucius and the concurrent Fifth Congress of the International Confucian Association (ICA) in September 2014. The government has also funded various research projects to study New Confucianism and established Confucius Institutions in multiple cities around the world, a signal of the determination of the government to revive traditional Chinese culture, especially Confucianism.

In the academic world, since the twentieth century, altogether four generations of Confucian scholars have made strenuous efforts to bring the research on Confucianism forward. They studied Confucianism in order to find some elements compatible with the Western modern values of freedom, democracy and human rights, and explored ways of tailoring Confucianism to facilitate China's entry into modernity (Tan, 2008). Among them, the fourth generation of scholars are intellectuals in Mainland China who attempt to rediscover the 'national essence' and value of Confucianism to meet the political and cultural needs of Contemporary China. Among the more recent scholars, Guo Qiyong (郭齐勇) and Zhen Jiadong (郑家栋) changed their position from 'regarding New Confucianism simply as an object of research to one of "sympathetic understanding"' (Makeham, 2008, p. 133); Jiang Qing (蒋庆) plans to use the Confucian revival as a platform for advancing political reforms in China (2003); Li Shen (李申) attempts to promote Confucianism as a religion (2004, 2005); Peng Guoxiang (2011) advocates taking Confucianism as a living tradition and guarding against the danger of commercialization and politicization of Confucianism in contemporary China; and Wu Zongjie (2011) calls for unveiling and renewing the authentic Confucian pedagogic discourse. These scholars contribute greatly to the reinvigoration of Confucianism in various ways.

Apart from these academic endeavours in the scholarly community various efforts to revive Confucianism are also found among the general public. The 'culture craze' (*wenhua re* 文化热) and the 'national learning craze' (*guoxue re* 国学热) have existed since the 1980s and Confucianism was seen as an indispensable cultural force that could usher China into the twenty-first century. Tutoring courses are offered to teach children classic readings of traditional Chinese culture. Old-style private Chinese schools are set up to offer children an alternative education or supplementary education, set apart from formal education. Various ceremonies are held to honor Confucius in Qufu, Confucius' hometown, and other localities. The aspirations for learning and understanding the Confucian tradition are a reflection of the popular demand from ordinary Chinese people 'who have felt a great vacuum in the value system after the collapse of communist ideology in the 1980s' (Peng, 2011, p. 226).

However, these efforts of reviving Confucianism somewhat are either politicized to serve nationalist purposes or commercialized, thus are superficial. The true value of Confucianism, which lies in its understanding of fulfilling humanity, has not been touched upon. How Confucianism can contribute to the contemporary moral education in China has not been sufficiently investigated. Moreover, the problems with contemporary moral education in China have not been sufficiently examined either. To diagnose the problems in moral education, I shall now review Chinese moral education in recent decades.

Contemporary moral education in China

Biesta (2009) argues that education generally performs three functions: qualification, socialization and subjectification, and the latter two functions cause tension. Subjectification refers to the process of individuation and becoming a subject, or person-making, and socialization is a process of citizen-making that socializes people to 'become members of and part of particular social, cultural and political "orders"' (p. 41), so the tension between subjectification and socialization is also the tension between person-making and citizen-making. Ever since the Enlightenment Age, multiple educational philosophers have argued that a good education 'should always contribute to processes of subjectification that allow those being educated to become more autonomous and independent in their thinking and acting' (p. 41). Among them Rousseau (1979) argues that making a man should be done before making a citizen. Once he is an autonomous man with moral judgement, he can develop his moral sense and become a good citizen. Then social stability will be secured, and there is little point of indoctrinating ideological education then. So the crux of the moral education is to cultivate an autonomous person with capacity for moral judgement, and that is exactly the main goal of person-making.

In essence, education has long been conceived of as a process of 'person-making' or self-formation (Zhao, 2013; also see Zhao and Deng, Chapter 1), which is true not only in Western culture but also in Chinese culture. In Western culture, person-making in education aims to cultivate rational, autonomous humans, which has been regarded as the major task of education ever since Kant (1906). This conception lays the foundations for the modern civilization of the Western world, and brings forth a rapid scientific, technological and sociocultural progress. Even though this modernist humanist notion of the self encounters crises and Western philosophers have tried different ways of mending and rescuing the modern subjects, their efforts still revolve around reconceptualizing the notion of the self. In the Chinese culture, person-making mainly refers to the process 'by which one returns to human nature, which is good and moral', and 'a process of becoming through self-cultivation' (Yang, 2006). Confucianism, the mainstream of traditional Chinese culture, has long believed that the main purpose of education is not to instil knowledge or skills in students, but to 'cultivate an ethical and relational self that brings harmony to the community and to the world' (Zhao, 2013, p. 498; Zhao and Deng, Chapter 1). Therefore, moral education has been the central task of Confucian education, and person-making has been the central task of Confucian moral education.

However, after Confucianism was declared as state orthodoxy in the Han Dynasty (202 BC–220 AD), it has been absolutized and monopolized, with unparalleled power and absolute domination in Chinese society. Consequently, certain original Confucian doctrines such as benevolence (*ren* 仁) and harmony were declared as moral norms that regulate people's moral life. These doctrines were then gradually developed into moral dogmas of loyalty, obedience, rites-observance and filial piety for maintaining social order and safeguarding the interests of the ruling class. As a result, Confucian morality was transformed into Confucian ideology,[2] and Confucian moral education into ideological education. And the original noble purpose of cultivating human nature and making man better gradually gives way to the instrumental purposes of maintaining social order and defending the ruling regime. For this reason, Tran (2002) argues that transforming morality into ideology is 'tantamount to the act of dogmatizing, monopolizing and manipulating human beings' (p. 129).

It is evident that contemporary moral education in China is in essence ideological education. After the People's Republic of China was founded in 1949, the CPC has upheld socialism as state orthodoxy, and moral education has been centred on cultivating socialist new persons (*shehui zhuyi xinren* 社会主义新人) who are both 'red' and 'expert' (*youhong youzhuan* 又红又专). Being 'Red' means shaping and guiding their lives with socialist ideology and being 'expert' means possessing the knowledge and skills needed for socialist economic undertakings (Baum, 1964). Confucianism and Western cultures were rejected generally. Moral education was essentially regarded as a means of political socialization, functioning in transmitting ideological and political values not only to the students, but also to the general public (Lee and Ho, 2005). According to the government's Common Framework for Chinese People's Political Negotiations issued in 1949, the task of moral education in China was mainly 'destroying feudalist, bourgeois and fascist ideologies, and to nurture such national virtues as loving the country, loving the people, loving labor, loving science and loving public property' (Cited in Lee and Ho, 2005). The moral education curriculum was thus directed towards ideological education, in which the growth of individuals was ignored.

After 1978, China switched from a planned economy to a market economy in order to rescue the national economy from collapse, and began to open up to the outside world. As a result, the moral education curriculum is more accommodative, with an aim to prepare students to live and function in a moderately prosperous China and in an increasingly competitive globalized world (Law, 2014; also see Law, Chapter 3). In 1981 the government reinstated the 'Behavioral Code for Primary and Secondary Students' (中小学生日常行为规范)

as a major measure to strengthen moral education. According to the Code, besides cultivating in students affectation towards the socialist motherland, the task of moral education also includes cultivating students' moral qualities including care and respect for people and nature, integrity and honesty, and responsibility, etc. The scope of moral education has been broadened from its original exclusive emphasis on the transmission of socialist values to include law education, psychology health, and knowledge of life. However, it remains deeply ideological as the primary concern is with preparing students for the society and the state.

With China's process of modernization intensifying and the irreversible powerful trend towards globalization in the first decade of the twenty-first century, the CPC government sees an urgent need to cultivate students' international horizons and personal qualities, such that would meet the need of market economy and international competitions. As a result, the development of personal qualities has become increasingly important in the moral education curriculum. Moreover, education on traditional culture is strengthened and students are encouraged to develop their creative ability, learning ability and practical ability (Ministry of Education, 2001, 2011a, 2011b, 2011c). The new moral education curriculum both prepares Chinese students to compete globally and also urges them to identify with and take pride in the nation's achievements and traditional culture, and develop their attachment to and love of their motherland and the CPC (Law, 2014; also see Law, Chapter 3), with a strong ideological overtone.

To implement the new curriculum, the government adopts a top-down model to ensure the practice of moral education. It develops socialist moral codes, and then requires Chinese students and the general public to observe them. Among these value systems are Five Stresses, Four Beauties and Three Loves (wujiang simei sanreai 五讲四美三热爱), Eight Honours and Eight Dishonours (*barong bachi* 八荣八耻), and the current socialist core values (*shehui zhuyi hexin jiazhiguan* 社会主义核心价值观). Currently, the socialist core values are widely taught in Chinese schools and students are required to recite them. In December 2014, the city of Wuhan, in Central China's Hubei Province, called upon all its residents, including students and kindergarten children, to recite the core socialist values and held mandatory recitation sessions (Cao, 2014). It is believed that this is an effective way for socialist moral education and the socialist moral values can take root in people's minds by recitation.

To improve the quality of moral education, the government also reforms the teaching methods of moral education. Schools and teachers are given more autonomy to explore new means of education (Cheung and Pan, 2006). More masters or doctoral degree programmes in Marxist Theories and Political Education are designed for moral education teachers to improve their teaching methods and pedagogy. Moreover, the government encourages schools to set up off-campus moral education bases in the local museums, public libraries and historic sites in order to conduct off-campus moral education (General Office of the General Committee, 2001).

The above brief review of moral education reform in China indicates that significant progress has been made concerning the policies, methods and practices in moral education. However, moral education in China remains ideological education, directed towards socializing students into socialist values for the purpose of building a harmonious socialist society, and lacks a concern for developing and perfecting human nature. Person-making, the central task of moral education, still has not received adequate attention in the current moral education curriculum.

Person-making and citizen-making in Confucianism

Confucian education in essence is moral education. Person-making, or the cultivation and perfection of the self, is at the core of Confucianism. This has been recognized by a number of scholars such as Tu Weiming, William T. de Bary, Roger T. Ames, Kwong-Loi Sun and Robert C. Neville. For example, Tu (1985) points out that 'to know oneself is simultaneously to perfect oneself' (p. 20) and 'to learn about the self is not only self-realization but also self-development' (p. 26). Therefore, Confucian understanding of person-making starts from the assumption that a self needs to be created, developed, and realized. It is important to note that Confucius is well aware that the self is imperfect and thus needs constant improving. In *The Analects*, the notion of 'I' (我) appears more than 45 times. In most cases the self is given negative connotations, understood as unfinished, imperfect, and even derogatory, indicating that Confucius is unsatisfied with the imperfect essence of the self. Since the self is insufficient and limited, the self needs constant developing and improving through self-cultivation. The self is not valued for what he is, but for what he becomes (Tran, 2002). During the process of becoming, the self is able to constantly improve himself. It is generally perceived that Confucian moral education is about acquiring virtues and observing rites and rituals; however, this is a misconception since acquiring virtues through learning and self-cultivation, obeying rules and assuming social roles and responsibilities are not the ultimate purpose of Confucianism, but a process of person-making. In this regard, the purpose of person-making is to cultivate human nature, assume social responsibility and become a morally ideal person of *Junzi* (君子).

In order to become a *Junzi*, a person must conduct self-cultivation. *The Great Learning* (*daxue* 大学) outlines eight steps of self-cultivation, namely, investigating things (*gewu* 格物), extending knowledge (*zhizhi* 致知), sincere thoughts (*chengyi* 诚意), rectifying hearts (*zhengxin* 正心), self-cultivation (*xiushen* 修身), regulating family (qijia 齐家), governing the state (*zhiguo* 治国), and making the world peaceful (*pingtianxia* 平天下). The eight steps of self-cultivation are all about making, developing and realizing an ideal Confucian self. During this process, the self is not a static object, but an evolving and expanding entity. Its final state is a unity of 'the world and the self' and 'heaven and person' (*tianren heyi* 天人合一). To be more specific, the first six steps are about person-making while the last two are about taking up social responsibilities, and therefore are citizen-making. Person-making is fundamental for a moral person's regulating family, governing the state and bringing peace to the world. After completing the first six steps and regulating the family, a person is able to govern the state and harmonize with the world, and become a sage ruler, which is referred to as Inner Sagehood and Outer Kingliness (*neisheng waiwang* 内圣外王). Therefore, Confucian understanding of an ideal person is someone who aims not only at achieving personal perfection, but also at striving for social prosperity and fully integrating himself into society. In this sense, person-making and citizen-making do not cause tension since they are not in dichotomy but closely interrelated. Person-making is the foundation and precondition of citizen-making and citizen-making is an indispensable part of person-making. Only when a person is morally and inwardly well-cultivated, is he capable of becoming a moral person and participating in state affairs. Only when a person both accomplishes the process of person-making and citizen-making, can he achieve the status of *Junzi*.

For Confucius, self-cultivation can be conducted through learning, practice and self-examination. Learning, which includes both learning the Confucian classical books and learning from others, is a process of the growth of the self, or the making of a person (Ames, 2011; Tu, 1989), so it is important in the process of person-making. According to *The Analects*, 'When I walk along with two others, they can always be my teachers' (三人行，必有我师, *The Analects*, 7.22). Furthermore, an authentic Confucian self is one living an examined life who constantly reflects on their daily life, employs constant self-examination and rectifies himself, or in Confucius' words, 'I examine myself three times a day' (吾日三省吾身, *The Analects*, 1.4). In this sense both learning and self-examination are autonomous actions and they are inseparable during the process of self-cultivation as Confucius holds that 'learning without thinking leads to confusion; thinking without learning ends in danger' (学而不思则罔，思而不学则殆, *The Analects*, 2.15). The Confucian self is valued for his autonomous nature. Lastly, practice of Confucian morality means practicing the five constant virtues (*wuchang* 五常), namely benevolence (*ren* 仁), righteousness (yi 义), propriety (*li* 礼), wisdom (*zhi* 智) and sincerity (*xin* 信). Confucian morality is mainly concerned about the fulfilment of these five constant virtues with *Ren*, or benevolence, as the central task. Only when a person acquires these five constant virtues through self-cultivation and constant learning, can he nurture a noble, righteous spiritual energy (*haoran zhengqi* 浩然正气) and finally become a *Junzi* who has discovered and developed his nature. The five constant virtues have been regarded as the foundation and core of traditional Chinese ethics.

The Confucian person-making is achieved mainly through two means: to cultivate human sentiments and to have close relations with community. While the modern Western understanding of person-making is founded on an appreciation of human beings' rationality and autonomy, traditional Confucian understanding of person-making is based on an appreciation of natural human sentiments (Zhao, 2013; also see Zhao and Deng, Chapter 1). Similarly, Tu (1989) argues that 'the person who realizes his nature to the full becomes a paradigm of authentic humanity' (p. 77). The very first sentence in *The Doctrine of the Mean* (zhongyong 中庸) relates that 'What Heaven imparts to man is called human nature. To follow our nature is called the Way, and to cultivate the Way is called education' (天命之谓性；率性之谓道；修道之谓教). This points out that one of the main goals of Confucianism is to discover human nature, and the learning and developmental processes cultivate the Way that follows human nature.

Confucianism advocates a relational self that has close relations with the family, the community, which means family clans (*shizu* 氏族) in most cases, and the state. Confucianism rejects any antagonism between the self and the community, as well as between self-realization and engagement with the world (Chen, 2014). The self is valued for the ability to develop a human's innate social nature, that is, to love other people and to live with them harmoniously (Bodde, 1953). Confucianism holds that a *Junzi* needs to reason from the self into others (*tuiji jiren* 推己及人) and take others into consideration. 'The man with *ren* wishes to establish himself and also seeks to help others to establish themselves; wishes to achieve something and also seeks to help others to achieve something.' (夫仁者，己欲立而立人，己欲达而达人, *The Analects*, 6.30). This is *Junzi*'s social responsibility and can be understood by Confucius as the perfect humanness. In other words, Confucian understanding of person-making is founded on a relational self and responsibility and care for others.

Confucianism regards the task of citizen-making as equally important. The citizens that Confucius understands are not obedient or passive persons. Nor should they follow the three cardinal guides (*sangang* 三纲) and the five constant virtues meekly. On the contrary, they should be autonomous since they are always ready to create, improve and fulfil themselves, and should be capable of taking social responsibilities and also possess critical spirits. The *Junzi* that Confucius envisions is someone who seeks harmony but not conformity (君子和而不同 *The Analects*, 13.26). Specifically, a *Junzi* seeks to maintain harmonious relations with others, but this does not mean that he should conform to others' opinion and refrain from raising different opinions. On the contrary, to have independent thinking is one important quality of *Junzi*. One example is that when Zilu asks Confucius how to serve the emperor, Confucius answers, 'Don't cheat him, but you should frankly remonstrate with him' (子路问事君，子曰:'勿欺也，而犯之. *The Analects*, 14.23). Therefore Confucianism advocates that officials need to have a politically critical spirit instead of being passive and obedient while serving their king.

Confucianism does not endorse cultivating passive and obedient citizens, and further advocates that rulers should develop their moral virtues through self-cultivation and practice benevolent ruling. According to *The Analects*, 'When a king's personal conduct is correct, his government is effective without giving orders. If his personal conduct is not correct, he may give orders, but they will not be followed' (其身正，不令而行；其身不正，虽令不从, *The Analects*, 13.6). Therefore, Confucius requires that rulers should first and foremost cultivate moral virtues. Only in this way can the people follow their orders. The art of ruling a nation does not lie in cultivating obedient and passive citizens, but lies in the continuous moral cultivation of the rulers. When the ruler does not behave morally, it is justifiable for his citizens not to obey him. In *The Great Learning*, Confucius argues that 'from the king to the ordinary people, everyone must take self-cultivation as the basis of their being' (自天子以至于庶人，壹是皆以修身为本). This indicates that self-cultivation, a means of achieving person-making, is everyone's central task and starting point for other undertakings, and even the king is no exception.

However, after Confucianism became the state orthodoxy, it gradually became an ideology and its focus on moral education has shifted to ideological education. The importance of person-making and citizen-making is fading out and the teaching of Confucianism focuses more on instilling the Confucian virtues of loyalty, filial piety, and abiding by rituals as the most important moral principles, in order to foster a passive, obedient and submissive citizenry with homogeneous thinking. One major approach of Confucian ideological education is to uphold the absolute authority and unconditional conformity to ancestors' laws and rituals and rites while discouraging independent thinking and innovative ideas. The imperial civil service examination system (*keju zhidu* 科举制度) is a case in point. The purpose of this imperial examination was to select candidates for the state bureaucracy, so the scholars with obedience, conformity and compliance, and respect for order and homogeneous thinking, were rewarded. Though Confucian classics are required testing materials, the examinees are not allowed to write freely and they must write standard eight-legged essays (*baguwen* 八股文). This imperial examination system stifled autonomous and critical thinking of the citizenry and cultivated officials who dared not defy authority. In this regard, Confucianism has been misused as a tool for maintaining social stability and securing ruling power. The effect of such misuse is that Chinese people generally lack rational and independent thinking. That is why Yu (2010) argues that there are two forms of Confucianism: the original Confucianism and the institutionalized Confucianism. The original Confucianism has a very profound understanding of human nature and human-society relations, as is analyzed above. If understood correctly, it can develop moral ideals with independent and autonomous thinking. However, when it is used for ideological control, it deviates from the original purpose of Confucius and became institutionalized Confucianism. Therefore, the central task of the revival of Confucianism should be to re-examine the essence of the original Confucianism and its understanding of person-making and citizen-making. A Confucian approach to moral education starts from person-making, with the acquiring of good human nature and becoming a moral person as the goals of moral education.

Suggestions for moral education in China and conclusion

In view of this brief review of the core values of Confucianism and the meaning of person-making and citizen-making in Confucianism, I offer several tentative suggestions on how to improve moral education in China.

First, we need to guard against a simple implantation of Confucianism in moral education. More emphasis needs to be given to moral development of students than to ideological and political education. Rote memorization of Confucian classical works and observance of Confucian rituals which are popular now in China are superficial, running the risk of cultivating passive, obedient people who are not capable of rational and independent thinking, thus falling into a vicious cycle that repeats failures. Mimetic, uncritical, passive and dogmatic teaching methods need to be avoided. It is imperative that we adopt the essential practices of person-making and citizen-making proposed by Confucianism. The school-based moral education should give students more freedom and more space for self-search, self-reflection and self-cultivation in order to cultivate students' independent, rational thinking and moral judgement. Specifically, schools can offer courses to teach students how to think logically and critically.

Next, we need to take Confucianism as an open and dynamic system that is open to continuous reinterpretation. In history various schools of thought including Buddhism and Taoism have enriched Confucianism. Both Yu Ying-shih and de Bary have repeatedly pointed out that some dimensions of democracy and liberal education can be detected in Confucianism as well (Peng, 2011). Therefore, we need to take a thorough examination of our cultural heritage, and reinvigorate Confucianism through recalibrating it to enrich today's moral education, rather than blindly inculcating Confucian teachings that have been wrongly interpreted or misused as tools for social control and ruling purposes.

Last but not least, more practice should be provided in school to develop students' moral values that are closely connected with their real life. The most salient and fundamental feature of Confucianism is its emphasis on practice. However, various efforts to reform the current moral education rarely go beyond taking the reform measures as a slogan. Instead of relying solely on the current top-down model, which means that the CPC government develops and modifies the moral codes and Chinese people can do nothing but recite and observe them, moral education in China needs to focus on cultivating rational and autonomous students in a bottom-up manner. The moral codes need to go beyond the slogan and be transformed into praxis. Slogan is conducive to producing homogeneous thinking, whereas praxis, which is defined as 'reflection and action upon the world in order to transform it' (Freire, 1970, p. 51), can lead to autonomous thinking and well-informed actions after reflection, so is therefore much more powerful than inculcating and classroom teaching. Instead of taking Confucianism simply as knowledge that can be instilled into students' minds, the moral education curriculum offers chances of praxis whereby students can reflect upon Confucian teachings and take well-informed moral actions.

Every nation needs solid philosophical and cultural foundations. The revival of Confucianism is both viable and imperative for us to re-envision moral education in this globalized world. We need to grasp the essence of person-making and citizen-making in Confucianism, and distinguish the humanist nature of Confucianism from its ideological nature, thus guarding against the misinterpretation and misuse of Confucianism. In this way we can avoid similar crises that Confucianism has encountered in history and rebuild a Chinese moral culture that is centred on person-making and citizen-making. Then we can envision a new moral education that cultivates rational, autonomous and responsible students who will grow to be autonomous and responsible Chinese citizens and fulfil China's dreams of freedom and prosperity.

Notes

1 This research is supported by Guangdong Social Sciences Co-Constructed Disciplines Research Grant for the National Twelfth Five-Year Plan, China (Project No. GD12XJY03).
2 *Morality* in the Confucian tradition refers to human nature tending towards its perfection (Tran, 2002), while *ideology* is defined as a system of norms that defends the *status quo* of social structures and serves the interests of a certain class or regime.

References

Ames, R. T. (2011). *Confucian Role Ethics*. Honolulu, HI: The University of Hawaii Press.

Baum, J. A. (1964). Diversity, Group Identity, and Citizenship Education in a Global Age. *Educational Researcher*, 37 (3), 129–39.

Biesta, G. (2009). Good Education in an Age of Measurement: On The Need to Reconnect with the Question of Purpose in Education. *Education Assessment, Evaluation and Accountability*, 21(1), 33–46.

Bodde, D. (1953). Harmony and Conflict in Chinese Philosophy. In A. F. Wright (ed.), *Studies in Chinese Thought* (pp. 19–75). Chicago: University of Chicago Press.

Cao, S. (2014). Wuhan rolls out 'Socialist Core Values' Recitation Campaign. *Global Times*, 26 December. Available online at: http://globaltimes.cn/content/898708.shtml (accessed 10 January 2015).

Chen, X. (2014). The Ethics of Self: Another Version of Confucian Ethics. *Asian Philosophy: An International Journal of the Philosophical Traditions of the East*, 24(1), 67–81.

Cheung, K. W. and Pan, S. (2006). Transition of Moral Education in China: Towards Regulated Individualism. *Citizenship Teaching and Learning*, 2(2), 37–50.

Freire, P. (1970). *Pedagogy of the Oppressed*. New York: The Seabury Press.

General Office of the General Committee of the Communist Party of China, and General Office of the State Council (2001). 关于适应新形势进一步加强和改进中小学德育工作的意见 *[Comments on Reinforcing and Reforming Moral Education in the New Era]*. Available online at: http://moe.gov.cn/publicfiles/business/htmlfiles/moe/moe_405/2004 12/4736.html (accessed 10 October 2014).

Jiang, Q. (2003). 政治儒学 – 当代儒学的转向、特质与发展 *[Political Confucianism: The Turning Point, Traits and Development of Contemporary Confucianism]*. 北京:三联书店 [Beijing, China: SDX Joint Publishing Company].

Kant, I. (1906). *On Education* (A. Churton, trans.). Boston, MA: D. C. Heath & Co.

Law, W. (2014). Understanding China's Curriculum Reform For The 21st Century. *Journal of Curriculum Studies*, 46(3), 332–60.

Lee, W. O., and Ho, C. H. (2005). Ideopolitical Shifts and Changes in Moral Education Policy in China. *Journal of Moral Education*, 34(4), 413–31.

Li, S. (2004). 中国儒教论 *[A Study of Chinese Confucianism as Religion]*. 郑州：河南人民出版社 [Zhengzhou, China: Henan People's Publishing House].

Li, S. (2005). 儒学与儒教 *[Confucianism and Confucianism as Religion]*. 成都：四川大学出版社 [Chengdu, China: Sichuan University Publishing House].

Makeham, J. (2008). *Lost Soul: 'Confucianism' in Contemporary Chinese Academic Discourse*. Cambridge, MA; London, England: Harvard University Asia Center.

Ministry of Education (2001). 基础教育课程改革纲要(试行) *[Guidelines on the Curriculum Reform of Basic Education, Pilot]*. Available online at: http://moe.edu.cn/public files/business/htmlfiles/moe/moe_309/200412/4672.html (accessed 10 October 2014).

Ministry of Education (2011a). 义务教育品德与社会课程标准 *[Curriculum Standards for Primary Education and Junior Secondary Education: Moral Character and Society]*. 北京：北京师范大学出版社 [Beijing, China: Beijing Normal University Press].

Ministry of Education (2011b). 义务教育品德与生活课程标准 *[Curriculum Standards for Primary Education and Junior Secondary Education: Moral Character and Life]*. 北京：北京师范大学出版社 [Beijing, China: Beijing Normal University Press].

Ministry of Education (2011c). 义务教育思想品德课程标准 *[Curriculum Standards for Primary Education and Junior Secondary Education: Thought and Moral Character]*. 北京：北京师范大学出版社 [Beijing, China: Beijing Normal University Press].

Peng, G. (2011). Inside the Revival of Confucianism in Mainland China: The Vicissitudes of Confucian Classics in Contemporary China as an Example. In *Oriens Extremus*, Hamburg, Germany, 49: 225–35.

Rousseau, J. J. (1979). *Emile* (A. Bloom, trans.). New York: Basic Books/HarperCollins.

Tan, S. H. (2008). Modernising Confucianism and New Confucianism. In K. Louie (ed.), *The Cambridge Companion to Modern Chinese Culture* (pp. 135–54). Cambridge: Cambridge University Press.

Tran, V. D. (2002). *The Poverty of Ideological Education. Council for Research in Values & Philosophy*. Available online at: http://crvp.org/book/series03/iii-2/chapter_vii.htm (accessed 10 October 2014).

Tu, W. (1985) *Confucian Thought: Selfhood as Creative Transformation* (SUNY Press).

Tu, W. (1989). *Centrality and Commonality*. Albany, NY: State University of New York Press.

Wu, Z. (2011) Interpretation, Autonomy, and Transformation: Chinese Pedagogic Discourse in a Cross-Cultural Perspective. *Journal of Curriculum Studies*, 43(5), 569–90.

Yang, C. F. (2006). The Chinese Conception of the Self: Towards a Person-Making Perspective. In U. Kim, K. Yang and K. Hwang (eds), *Indigenous and Cultural Psychology: Understanding People in Context* (pp. 327–56). New York: Springer.

Yang, S. (2013). On the Historical Development of Confucianists' Moral Ideas and Moral Education. *Ethics in Progress*, 4(1), 34–47.

Yu, Y. (2010). *Modern Confucianist Theory.* Shanghai: Shanghai People's Press.

Yuan, Z. (2001). The Status of Confucianism in Modern Chinese Education 1901–49: A Curricular Study. In G. Peterson, R. Hayhoe and Y. Lu (eds), *Education, Culture, and Identity in Twentieth-Century China* (pp. 193–216). Hong Kong: Hong Kong University Press.

Zhao, G. (2013). Rebuilding the Chinese Soul: Some Considerations for Education. *Frontier of Education in China,* 8(4), 498–517.

8   Rediscover lasting values
Confucian cultural learning models in the twenty-first century

Jin Li

In *Meno*, the renowned dialogue by Plato (1981), Socrates tutored an illiterate slave boy about geometric principles, as typified in the following exchange:

> S (Socrates):   Is this square then, which is four times as big, its double?
> B (Slave boy):   No, by Zeus.
> S: How many times bigger is it?
> B: Four times.
> S: Then, my boy, the figure based on a line twice the length is not double but four times as big?
> B: You are right . . .
>
> (p. 72)

As the dialogue continues, it becomes clear that the Platonic Socrates pronounced the view that human knowledge is not taught and learned but born and recalled. In *Meno* as well as in other writing by Plato, six themes pertaining to learning are central:

- The external world is the object of learning.
- Learning is inquiring into the world for oneself.
- The human mind is supreme in this inquiry.
- Perplexity about the world is the drive for knowledge.
- One derives intrinsic enjoyment and pleasure in this process.
- The purpose of such learning is to produce objective knowledge – truth.

During the same period, China was also blessed with thinkers. Mencius, regarded as the second sage after Confucius, was known for his tutoring of people, too. However, instead of powerless people, he tutored the nobles, kings and dukes. One summary excerpt illustrates the kind of teaching Mencius offered:

> M (Mencius):   Your Majesty, is it true that you spared an ox from being sacrificed because you couldn't bear to see it shrink in fear?

K (King Xuan of Chi):   Yes, it was like an innocent man going to the place of execution.

M: Then, your Majesty possesses compassion!

K: Do you really think so?

M: Yes, but you should extend it to care for your people instead of waging wars against other states. You will gain respect and a following and become a true king.

K: Marvelous! I'd like to learn more about this . . .

(Mencius, 1970, pp. 54–5)

The king seeks advice from Mencius on how to secure his political dominance over other states. This excerpt illustrates that while the king used to believe the only way to be king was to be ruthless, he now contemplates his goodness and perhaps a different and humane way to be king. Throughout Confucian and Mencian discussions, also, six themes can be extracted:

- Self (not the external world) is the object of learning.
- This learning begins at recognizing one's constant need to become a better person; no one, not even the king is exempt.
- The pursuit of learning enables and dignifies powerless individuals (who are legitimized to challenge the otherwise powerful).
- Learning is a lifelong process.
- It requires continuous commitment.
- The purpose of learning is not to produce objective knowledge but to cultivate/perfect oneself morally.

As it turned out, these two ancient teaching and learning exchanges are not casual recordings of history, forgotten or collecting dust in libraries, but represent profound and long-lasting values in the West and East Asia, respectively.

These values form what I term (Li, 2003) the 'cultural learning models' that outline two visions of learning. These visions concern the respective person-making processes (Biesta, 2009) that the two cultures hold as fundamental for learning and education. In this chapter, I present Western mind and Confucian virtue-oriented learning models based on decades of research. I then show children's learning beliefs and parental socialization at home. I claim that, like their Western counterparts, the Confucian learning values are also enduring thanks to their entrenchment in families. Next, I describe the need for an urgent and effortful restoration of these values because they have been unfortunately tarnished for 150 years. Towards such values, adults and children in Confucian-heritage cultures (CHCs) feel ambivalent and often self-loathing. I argue that a concerted grounding in one's own cultural heritage is the unalienable foundation for children's cultural identity and self-confidence. Only with this development secured can children truly learn from other cultures, irrespective of globalization.

Cultural learning models from research

Empirical research on culturally-based learning conceptions and beliefs, using many different methods and from many disciplinary conceptual frameworks, has been conducted over past decades (Gao and Watkins, 2001; Huntsinger and Jose, 2009; Li, 2002, 2003, 2004, 2006; Li and Wang, 2004; Li, Fung, Bakeman, Rae and Wei, 2014; Tobin, Hsueh and Karasawa, 2009; Wang, 2013). These methods include but are not limited to, collecting lexicons referring to learning, describing the model learner images people hold in their minds and self as a learner, endorsing learning statements, responding to experimental manipulations, face-to-face interviews, portraying images of good teachers, eliciting teacher beliefs, classroom observations, children's story completions, recording mother–child conversations, videotaping parents-teaching child sessions, and mothers writing diaries on their activities with children. The disciplinary frameworks range from cognitive science, psychology, anthropology, education and sociology. This body of research resulted in the development of two different cultural learning models (Li, 2012): Western mind-oriented and Confucian virtue-oriented. Below I detail each.

The Western mind-oriented learning model

As discussed elsewhere (Li, 2012), the person-making purpose of the Western learning model is characterized as mind-oriented because it emphasizes the person's cognition, that is, his or her mind, in both its development and its function. This learning model has at least five characteristics. First, understanding of the world is the central goal of learning. Originating from Greek antiquity, Western learning aims at cracking the code of the physical universe (Russell, 1975). Later this purpose incorporated the pursuit of understanding the Christian notion of divine power and manifestations. Through the modern age until the present, these traditional objects of learning/studies have expanded to include social, economic, organizational and psychological realms. Scientific achievement is the clearest testimony to this characteristic of Western learning.

The second characteristic is seeking certainty of knowledge. Again from Greek antiquity, through religious devotion, to modern science, and to the present era, the West goes about living, working, scholarship, governance and business with a great deal of effort to seek truth and the derivative of accurate facts, information, processes and efficiency. In order to achieve the goal, math was developed and perfected as an approach to knowledge (Russell, 1975). Despite doubt cast on absolute truth and certainty in modern times (Hecht, 2003), it would be hard to imagine how the West could continue to operate without reliance on the certainty of math and accuracy of knowledge.

The third characteristic is the emphasis on the mind and its functions (Gardner, 1983). Mind is the human intellect that does all the knowing and thinking. Reason or rational thought is possible because humans possess a mind. Since ancient times, the inner workings of the mind have been the subject of

philosophical contemplation and debate. Modern cognitive science, neuroscience, and psychology have focused on the detailed mechanisms of the mind
and its functions. Childrearing and education are seen as the process of
cultivating children's minds so that they can put their minds to good use in
further learning and intellectual work.

Inquiry by curiosity about and personal interest in the world is the fourth
characteristic. Curiosity about and interest in the world are the two personal
predispositions that drive human inquiry. Inquiry then leads to discovery.
From antiquity to the present, children's natural curiosity and interest are
regarded as the most important motivational qualities in learning and further
intellectual activities (Edwards, Gandini and Forman, 1998). Without these
predispositions, one is not believed to learn well, let alone to achieve creativity.
Western scientific breakthroughs evidence the power and efficacy of personal
curiosity and interest.

The final characteristic of the Western learning model is self-expression,
particularly verbal self-expression. This is both a natural talent and a developed
skill. Since Greek antiquity, the West has valued and promoted eloquence of
speaking (Todd, 2000). Much of political, legal, religious and social life requires
public speaking. The West has a long and impressive list of great orators and
leaders, from Demosthenes to Cicero, from Lincoln to Churchill, and from
Kennedy to Martin Luther King. Because of their eloquence (in addition to
their leadership skills), these leaders influenced the world significantly. Children
from early on are socialized to express themselves to present their ideas,
opinions, preferences and feelings (Minami, 1994). They are also taught to argue
and defend their positions verbally at home and throughout their schooling
(Goffman, 1981; Hewitt and Inghilleri, 1993; O'Connor and Michaels, 1993).

These five characteristics form the core of the Western learning model. It
serves as a cultural goal and ideal towards which children develop under
concerted socialization by parents, teachers, community and society at large.[^ii]

The East Asian virtue-oriented learning model

Five core components can also be identified for the Confucian learning model.
The first and most pivotal is the purpose of learning. As alluded to earlier, this
purpose was outlined by Confucius, and later Confucians, as a worthy goal of
any human being to pursue (Ames and Rosemont, 1999; Lee, 1996). Human
lives are not isolated but deeply entangled with others, particularly those on
whom one depends for survival and flourishing, such as parents, siblings,
grandparents, relatives, friends and ever larger social acquaintances throughout
one's life. This very social condition for life requires that one learn to relate to
others and to take on roles and responsibilities (Rosemont, 1992). How to
become the best person one can become in his or her entire existence is the
question for one to face. Thus, to Confucian thinking, learning is tantamount
to learning to self-cultivate morally and socially (修身). Since the introduction
of Western learning, CHC people have also incorporated it with their traditional

moral self-cultivation. Thus, perfecting self also gears towards learning academic subjects well.

Second, related to the first purpose, Confucian learning aims strongly at making social contribution above and beyond personal relationships and fulfilment of roles and responsibilities. Rosemont (1992) explains that at the beginning Chinese children are beneficiaries of the support and dedication of their family and community. As they grow older and mature more, they become benefactors who take on the role to care for and support the family and community. The latter part has been referred to as 'take the world upon oneself' (以天下為己任), a process by which all learners ideally learn to understand and practice this social cause (Li, 2012).

The third feature is that learners are encouraged and guided to develop what has been referred to as a set of learning virtues (Li, 2012). These include sincerity/seriousness, self-exertion, endurance of hardship, perseverance and concentration. These virtues have cognitive, moral and affective elements. When cultivated, these virtues become enduring traits of a person because they regularly enable the person to learn with standards guided by the virtues in order to achieve personal excellences (Zagzebeski, 1996). Each of these virtues is acquired and used to address a specific part of learning motivation and process, particularly when the learner is faced with challenges of different sorts (Li, 2002). When displaying these virtues, there is much social reward and admiration. However, a lack of them in a learner is cause for concern and remediating effort from parents and teachers.

Related to the above five learning virtues, there are two additional dispositional qualities that all learners in CHCs are to develop and exercise: humility and respect for teaching authority. In the West, humility is regarded as a disposition that keeps one's ability and accomplishment in perspective, enables one to acknowledge one's limitations and shortcomings and to be in touch with one's need to learn from others (Tangney, 2000). However, the West emphasizes intellectual humility that is conducive to truth seeking (Spiegel, 2012). In CHC cultures, humility is highly, probably more, valued, especially in reference to learning and achievement. Unlike the West, the stress is on the presumed never-fullness of the self, but not on the fallibility of the self or truthfulness of one's beliefs (Li, 2014). Respect goes in tandem with humility. In CHCs, respect is a positive self-conscious emotion felt when one recognizes another's qualities, talent, or skills that one may wish to possess him or herself (Li and Fischer, 2007). Teachers are generally held not only as models of learning but also as embodiments of moral character. Students are socialized to respect teachers, who are, conversely, held accountable for their teaching and conduct. This emotion/attitude is similar to Western admiration towards another. However, the CHC tendency of teacher respect has often been equated to passivity in pupils. Counter to this portrayal, research on respect among CHC schoolchildren does not support this view. Instead, respect enables children to make great efforts to learn with the virtues outlined above (Hsueh, Zhou, Cohen, Hundley and Deptula, 2005).

The final emphasis of the Confucian learning model is on doing over speaking. Contrary to Western self-expression, the Confucian tradition devalues verbal eloquence (Chang, 1997; Gao, 1998). Because the model values moral and social self-cultivation, the standard of learning falls on what one does, not what one says. In fact, it is much easier to talk, even to verbalize resolve than actually practicing, delivering, and acting upon one's resolve. For this reason, the Confucians do not regard verbal eloquence as a viable way to achieve worthy ends. Thus, learners are urged to do, show, and practice both while learning (e.g., earnest study) and in their application of what they have learned.

Like the Western model, these five components form a coherent whole that guides children in their daily learning, parents in their home socialization and teachers in their teaching.

Developmental evidence for lasting values

Research also documents that just like the Western model, the Confucian model has lasting power. Two lines of research provide evidence for this claim: (1) children's learning beliefs and (2) parental socialization of children's beliefs.

Children's learning beliefs

Children in both the West and CHC cultures are able to express learning beliefs regarding at least four areas, purposes of learning (e.g., to make oneself smart or to help others), the learning process (i.e., what it takes for one to learn something, e.g., thinking well or persistence), learning affect (e.g., fun or dread), and social aspects (e.g., how learning peers are regarded and parental expectations). Research using children's stories about learning scenarios (Li, 2004; Li and Wang, 2004) found Western children to mention more ideas about mental and intellectual purposes (e.g., 'learning makes me smart'), more positive feelings for self, more ability and strategy use (e.g., 'you have to grow bigger to learn', and 'the bear can practice swimming first, then you can catch fish'), and more peer negativity towards high achievers (e.g., 'other children don't like her [high achiever] because she is better than them'). By contrast, Chinese children elaborated more on social purposes (e.g., being liked by and helping others), learning virtues for the process (e.g., 'he practices so much' and 'he should keep trying until he catches a fish'), and desire to emulate achieving peers. Additionally, they voiced concerns about high achievers being too proud of themselves to continue to self-improve and their greater need to comply with parental expectations. Clearly, these findings confirm that preschool children have already begun to internalize their cultural learning models.

Inescapable role of parental socialization

Children are certainly not born with set beliefs, but they develop them as they grow older. Still, they do not develop in a vacuum but in their specific sociocultural context. Based on Vygotskian theory (Vygotsky, 1978), children internalize the outside knowledge by the process of adult guidance understood as socialization. The most powerful socializing agents in children's formative years are parents because they spend the most time caring for and guiding their children. Moreover, the transmission of any cultural values is actually not primarily through school but in the home. Everything parents do and say conveys culturally-informed thoughts, feelings and norms. Parents socialize their children tirelessly because they love their children and want the best for them. All parents possess values that are dear to them; therefore, they cannot help wanting to give those values to their offspring. Useful knowledge and effective ways to learn are such values (Rogoff, 2003). Interesting is the fact that although highly successful, parents are generally unaware of their role in cultural transmission. The degree of their unawareness reflects the degree of the implicitness such values are learned by their children. Based on anthropological research, values acquired in this way are deep-seated and difficult to change (Harkness and Super, 1996).

Research (Li *et al.*, 2014) indeed demonstrates that European American (EA) and Taiwanese mothers of elementary schoolchildren talk very differently with their children about their learning attitudes and behaviours. EA mothers stress mental and intellectual activities (e.g., analyzing math steps), and positive effect (e.g., curiosity, fun and pride in achievement) more than learning virtues and negative effect (e.g., disappointment and guilt). By contrast, Taiwanese mothers converse more about learning virtues (e.g., seriousness about learning) and negative effect (e.g., feeling self-reproach about lack of learning virtues). These parental socialization patterns cohere with their respective learning models.

Resurging Confucian learning but lingering challenges

China (along with other CHCs) has been suffering a self-loathing mindset towards its learning tradition for over 150 years. This very troubling self-attitude came about as their millennia-long dynastic system collapsed under the attack of Western powers during the turn of the twentieth century. Dreaming of the rebirth of a new culture, China, for example, engaged out of desperation in a massive abandonment of their own learning tradition to zealously embrace Western learning. The elements that CHCs sought to adopt from the West were creativity, independent/critical thinking and self-expression, elements that their own tradition lacked (Yue, 2009). Today, this wave for Western education has not only not subsided, but it has also surged higher due to rapid economic growth. This type of West-envy while self-denouncing has yet to reach its pinnacle because more and more people now can afford a Western education. Within CHCs, education reform has also been deepening. For example, whereas initial learning from the West was an awkward imitation, preschools are now making children enjoy and explore and become 'story kings/queens' to increase their self-expression (Tobin *et al.*, 2009). Another example is the profound penetration of Western language and epistemology into Chinese classroom teaching (Wu, 2011). This continuous trend does project, quite unequivocally, the belief that the ultimate solution to CHCs' educational challenges ought to be found in the West.

Under such a long and intensive shedding force, we would assume that their learning tradition would have perished by now. However, the research reviewed in this chapter indicates that the Confucian learning model is not dead but alive and well (Cheng, 2011; Curran, 2013; Hayhoe, 2014). Even more interesting are most recent signs for restoration of Confucianism. For example, Taiwan, after decades of not requiring schoolchildren to study Confucian texts (presumably in response to internal struggles between tradition and modernity as well as political strife), has a new curricular policy that requires all high school students to study Confucian texts (Taiwan Center for Chinese Curriculum (TCCC), 2014). Part of the reason for such a requirement was to improve Taiwanese children's 'declined' moral education, as seen in the deteriorated student–teacher relationships and increasing bullying in school. Even China, after denouncing Confucian values during the Cultural Revolution (1966–1976) and several decades of ambivalent exploration into the past, somewhat clandestinely erected (in early 2011) a large Confucius statue on its Tiananmen Square, the utmost political centre of China. Confucian excerpts are also found in their language arts curriculum for their nine-year compulsory education (Hong, 2004). Moreover, China began a national award called the 'Award for Moving China' (*gan dong zhong guo* 感动中国) in 2002 and has been granting such awards annually. They are conferred on people who make great contributions to society, but also to exemplars of filial piety, loyalty to friendship, and perseverance to learn despite great personal challenges (Baike, n.d.). Most unexpected was China's newest selection of 40 'exemplary elementary and secondary schools for their teaching of traditional cultural values' out of some 650,000 schools (EDUFZ, 2014). All of these changes are thrown into sharper light when we bear witness to the declining trust in society, surging fraud and corruption, and the towering material wealth in East Asia.

In addition, a large body of research in human development, psychology, education, sociology, cultural studies and East Asian studies over several decades has also yielded overwhelming evidence that Confucianism seems tenacious, reincarnating across time (e.g., repossession and rediscovery in China's Song and Ming era) and space (in Asia or among East Asian diaspora across the world), no matter how it has been attacked. It appears that the more we attempt to eliminate it, the stronger it becomes, demonstrating its time-tested vitality. But in actuality, no researcher in these research fields is really surprised. As in all cultures, the validity depends on one important cultural force: most of what people do to express their values is often second nature to them without their explicit awareness. As stated previously, this taken-for-granted nature makes parents the most willing and effective transmitters of their cultural values (Shweder, 2011). So long as childrearing routines are left alone, families operate based on the basic values and principles of their cultural model.

However, educators in practice and the general public may not be aware of the essential meaning of research findings. The main problem, as I see it, lies in the fact that CHCs, particularly China, still view Confucian learning with trepidation. Looking in from outside, it seems quite strange that these cultural groups would engage in self-condemnation in public discourse for so long, wishing to become somebody else. But at the same time, these same people implicitly still uphold and operate based on the same cultural heritage. This is to say, the people hate it in their open discourse but thrive on it unconsciously. If this were an individual, we would classify him or her as having a classic case of mental illness. It is too unfortunate that Chinese educators have been subject to this kind of schizophrenic state for more than a century. As a result, their formal education system still suffers much ambivalence towards their cultural heritage.

This strange state continues because political ideology has been supplanting cultural beliefs in the official discourse. Many people are confused about the two, mistaking them as being the same. So long as these two symbolic systems are mixed, it would be difficult for Chinese educators to tease apart what is a governing realm and what is a deep-seated cultural belief system. Governing success is measured by how well the government manages the country by standards of a strong state, a rule of law, accountability (Fukuyama, 2012), and I might add how well they provide care and humane treatment to their people. But cultural heritage is a completely different sphere. This sphere, as long-known by anthropologists and psychologists, is above and beyond the political because it deals with lives of individual people, families and communities. The cultural pertains to what people regard as good, true and beautiful versus that which is immoral, false and despised (Shweder, 2011). Cultural heritage is essential for people's personal identities, life aspirations and related pursuits. This is probably why culture tends to endure irrespective of political, social and economic changes. But when the two are constantly mixed and told to people as the same, people end up confused. This may explain why they blame their culture for political and social ills when in fact people are frustrated about their governing system.

In light of this, it seems that the vitality of the Confucian learning model has been underestimated by both the radical revolutionaries and more rational reformers. Thus, cultural reform, that is, an attempt to alter deep-seated cultural values, cannot be achieved with a simple declaration made by politicians, social engineers, educators, or even parents (Curran, 2013; Li, 2012; Nisbett, 2003). This is so because cultural reform is not a matter of sheer will by bold thinking and radical acts, but only possible through a gradual process. And this process is conditioned by the actual change in thinking, feeling and behaviour of the socialization agents such as parents and school. Yet, research on East Asian immigrants, including those who have lived in the West for generations, attests to their tenacity to hold on to their home cultures' core values (Schneider, Hieshima, Lee and Plank (1994). If such immigrants who are immersed in the West daily do not seem to change much, how can people in CHCs, who are not under another culture's force on a daily basis, change?

Premature cross-cultural learning among young children: further cause for concern

The long educational exodus from East to West has resulted in many East Asians now living, receiving education, and raising their children in the West. Today, these early waves of immigrants are joined by millions more who go to the West to study (Institute of International Education (IIE), 2014). Even more surprising is the fact that the age of such education emigrants is becoming younger and younger (Zhou, 2009). Some parents and teachers believe that they ought to send their preschool children to the West for better education (by the count of hands at a lecture I gave to a large Chinese audience in 2012).

Yet, very little research exists to verify if this widely accepted premise holds true. We have reasons to believe that the first adult generation of immigrants might have benefited from their Western learning because many successful examples can be cited (e.g., the Nobel Laureates in science). However, we must ask a very simple question: Are their children more creative, more critical-thinking, and more self-expressive than their counterparts who have never left East Asia? Unfortunately, the answer to this question, based on emerging evidence, is likely no. Thus, there may be a hitherto unseen dark side of this dashing education exodus. If so, then what is the nature of this dark side? What new light does such an inquiry throw on human children's need to be enculturated by their parents' home culture first without disturbance? Finally, is there a developmental risk to exposing young children to two or more very different cultures' socializations simultaneously but prematurely?

These questions are spawned by an important new line of research on how immigrant children of non-European heritage fare in the West. The most important discovery is that the first generation immigrants achieve relatively well. One would assume that their progeny would do the same if not better, given the West-born children's acculturative advantage over their culturally, linguistically and educationally disadvantaged parents. But the data do not support this assumption. Instead, they show a downward trend, with worsening development in each succeeding generation. Scholars term this general and strange phenomenon 'the immigrant paradox' (Garcia Coll and Marks, 2012; Suárez-Orozco, Suárez-Orozco and Todorova, 2008).

Initially, this startling discovery did not catch the attention of East Asian scholars because the group studied were not East Asian but Latino children (Suárez-Orozco and Suárez-Orozco, 1995). On the surface, East Asians may have good reasons to reject the idea that their children might experience stunted intellectual growth and psychological difficulties. Indeed, these children often display impressive achievement (Portes, 1999). However, more recent data on East Asians show an undeniable tendency towards the same downward patterns. For example, as Chinese families live longer in the US, they become less motivated and achieve less well (Han, 2012; Kao, 1999; Pong and Zeiser, 2012; Qin, 2008).

My own longitudinal research on US-born preschool children of Chinese immigrant (CHI) and European American (EA) children revealed findings

(Li, Yamamoto, Luo, Batchelor and Bresnahan, 2010) that mirror the same paradoxical trend. Accordingly, CHIs are far behind their EA peers in oral expression despite their faster growth in math and reading. Oral expression, or simply verbal expressivity, is an index measuring children's complexity of speech development that includes 'mean utterance length' (means of the smallest units of speech, bounded on either end by a pause), tokens (total number of words), types (different kinds of words), number of utterances, rare words (beyond the most common words for their age), dependent clauses (a measure of complexity), quotes (a measure of language sophistication), and holistic rating of educated native speakers (Qin, 2013; Rice *et al.*, 2010; Rivera and Rogers-Adkinson, 1997; Uccelli and Páez, 2007). Juxtaposing CHIs' reading and math with their thwarted oral expression, a clear picture emerges: they are developing intellectually well but only *silently*. Thus, CHIs are not developing into well-rounded individuals by Western standards, as the deep belief driving their parents' educational exodus would predict.

According to developmental theory, preschool children undergo steady growth in productive language and narratives (Bates, Thal, Finlay and Clancy, 2002; Peterson and McCable, 2004), yet, these CHI children do not show this pattern. This counterintuitive finding led us to explore further CHIs' stunted oral expression with children's free expressions in storytelling. Our analysis of fluent English speaking CHIs showed that they were similar to EA children in oral expression at age four but diverged dramatically afterwards. Specifically, while EA children, particularly girls, increased linearly and dramatically, their CHI counterparts decreased sharply, displaying the opposite developmental trajectory. It seems that the linguistically talented and eager talking four-year-old CHIs were no longer expressive by six. It is important to note that over the same period, their English proficiency reached the ceiling of native fluency. Apparently, their thwarted expressivity cannot be explained by their lack of English proficiency, but by something else.

These emerging findings are perplexing. It is even more puzzling to consider the fact that CHIs live in a culture that heavily emphasizes verbal self-expression. Yet, their poor oral expression does not cohere with this very core cultural value of the West. It appears, quite strangely, that living and being educated in the expressive West takes a toll on CHIs' verbal expression. Since self-expression in the West is a hallmark of children's critical, independent thinking and creativity (Edwards *et al.*, 1998; Gardner, 1993), these developments are also likely compromised. Nevertheless, sceptics might cite the well documented verbal reticence in East Asian cultures as the cause of the observed trend of CHIs. Admittedly, this is a legitimate counterargument. To entertain this possibility, we compared CHIs' expressivity with their peers who never lived outside China. Preliminary analysis of the same storytelling data showed even more surprising but confirming results. The latter group's oral expression actually increased, not decreased, in each older age group, resembling the growth trajectory (if not the magnitude) of their EA peers! Hence, if children in China, where oral expression is indeed devalued (Li, 2012), become more self-expressive, then something in CHIs' intellectual development might have gone awry (Qin, 2006, 2008; Tseng and Fuligni, 2000).

Some steps towards restoring cultural values

More research is clearly needed to document the developmental process of CHI children's quieting process regarding their oral expression and associated effects on their general development. Nonetheless, research also shows positive effects of speaking the home language well and having a strong cultural/ethnic identity while learning English and the Western cultural norm (Phinney and Ong, 2002; Qin, 2008; Rumbaut, 1995; Tseng and Fuligni, 2000). Thus, it seems that trying to abandon one's cultural heritage is a bad idea. If children are unable to acquire the basic linguistic skills to communicate with the very people who care for them (i.e., family) and if they do not develop a strong life-sustaining cultural/ethnic identity, upholding their core native cultures' values, then they are unlikely to grow well, let alone to learn from another culture. It is time for CHC educators to think deeply but calmly about how to break the spell of the vicious cycle. To be sure, there is no panacea that anyone can offer to make the distorted self-perception formed over nearly two centuries magically vanish. But our moral obligation suggests that, in light of research evidence (Phinney and Ong, 2002; Qin, 2008; Rumbaut, 1995; Tseng and Fuligni, 2000), education in CHCs may be better served to restore their native cultural heritage. Towards this end, I outline three general steps, focusing on CHC regions, particularly China, because it may face greater challenges.

The first step is to engage in a thorough understanding of their own heritage, particularly in relation to individual families and people. Due to the political turmoil and massive economic development, Chinese educators have not been afforded the opportunity to learn and study their own cultural heritage. For example, universities and professional training rarely offer teachers opportunities to study their culture. Over the past few years, I have interacted with many K-12 principals from China. However, very few have ever read *The Analects*, *Mencius* and other classical texts. To me, this is alarmingly clear how little the educational leaders are prepared to restore their cultural heritage. If teachers do not know, they cannot possibly teach children. It is one thing to live daily lives the Chinese way. It is an entirely different matter to learn *about* and contemplate one's own cultural heritage. Towards more effective learning, I would argue for separating studying Chinese cultural heritage from government and political ideology. This is not to say that government and political ideology should not be discussed or even presented to schoolchildren for discussion. The separation is likely to do much good, even for better governance. Let culture be culture, and let political ideology be that. Mixing has done more harm than good for both.

After the self-study of culture, educational efforts to create the appropriate curriculum could be the next step. One excellent but hitherto untapped resource for Chinese educators is the wealth of overseas scholars who have contemplated deeply and written about the distinct nature of Chinese cultural heritage in comparison with that of the West/other cultures. The work by esteemed scholars who traverse freely between the Chinese and Western world such as Wei-ming Tu on Confucianism and David Wong, on both Confucian and Taoist insights into nature and the universe, Francois Chang on Chinese literature and visual art, and Tan Dun on Chinese music, all offer profound perspectives. They do so precisely because their work is comparative in nature. Children learning both their native material and comparative material would be able to sharpen their minds, hone their sensibilities, and enrich their aesthetic cultivation. Such learning can not only instil in children the broad knowledge about Chinese culture but also connect their daily experiences to the deeper levels of understanding. This kind of learning coupled with their reading and discussion of original texts and art is likely to build the kind of pride that Chinese children are in great need to develop.

At the same time, they are also learning about Western cultures. I disagree with the idea that we need to return to the ancient language in which the great Chinese sages outlined their wisdom and aesthetics (Wu, 2011). Although the ancient Chinese language is very beautiful, expressive, and unique, and contemporary children should learn to read it, there is no reason to believe that only that language can possibly express Confucian and Taoist concepts (putting aside any chance of return to an ancient language no longer spoken or used by current humans). In fact, I would even go so far as to suggest that Chinese students, after mastering English well, should be afforded the opportunity to read ancient Chinese texts in English translation. Such exposure offers a unique perspective for understanding both the Chinese heritage and possible ways to express it in English (or any other foreign languages). An added value is to learn how their cultural wisdom has been apprehended by non-Chinese people. Such learning would enable Chinese children to gain a deeper appreciation of their own cultural heritage. When grown up, they are also more empowered to pass on their own heritage to the next generation, as well as to bridge cross-cultural understanding.

A third step would be to use effective pedagogy tested by educational psychology, human development, and neuroscience to engage children with the curricular material. There are many innovative techniques to help children (of course, many traditional ones have also proven effective). But the most effective is to link their daily experiences that reflect Confucian or Taoist teaching to their classroom learning. For example, children could be asked to bring real life examples of what they observe or do to show parents and grandparents filial piety. Common family discord could also be collected and presented (e.g., a grown-up child is too busy at work to visit his parents) both from well-known historical or contemporary cases. For example, a top scholar during the Ming Dynasty passed the Civil Service Examination after years of study. Yet, when receiving an appointment to serve the emperor, he refused to leave his ill mother behind. Instead, he served by his mother's side until she passed away, and then accepted the emperor's post. The emperor was initially angered by his refusal to serve but was moved by his deed upon learning the truth. The emperor not only did not punish the scholar but erected a monument in his home village to honour him instead. Children could be asked to discuss if the scholar did the right thing, missing the opportunity for personal advancement and why the emperor who had the power to demand him to his post did not do so. Children could also read the relevant passages in *The Analects*, *Mencius*, *Family Reverence*, and other texts and discuss, write about, and observe their own family interactions regarding filial piety. Such thought-provoking pedagogy, commonly used in the West, is more potent in making children empathize with and appreciate the great sages of Chinese culture. Such methods enable children to come to own these values willingly, gladly and effectively without being mired in the problem of memorizing ancient texts without understanding.

Concluding note

The Confucian learning model for person-making through learning has survived. However, it has also been marred for nearly two centuries, due to political and social turmoil and recent, sudden economic growth in the region. Families, children and educators all have been subject to the unfortunate denunciation of their cultural heritage but at the same time depend and thrive on it. This tormenting psychology has harmed generations of Chinese and CHC people. It must not continue. Restoration of their cultural heritage is urgent.

Surely, the three steps towards this restoration, and many more steps that could be listed, cannot be achieved overnight. The restoration requires the whole society's recognition, commitment and careful planning over a much longer time. Chinese and other CHCs' education could benefit from a new generation to start the process. We hope that, over time, children will not just live their cultural heritage but will also know about it, reflect on it, guard it and be proud of it. And then these children can truly learn from other cultures from a position of confidence and strength.

References

Ames, R. T. and Rosemont, H., Jr. (1999). *The Analects of Confucius: A Philosophical Translation*. New York: Ballantine.

Baike (n.d.). Available online at: http://baike.baidu.com/view/14280.htm#sub14280 (accessed 15 June 2014).

Bates, E., Thal, D., Finlay, B. and Clancy, B. (2002). Language Development and its Neural Correlates. In I. Rapin and S. J. Segalowitz (eds), *Handbook of Neuropsychology* (pp. 109–76). Amsterdam: Elsevier.

Chang, H. C. (1997). Language and Words: Communication in the Analects of Confucius. *Journal of Language and Social Psychology*, 16, 107–31.

Cheng, K. M. (2011). Pedagogy: East and West, Then and Now. *Journal of Curriculum Studies*, 43(5), 591–9.

Curran, T. D. (2013). A Response to Professor Wu Zongjie's 'Interpretation, Autonomy, and Transformation: Chinese Pedagogic Discourse in a Cross-Cultural Perspective'. *Journal of Curriculum Studies*, 46(3), 305–12.

EDUFZ (China Education Development Network) (n.d.). Available online at: http://edufz.net/news_detail.asp?id=39 (accessed 4 January 2015).

Edwards, C., Gandini, L. and Forman, G. (eds) (1998). *The Hundred Languages of Children: The Reggio Emilia Approach – Advanced Reflections* (2nd edn). Westport, CT: Ablex.

Fukuyama, F. (2012). *The Origins of Political Order: From Prehuman Times to the French Revolution*. New York: Farrar, Straus and Giroux.

Gao, G. (1998). 'Don't take my word for it': Understanding Chinese Speaking Practices. *International Journal of Intercultural Relations*, 22, 163–86.

Gao, L.-B. and Watkins, D. (2001). Identifying and Assessing the Conceptions of Teaching of Secondary School Physics Teachers in China. *British Journal of Educational Psychology*, 71, 443–69.

Garcia Coll, C. T. and Marks, A. K. (eds) (2012). *The Immigrant Paradox in Children and Adolescents: Is Becoming American a Developmental Risk?* Washington, DC: APA Press.

Gardner, H. (1983). *Frames of Mind*. New York: Basic Books.

Gardner, H. (1993). *Creating Minds: An Anatomy of Creativity Seen Through the Lives of Freud, Einstein, Picasso, Stravinsky, Eliot, Graham, and Gandhi*. New York: Basic Books.

Goffman, E. (1981). *Frames of Talk*. Philadelphia, PA: University of Pennsylvania Press.

Han, W-J. (2012). Bilingualism and Academic Achievement: Does Generation Status Make a Difference? In C. T. Garcia Coll and A. K. Marks (eds), *The Immigrant Paradox in Children and Adolescents: Is Becoming American a Developmental Risk?* (pp. 161–84). Washington, DC: APA Press.

Harkness, S. and Super, C. M. (eds) (1996). *Parents' Cultural Belief Systems: Their Origins, Expressions, and Consequences*. New York: Guilford.

Hayhoe, R. (2014) Hopes for Confucian Pedagogy in China? *Journal of Curriculum Studies*, 46(3), 313–19.

Hecht, J. M. (2003). *Doubt, A History: The Great Doubters and Their Legacy of Innovation from Socrates and Jesus to Thomas Jefferson and Emily Dickinson*. New York: Harper Collins.

Hewitt, R. and Inghilleri, M. (1993). Oracy in the Classroom: Policy, Pedagogy, and Group Oral Work. *Anthropology & Education Quarterly*, 24(4), 308–17.

Hong, Z.-L. (2nd edn) (2004). 義務教育課程標准實驗教科書:《語文》九年級.江蘇教育出版社 *[Chinese for 9th Grade: Standard Experimental Textbook for Compulsory Education]* (ed.), Jiangsu Province: Jiangsu Education Press.

Hsueh, Y., Zhou, Z.-K., Cohen, R., Hundley, R. J. and Deptula, D. P. (2005). Knowing and Showing Respect: Chinese and US Children's Understanding of Respect and its Association to their Friendships. *Journal of Psychology in Chinese Societies*, 6(2), 89–120.

Huntsinger, C. S. and Jose, P. E. (2009). Parental Involvement in Children's Schooling: Different Meanings in Different Cultures. *Early Childhood Research Quarterly*, 24, 398–410.

IIE (Institute of International Education) (2014). Available online at: http://iie.org/en/Research-and-Publications/Open-Doors (accessed 1 April 2014).

Kao, G. (1999). Psychological Well-being and Educational Achievement Among Immigrant Youth. In D. J. Hernandez (ed.), *Children of Immigrants: Health, Adjustment, and Public Assistance* (pp. 410–77). Washington, DC: National Academy Press.

Lee, W. O. (1996). The Cultural Context for Chinese Learners: Conceptions of Learning in the Confucian Tradition. In D. A. Watkins and J. B. Biggs (eds), *The Chinese Learner* (pp. 45–67). Hong Kong: Comparative Education Research Centre.

Li, J. (2002). A Cultural Model of Learning: Chinese 'Heart and Mind for Wanting to Learn'. *Journal of Cross-Cultural Psychology*, 33, 248–69.

Li, J. (2003). US and Chinese Cultural Beliefs About Learning. *Journal of Educational Psychology*, 95(2), 258–67.

Li, J. (2004). Learning as a Task and a Virtue: US and Chinese Preschoolers Explain Learning. *Developmental Psychology*, 40(4), 595–605.

Li, J. (2006). Self in Learning: Chinese Adolescents' Goals and Sense of Agency. *Child Development*, 77(2), 482–501.

Li, J. (2012). *Cultural Foundations of Learning: East and West*. Cambridge: Cambridge University Press.

Li, J. (2014). *Humility in Learning: A Confucian Perspective. Presentation at the Conference: Developing Virtue: Empirically-Informed Perspectives from East and West*, California State University Fullerton.

Li, J. and Fischer, K. W. (2007). Respect as a Positive Self-Conscious Emotion in European Americans and Chinese. In J. L. Tracy, R. W. Robins and J. P. Tangney (eds), *The Self-Conscious Emotions: Theory and Research* (pp. 224–42). New York: Guilford.

Li, J. and Wang, Q. (2004). Perceptions of Achievement and Achieving Peers in US and Chinese Kindergartens. *Social Development*, 13(3), 413–36.

Li, J., Fung, H., Bakeman, R., Rae, K. and Wei, W.-C. (2014). How European American and Taiwanese Mothers Talk to Their Children About Learning. *Child Development*, 84, 1–16.

Li, J., Yamamoto, Y., Luo, L., Batchelor, A. and Bresnahan, R. M. (2010). Why Attend School? Chinese Immigrant and European American Preschooler's Views and Outcomes. *Developmental Psychology*, 5, 1–14.

Mencius (1970). *Mencius* (D. C. Lao, trans.). Harmondsworth: Penguin Books.

Minami, M. (1994). English and Japanese: A Cross-Cultural Comparison of Parental Styles of Narrative Elicitation. *Issues in Applied Linguistics*, 5, 383–407.

Nisbett, R. E. (2003). *The Geography of Thought*. New York: Simon & Schuster.

O'Connor, M. C. and Michaels, S. (1993). Aligning Academic Task and Participation Status Through Revoicing: Analysis of a Classroom Discourse Strategy. *Anthropology & Education Quarterly*, 24(4), 318–35.

Peterson, C. and McCabe, A. (2004). Echoing our parents: Parental influences on children's narration. In M. W. Pratt and B. H. Fiese (eds), *Family Stories and the Life Course: Across Time and Generations* (pp. 27–54). Mahwah, NJ: Lawrence Erlbaum.

Phinney, J. S. and Ong, A. D. (2002). Adolescent–Parent Disagreements and Life Satisfaction in Families from Vietnamese- and European-American Backgrounds. *International Journal of Behavioral Development*, 26(6), 556–61.

Plato (1981). *Five Dialogues* [trans. by G. M. A. Gruber]. Indianapolis, IN: Hackett.

Pong, S.-L. and Zeiser, K. (2012). Student Engagement, School Climate, and Academic Achievement of Immigrants' Children. In C. T. Garcia Coll and A. K. Marks (eds),

The Immigrant Paradox in Children and Adolescents: Is Becoming American a Developmental Risk? (pp. 209–32). Washington, DC: APA Press.

Portes, P. R. (1999). Social and Psychological Factors in the Academic Achievement of Children of Immigrants: A Cultural History Puzzle. *American-Educational Research Journal*, 36(3), 489–507.

Qin, D. B.-L. (2006). 'Our child doesn't talk to us anymore': Alienation in Immigrant Chinese Families. *Anthropology and Education Quarterly*, 37(2), 162–79.

Qin, D. B.-L. (2008). Doing Well vs. Feeling Well: Understanding Family Dynamics and the Psychological Adjustment of Chinese Immigrant Adolescents. *Journal of Youth and Adolescence*, 37(1), 22–35.

Qin, W. (2013). *Cohesion Markers in 4th and 6th Graders' Argumentative Writing*. Poster presented at the Twentieth Annual Meeting of Society for the Scientific Study of Reading, July, Hong Kong.

Rice, M. L., Smolik, F., Perpich, D., Thompson, T., Rytting, N. and Blossom, M. (2010). Mean Length of Utterance Levels in 6-Month Intervals for Children 3 to 9 Years With and Without Language Impairments. *Journal of Speech, Language & Hearing Research*, 53(2), 333–49.

Rivera, B. D. and Rogers-Adkinson, D. (1997). Culturally Sensitive Interventions: Social Skills Training with Children and Parents from Culturally and Linguistically Diverse Backgrounds. *Intervention in School and Clinic*, 33(2), 75–80.

Rogoff, B. (2003). *The Cultural Nature of Human Development*. New York: Oxford University Press.

Rosemont, H., Jr. (1992). Rights-Bearing Individuals and Role-Bearing Persons. In M. I. Bockover (ed.), *Rules, Rituals, and Responsibility: Essays Dedicated to Herbert Fingarette* (pp. 71–101). La Salle, IL: Open Court.

Rumbaut, R. G. (1995). The New Californians: Comparative Research Findings on the Educational Progress of Immigrant Children. In R. G. Rumbaut and A. C. Wayne (eds), *California's Immigrant Children: Theory, Research and Immilication for Educational Policy* (pp. 17–70). La Jolla, CA: Center for U.S.-Mexican Studies, University of California, San Diego.

Russell, B. (1975). *A History of Western Philosophy and its Connection with Political and Social Circumstances from the Earliest Times to the Present Day*. New York: Simon & Schuster.

Schneider, B., Hieshima, J. A., Lee, S. and Plank, S. (1994). East-Asian Academic Success in the United States: Family, School, and Cultural Explanations. In P. M. Greenfield and R. R. Cocking (eds), *Cross-Cultural Roots of Minority Child Development* (pp. 332–50). Hillsdale, NJ: Erlbaum.

Shweder, R. A. (2011). Commentary: Ontogenetic Cultural Psychology. In L. A. Jensen (ed.), *Bridging Cultural and Developmental Psychology: New Syntheses in Theory, Research and Policy* (pp. 303–10). New York: Oxford University Press.

Spiegel, J. S. (2012). Open-Mindedness and Intellectual Humility. *Theory and Research in Education*, 10, 27–38.

Suárez-Orozco, C. and Suárez-Orozco, M. (1995). *Transformations: Immigration, Family Life, and achievement motivation among Latino adolescents*. Stanford, CA: Stanford University Press.

Suárez-Orozco, C., Suárez-Orozco, M. and Todorova, I. (2008). *Learning a New Land: Immigrant Students in American Society*. New York: Belknap.

Tangney, J. P. (2000). Humility: Theoretical Perspectives, Empirical Findings and Directions for Future Research. *Journal of Social and Clinical Psychology*, 19(1), 70–82.

TCCC (Taiwan Center for Chinese Curriculum) (2014). Available online at: http://chincenter.fg.tp.edu.tw/cerc/98ke.php (accessed 1 July 2014) for required study of Confucian texts by Taiwan's Ministry of Education.

Tobin, J., Hsueh, Y. and Karasawa, M. (2009). *Preschool in Three Cultures Revisited: China, Japan, and United States.* Chicago: The University of Chicago Press.

Todd, S. C. A. (2000). *The Oratory of Classical Greece: Volume 2.* Austin, Texas: University of Texas Press.

Tseng, V. and Fuligni, A. J. (2000). Parent–Adolescent Language Use and Relationships Among Immigrant Families with East Asian, Filipino, and Latin American Backgrounds. *Journal of Marriage and the Family,* 62, 465–76.

Uccelli, P. and Páez, M. (2007). Narrative and Vocabulary Development of Bilingual Children from Kindergarten to First Grade: Developmental Changes and Associations Among English and Spanish Skills. *Language, Speech, and Hearing Services in Schools,* 38, 225–36.

Vygotsky, L. S. (1978). *Mind in Society: The Development of Higher Psychological Processes.* Cambridge, MA: Harvard University Press.

Wang, J.-J. (2013). Understanding the Chinese Learners from a Perspective of Confucianism. In M. Cortazzi and L.-X. Jin (eds), *Researching Cultures of Learning: International Perspectives on Language Learning and Education* (pp. 61–79). New York: Palgrave Macmillan.

Wu, Z. (2011) Interpretation, Autonomy, and Transformation: Chinese Pedagogic Discourse in a Cross-Cultural Perspective. *Journal of Curriculum Studies,* 43(5), 569–90.

Yue, N. (2009). 陳寅恪與傅斯年 *[Chen Yinke and Fu Sinian].* Taipei, Taiwan: Yuan-Liou Publishing.

Zagzebeski, L. T. (1996). *Virtues of the Mind: An Inquiry into the Nature of Virtue and the Ethical Foundations of Knowledge.* New York: Cambridge University Press.

Zhou, M. (2009). Conflict, Coping, and Reconciliation: Intergenerational Relations in Chinese Immigrant Families. In N. Foner, *Across Generations: Immigrant Families in America* (pp. 21–46). New York: New York University Press.

9 Huang Yanpei's view of folk culture as a person-making tool

Thomas D. Curran

Observers of the Chinese educational scene have commented recently that the nation's schools tend to concentrate on the instrumental objectives of preparing students for employment or socialization rather than the goal of developing 'well-rounded, self-aware ethical and spiritual beings' who have 'a genuine passion for and interest in learning' (Zhao, 2013a, p. 492; also see Zhao and Deng, Chapter 1). As Professor Zongyi Deng has put it, employing terminology that was developed in 2008 by Gert Biesta in an important essay calling upon educators to re-examine the ultimate purposes of education, the '*subjectification* function' of schooling, the act of forging a unique individual 'with autonomy, critical thinking, and creativity,' has been neglected as Chinese educators have focused primarily on fostering the 'acquisition of knowledge, skills and attitudes required for jobs' (the *qualification* function of schooling) and encouraging the 'development of values and norms necessary for becoming a member of existing social and cultural orders' (the *socialization* function) (Deng, 2013, p. 560; Biesta, 2009, pp. 39–41; also see Deng, Chapter 11).[1] The antidote to this imbalance that is often proposed is to re-focus schooling on its *subjectification* or person-making function; that is, its major objective should be the cultivation of individuals whose intellectual, moral and spiritual qualities are fully developed.

It will not surprise historians to find that the disjunction between the instrumental and other purposes of schooling was well understood in the early days of China's educational modernization effort. The first several decades of the twentieth century spawned a wide variety of reform initiatives, one especially prominent fault line being that which divided those aimed primarily at job preparation and those targeted at the cultivation of liberally educated individuals.[2] Many of the reformers were particularly well acquainted with the problems associated with schooling meant exclusively for qualification, and they experimented with a number of 'developmentalist' models derived from the theories of Western pedagogues such as Johann Heinrich Pestalozzi (1746–1827) and Johan Friedrich Herbart (1776–1841) who sought to expand their students' intellectual horizons by capitalizing on their natural curiosity and exposing them to the realities of life (Curran, 2005, pp. 128–34).[3]

Although there was always a strong current of pragmatism in these reformers' thinking regarding graduates' need to secure employment and adapt to a rapidly changing social field, they were also deeply concerned about the moral and spiritual development of China's youth, and one might imagine that the language of personhood or person-making that today's critics employ would be instantly recognizable to them. It is important, however, to note that by and large the developmentalist projects failed. Not only were the new schools expensive, but their curricula and pedagogy were based on Western models that in the final analysis could not survive the process of transplantation into Chinese cultural soil. At the elementary level they were sufficiently exotic to prevent ordinary Chinese from considering them attractive places to send their children, while at higher levels their high costs and foreign curricula virtually guaranteed that they would be accessible primarily to urban elites who had already acquired Western habits and tastes that significantly alienated them from the mainstream of Chinese life. Education which adopted Western principles proved to be difficult for Chinese society to digest (Curran, 2005, pp. 235–87, 458–68).

This chapter will review some of the reform ideas of one of the early twentieth century's most influential Chinese educational reformers, Huang Yanpei 黄炎培 (1878–1965). As the founder and head of the Chinese Vocational Education Association, Huang led a major reform initiative that struggled with the dual objectives of career preparation and person-making. After he launched the movement for vocational schooling in 1917 he spent most of his time during the next decade pursuing reforms that he hoped would endow school graduates with the skills and temperament to launch successful careers in business, industry, or finance.[4] By the 1930s, however, he had come to consider the goal of education to be significantly broader than that; he had come to believe that its proper function is to nurture citizens who not only possess the basic requirements for employment but also have moral qualities and character traits that will prepare them for life well beyond the workplace.

It is important to note that Huang's thinking on the subject of person-making was powerfully influenced by historical circumstances that made education a matter of intense national security interest. Responding to the crises that plagued China in the 1930s and 1940s, he and most other reformers believed that education should serve first and foremost the cause of national salvation – as a popular slogan of the day put it, education must 'save the nation'. For patriotic reasons, they were deeply concerned with the socialization function of schooling, and they were determined to build school systems that could graduate citizens who were both able and willing to serve the national interest as well as their own. They also believed, however, that the nation's welfare demanded morally cultivated individuals who possessed a set of ethical principles that were entirely compatible with their needs as individuals. Few of the reformers would propose that a graduate could serve either his country or himself by mere technique alone. Thus, one could argue that their interest in the cultivation of character brought them a bit closer in spirit to educators today, whose primary concern is to train 'well-rounded, self-aware ethical and spiritual beings', than might appear to be the case were we only to notice their intense desire to socialize Chinese students into the role of citizen.

What makes Huang Yanpei particularly interesting is that while most other intellectuals of his generation were iconoclastic in their critique of Chinese culture, blaming China's contemporary problems in part upon the nation's Confucian traditions, he believed that the nation's ancient cultural heritage continued to be of great value. He accepted Social Darwinist premises and the telos of modern nationalism that many of his generation shared, yet unlike most of his colleagues he was unwilling to deny the contemporary relevance of China's heritage. As Irwin Schwintzer points out, he was a member of a class of 'Confucian Protestants' who were troubled by the decay of Confucian institutions yet reluctant to jettison the conventional moral principles upon which they were built (Schwintzer, 1992, pp. 4–5).[5] One senses in his writings that were he alive today he would find himself substantially in sympathy with calls for a revival of the Confucian tradition of self-cultivation that contemporary scholars, such as Huajun Zhang, have made (Zhang, 2013, p. 555; also see Zhang, Chapter 5).[6] On the other hand, while he was conservative in many respects he did not propose to restore the Confucian classics to the central place they had occupied in Chinese education during imperial times. Also, unlike the developmentalists, he sought conscientiously to avoid tying schooling so closely to Western models that Chinese students might find them alienating. Rather, as he pondered the role of education in the 1930s and 1940s he paid particular attention to the country's repertoire of popular traditions and values, finding in them elements that he believed could serve Chinese youth well in their modern incarnation. He believed that within the nation's folk heritage there lay resources that could be used to inspire Chinese students to discover for themselves the moral and spiritual qualities that he believed would serve both them and their nation well. At the present time, when China's reformers may be tempted to turn once again to the West for inspiration, one might regard Huang's argument as a suggestion that in their effort to strike a balance between instrumental education and the cultivation of well-rounded individuals they might still find value in their nation's ancient cultural heritage.

Huang re-envisions education

Huang Yanpei began his career as an educator thinking almost exclusively about China's employment problems and the need to match schooling to the country's need for trained manpower. A practical man who chose to call the set of reforms he championed in the mid-1910s 'pragmatic education' [*shiyong zhu-i jiaoyu* 使用注意教育], he devoted most of his energies to rectifying what he considered to be an imbalance between a conventional academic curriculum and one focused more directly on the job market.[7] On the other hand, as he pondered the future of China's youth he was also deeply concerned about the fate of his country, and some of his early writings shed light onto the direction his thinking would take later in his career when he spoke and wrote more purposefully about the role schooling might play in crafting the type of person he hoped Chinese schools would produce.

Unsurprisingly, his views were influenced by comparisons he drew between China and the West. In one of his earliest writings on the subject, a January 1916 piece published in the Chinese Educational Review (*Jiaoyu zazhi* 教育杂志), he offered a damning indictment of China's contemporary culture by drawing comparisons between it and that of the West. In the West, he maintained, the core values were naturalness and spontaneity, diversity, creativity and service to society.[8] By contrast, he argued, Chinese culture in its modern form prized coercion and control of the individual, uniformity, imitation and self-gratification. As a result, China's schools suppressed the spontaneous expression of opinions and sentiment, taking as their primary objective the enforcement of social norms which encouraged the individual student to focus more or less single-mindedly upon the pursuit of material self-interest. Rather than to encourage student self-discovery, moral development, or any other form of personal self-cultivation, the schools emphasized the mere transmission of basic skills and knowledge (Huang, 1916, pp. 49–51).

Having taken this short step towards crafting an educational vision that encompassed a concept of person-making that approaches what today's commentators appear to have in mind, Huang returned to his main concern, unemployment and underemployment among China's youth, and during the next decade he spent most of his time promoting his pet interest in vocational schooling. By the early1930s, however, events had occurred which revived the concern he had expressed in his 1916 essay for learning that would reach beyond the narrow borders of vocationalism. In particular, by 1931 he had become acutely aware that the rise of Japanese militarism posed a serious threat to his country, and when his fears were confirmed a year later by the Japanese attack on Shanghai he began to reconstruct his educational vision. From this point and for the remainder of the 1930s one senses in his writings a nagging fear that the Chinese people lacked the patriotic spirit that he believed was necessary if they were to avoid a national catastrophe, and his comments on education make it clear that he had come to believe that one of its major objectives was to overcome students' customary self-absorption and lead them to perceive the mutuality of interests they shared with their compatriots. Probably the most direct expression of this view came in a 1938 piece in which he presented an argument somewhat akin to Aristotle's assertion that a human being cannot exist as an autonomous being in isolation from his state (Huang, 1939, pp. 335–9).[9]

Obviously, there is nothing in this message that suggests Huang was concerned that students acquire a passion for learning for its own sake or a self-conscious recognition of the individual's potential for self-directed growth; such a version of education would probably have appeared to him as a dangerous distraction from the need to unify the Chinese people during a time of acute national emergency. On the other hand, as he reflected upon what would best serve the interests of the nation and the individual he turned inevitably to the question of character and what sort of education could best cultivate it. In the summer of 1942 he gave a series of ten public addresses at Chengdu's China Western (Huaxi 华西) University in which he presented what was probably the most coherent summary of his educational vision of his entire career (Huang, 1944, passim). As we shall see, while in these talks he never deviated from his objective of bringing the ambitions of China's youth into harmony with the nation's needs, he nevertheless paid considerable attention to the problem of how best to shape individual character and behaviour. Interestingly, unlike his fellow reformers who were attracted to foreign educational theories and models, he turned his gaze inward, finding that China's folk culture contained the most promising sources of insight into the question of what sort of education would lead young people to fulfil their potential as both patriotic citizens and refined human beings.

Expressing his confidence in China's future, he began the series by noting that, although China remained cut off from its allies and imperilled, he was optimistic that it would eventually weather the storms that beset it. Employing a Shanghai expression roughly analogous to the English phrase 'It is darkest just before the dawn,' he said that China was at present 'in the darkness when people steal cattle' [*tou niu hei* 偷牛黑] – the situation was not good, but there was good reason to anticipate improvement (Huang, 1944, p. 5). Of particular significance, he asserted, was that unlike Europe where class struggle had become a divisive phenomenon, there was nothing in China of a historical or structural nature standing in the way of building a well-integrated national community; there were no 'latent sources of turmoil,' no organic obstacles to national integration (Huang, 1944, pp. 24–5).[10] Rather, there were many factors present in Chinese culture that had helped China's civilization thrive for several thousand years. The greatest of these resources, he believed, was China's national character, its 'national soul,' a spirit or essence that includes a set of shared values (Huang, 1944, pp. 72–3).

Two components of the national mentality that Huang believed were especially important in light of the desperate times were a spirit of devotion to the nation and persistence in the face of adversity – habits of mind that he believed were core elements of Chinese popular psychology. To illustrate the former he cited an incident during the Shanghai War of 1932 in which a Chinese driver plunged his truck into the Huangpu River rather than allow his deadly cargo of Japanese munitions to be used against the city's defenders. Occurrences such as this, he claimed, were very common in wartime China, proving that within Chinese culture there existed a spirit of devotion to one's country (Huang, 1944, pp. 57–8). As for persistence, he quoted from one of Sun Yat-sen's lectures on the principle of nationalism in which Sun declared that 'When we do something, we must follow it through to completion; if we do not succeed, then even to sacrifice our lives trying would be no pity' (Huang, 1944, p. 67).

Aside from considering the behaviour of patriotic Chinese or consulting the writings of leaders such as Sun Yat-sen, Huang believed that a fruitful source for insight into the nature of China's national soul was its folklore, the concrete manifestations of belief one finds among the Chinese people, and he suggested that educators searching for inspiration might begin by asking which personalities from China's past were most well-known among the people. Of course, he told his audience, the first name that came to mind was Confucius. However, since the sage and his philosophy may not be well understood by most citizens, he thought a better choice would be three famous generals of Chinese history and legend, Guan Gong 关公,[11] Zhuge Liang 诸葛亮[12] and Yue Fei 岳飞,[13] each of whom ended his life tragically in a losing cause while exemplifying virtues that Huang believed lay deeply embedded within China's popular culture: selflessness and perseverance in the face of near certain death. The Chinese people, Huang pointed out, could have reserved their admiration for the winners of the conflicts in which each of these heroes had given his life. Instead, however, they venerated these three who had died in defeat. Why? he asked. While some might ascribe this legacy to their dramatic life stories, each of these heroes having been memorialized in a great work of fiction, there were many other legendary figures who did not evoke a similar response in the hearts of the Chinese people. No one, for example, worshipped Tang Seng 唐僧 or Jia Baoyu 贾宝玉, the protagonists in *The Journey to the West* and *The Dream of the Red Chamber*. The reason for this discrepancy, Huang asserted, was that while characters such as Tang and Jia were of interest to the literate elite they did not appeal strongly to common people who themselves possessed a basic nature, a distinct spirit and character, akin to that which was reflected in the life stories of the three great generals. To Huang, it was the fact that the generals had been willing to give their lives for the causes they served that made their stories compelling. Such selflessness, Huang suggested, was something China needed in its current state of emergency, and fortunately it was a key component of China's national soul (Huang, 1944, pp. 74–6).

Conversely, Huang pointed out, in the public mind the self-serving and ambitious were despised. He related a story he had heard about a rural performance of a folk play featuring Guan Gong and Cao Cao 曹操.[14] When the Guan Gong character mounted the stage the audience responded by solemnly standing up and bowing to show respect, but when the actor playing the despised Cao Cao appeared a tanner in the audience leapt onto the stage and cut the unfortunate actor down with a knife while the audience cheered in righteous approval (Huang, 1944, p. 79). Huang, of course, was not about to endorse the murderous behaviour of the tanner or the crudeness of the audience. What he thought offered hope to China, rather, was the villagers' reverence for Guan Gong. Such admiration for a loyal defender of his patron, Huang believed, was universal in China, a core element of the Chinese code of ethics and something that distinguishes Chinese culture from others. 'This,' he asserted, 'is the place where foreign countries and China differ the most' (Huang, 1944, p. 80).

Closely associated in Huang's mind with perseverance and selfless devotion to one's country were the virtues of moral integrity and courage, and for evidence that they were important elements of China's national soul he turned to the standard dynastic histories. There, in the biographical sections in particular,

Huang noted that one finds numerous examples of individuals who demonstrated the courage to stand up for right principles regardless of the consequences. These values were not limited to the elites, since the histories recorded many cases in which knights-errant and even assassins were admired by historians; even though these heroes had violated the laws, they had done so in order to oppose or avenge injustices. 'If to record the meritorious deeds of principled individuals was a unique feature of Chinese historiography,' Huang insisted, 'even though at times the individuals may have been crude, such an appreciation for individuals who risk everything for righteousness must also be a unique characteristic of China's national essence.' Perhaps, he mused, that explains why during the present world war, while other countries had surrendered to the overwhelming power of their enemies, the Chinese continued to fight even after five years of misery (Huang, 1944, pp. 76–8).[15]

Loyalty was another virtue that Huang found to be embedded within China's folk culture. Curiously, to demonstrate the popular commitment to it Huang cited the example of secret societies, the progenitors of some modern-day gangs that were organized following the collapse of the Ming dynasty. During the nineteenth century, Huang noted, even such a powerful official as Zou Zongtang 左宗棠 (1812–1885) found his authority seriously undermined by the secret society leaders who commanded some of his troops.[16] Similarly, in the factories of modern Shanghai managers could not secure the cooperation of their workers without first dealing with gang bosses. The glue that held both the societies and the gangs together, Huang maintained, was loyalty. It was a value that been part of the Chinese national character for centuries (Huang, 1944, pp. 80–4).

Next on Huang's list of virtues was filial piety, an integral component of China's cultural heritage that had very deep roots. Huang took the story of the founding of the Zhou dynasty (1046–256 BCE) by Kings Wen 文 and Wu 武 as an example. According to ancient legend, lacking virtue himself the last ruler of the Shang dynasty (c. 1600–1046 BCE), King Zhou 周, had placed King Wen in prison where he subsequently died. Wen's son, King Wu, thereupon led his army against King Zhou, mounting upon his chariot a spirit tablet in memory of Wen to indicate to the enemy forces that he had no ambition to become emperor; he merely sought righteous vengeance for the death of his father. At the same time, Wu hoped to convince the common people of the Shang state that he was a man of virtue; surely, he reasoned, they would submit willingly to such a man. As it turned out, according to the legend, the spirit tablet was King Wu's most powerful weapon and was the real reason why his armies prevailed over the Shang. The lesson Huang chose to derive from this story was that filial piety had been an elemental component of China's popular psychology since ancient times. It and two other virtues that Huang closely associated with it, faithfulness and mutual trust, could be readily found in contemporary life, notably in the relationships between parties in business where the Chinese habit was to take other people at their word and rely on verbal commitments when conducting transactions. These values, and the traditional reliance on human relations that each of them imply, were in Huang's mind uniquely Chinese assets that should be preserved and strengthened in the schools (Huang, 1944, pp. 82–4).

Huang pointed out that it was also extremely important that the schools cultivate among young people the habit of obedience to laws and the principle that all people, regardless of their stations in life, are equal before them. He admitted that China's recent history in this regard had not been encouraging. In particular, after the rise of militarism in China during the 1910s laws had simply ceased to function; even after the national government was instituted in Nanjing it found itself preoccupied with preparations for war and had been unable to make much progress towards the re-establishment of legal bases for the exercise of authority. Nevertheless, Huang argued, even as the Chinese people waged resistance war they needed to conduct themselves lawfully; they had to 'follow the proper path' (Huang, 1944, p. 104). Fortunately, he argued, the nation's educated citizens possessed a venerable tradition of respect for law and were in a position to play a leading role in cultivating it among the people. As 'models for the people' – that is, those to whom the people looked for leadership – China's intellectuals had a special obligation to set an example by upholding the laws themselves in a self-conscious and conspicuous way. He likened an educated person's role to that of a county magistrate he had encountered in 1934 who decided to forbid the residents of his county to smoke cigarettes. The official's strategy was to make the prohibition clear to all by setting a personal example, and during the first month he applied the law only to himself. During the next month he extended it to cover all of his subordinates in the county government. The following month he implemented the policy within the entire county capital, and in the final month he applied it to the entire county. Huang left the county during the second month, and by then with the county government in compliance it had become generally understood that the law would be enforced and was to be obeyed by all citizens. Huang noted that he himself had attempted to lead this way by insisting that those who worked in his service or on his behalf adhere strictly to local ordinances and regulations. While on a 1939 tour of inspection in southern Sichuan as a member of the National Political Council, for example, he insisted that his staff, which included nearly one hundred people from clerks to litter bearers and even grooms for his horses, refrain from taking advantage of his high status to evade local customs. When a messenger and a cook were found with opium he unceremoniously turned them over to the local court for punishment. Thus, he reasoned, when he lectured the public on the role that law ought to play in rectifying private behaviour he could do so without fear of contradiction (Huang, 1944, p. 104).

Finally, Huang argued that Chinese schools should conduct military training for their pupils. One very important reason China had survived the Japanese onslaught for so long, he reasoned, was that many school curricula already included military drill. Not only were the theoretical and technical aspects of a military education beneficial to graduates who might be called upon to fight for their country, but so were the habits of discipline and the solemn frame of mind that drill would induce. Importantly, these habits of mind would not only be of benefit in time of military emergency; they would also contribute greatly to success in one's private life (Huang, 1944, p. 105).

These virtues – selflessness, persistence, moral integrity and courage, loyalty, filial piety, faithfulness, obedience to law and a martial spirit – Huang maintained, were at the heart of what it meant to be Chinese in the past, and it was to these traditional aspects of the Chinese character that he turned when he considered the sort of education the nation and its youth needed. As he put it, together they constituted 'the firmest plinth upon which to establish a nation' (Huang, 1944, p. 88).

In Huang's final two lectures the troubled educator discussed ways by which he proposed to make use of these salient elements of China's national personality to rescue China from its contemporary troubles. Since the values that he believed could save the nation were within the common vocabulary of the Chinese people, Huang argued, it should be possible for Chinese educators to locate and make use of them to awaken the people – to revive China's 'half buried national soul.'

China's reformed school systems, Huang noted, were not necessarily the best vehicle for accomplishing this task because in large part they were a foreign import, a product of foreign models that did not necessarily promote the virtues he sought to instil in China's youth. 'Not to mention Western political ideologies,' Huang complained, 'even the education of Western countries rarely emphasizes these values' (Huang, 1944, p. 85). What needed to be done, rather, was to find the ingredients of China's national character within popular culture and develop ways to lead people to a greater understanding of and appreciation for them. China's educators, and the nation's educated elite in general, should seek to develop techniques to identify, explain and popularize elements of China's national heritage. One technique was to tell the people inspiring stories of the sages and worthies of China's past who devoted themselves, often with tragic consequences, to the values that Huang wished young Chinese to have. Another was to publicize as much as possible incidents of Japanese brutality in order to awaken the people to their identity as Chinese and to activate the self-sacrificing, heroic spirit that lay dormant within the Chinese mind. Always conscious of the power of a story as a rhetorical devise, Huang told his listeners of a case in Guilin in which a wounded army officer returned to his home in the city to recuperate from his injuries. While there, his wife and mother begged him not to return to the front; he had, they asserted, already fulfilled his obligations to the country. In reply, the soldier described to them, incident by incident, some of the horrors he had personally seen the enemy inflict upon Chinese victims. Before he could finish, his mother broke into tears and said, 'Then you go! You go!' His wife added, 'If this is really true, then I too will go!' This story, Huang noted, was sufficient to illustrate the uniquely Chinese virtue of resistance to enemy outsiders and the natural instinct of every person for self-preservation. This capacity to set aside the 'small self' and treasure the 'large self,' he wrote, is 'what makes a man a man. It is why a human being has the capacity for nobility' (Huang, 1944, pp. 99–101).

As the above discussion makes clear, by the 1940s Huang had come to conclude that the ultimate objective of education was to advance a national agenda. Significantly, however, he was also convinced that the interests of the nation and the individual were in many respects the same. His conception of person-making was deeply coloured by the need he felt to promote the convergence of individual and national identities, and his recommendations for the reform of education were influenced by his desire to use the schools to equip youth with skills, values and attitudes that would serve the interests that individuals shared with their compatriots. As he closed the lecture series he turned briefly to what he considered private behaviour, but it is important to keep in mind that he believed that even private behaviour directly affected the public welfare. In his mind, if the behaviour of the individual were incorrect, social practices in general would be perverted, the productivity of labour would decline, and the national soul would die. Since very little was truly private, person-making through education was a matter of intense public interest.

On the other hand, Huang also believed that certain personal behaviours were prerequisites for individual vocational success and both physical and moral health, and in his final lectures it is clear that he had three particular sets of behaviours in mind. First, be truthful: The student must learn to be practical and realistic in everything he says and does. In the case of physical exercise, for example, to make one's body strong and healthy requires that one acknowledge the need for constant exercise; one must face the fact that sporadic or infrequent training is unlikely to produce the desired results. Similarly, in choosing one's clothing 'one does not ignore the fact that in the winter it is cold and in the summer it is hot.' In each of these examples one must 'seek truth from facts,' that is, live one's life in accordance with what is realistic (Huang, 1944, pp. 106–7). Second, one must work hard and exercise economy in the use of resources and energy, as China's peasants had understood very well for thousands of years. Finally, one must train one's body and mind to lead an orderly and self-disciplined life. One must exercise punctuality and follow appropriate fashions in all that one studies and does; one must live simply, avoiding extravagance, and take one's meals following an orderly schedule; and, above all, one must learn through self-cultivation to overcome one's fears. Drawing once again upon China's folk heritage, he wrote: 'In ancient times there was a scholar who had a method of developing his courage. He kept a dagger in his desk and every day he would stare at it intently. At first he feared it but later, no matter how sharp it was, he had lost his fear. In other circumstances, if he had used a weapon in battle he would have feared its sharpness and not have had the courage to strike. Now, however, because of his effort to train his mind, not only did he no longer fear the knife, he was not even afraid of bombs' (Huang, 1944, p. 110).

Conclusion

This chapter has focused on the ideas of one of the most influential educators of China's Republican and Nationalist eras, Huang Yanpei. As the leader of a movement to promote vocational education, he spent some twenty years attempting to reform Chinese schooling so as to make it serve primarily the vocational needs of the nation's youth. Much like today's critics of Chinese education, however, by the 1930s he had come to conclude that the narrow careerism being fostered in the schools was in neither his students' nor the nation's best interests, and he began to direct his activities towards the reorientation of education so as to bring it into closer alignment with what he now believed both Chinese youth and a nation seeking salvation from the twin threats of internal disintegration and foreign aggression needed.

Obviously, the times are very different now. The unequal treaties have been gone for seventy years, China no longer suffers from the humiliation of imperialist aggression, and the memory of Japanese occupation is fading as the generation that experienced it passes from the scene. Huang's answers to China's educational problems were powerfully influenced by circumstances that, fortunately, no longer exist, and one could argue that his solutions have little to teach the current generation of reformers. On the other hand, for those who may be considering the adoption of foreign models, Huang's experience may have something important to teach. After all, when one encounters his writings one comes face-to-face with an image of China formed by a fully engaged practitioner of reform (and, incidentally, a very careful observer). It is an image that was generated through both intense involvement with the educational reform movement and direct exposure to its results and consequences, and it conveys an impression of immediacy, perhaps even maturity, which may be worth considering even in today's altered circumstances.

After two decades attempting to construct a school system that satisfied the demand of career-minded students for vocational training, Huang had reached the conclusion that what young people needed most was moral and spiritual cultivation, and that the best way to reach students would be to tap into the cultural resources and moral vocabulary that were already important elements of their heritage. Much like the developmentalist reformers, he discovered that reform programmes were likely to fail if they were crafted without careful attention to Chinese realities, and if there is wisdom to be gained from that insight one aspect of it is that today's reformers may want to keep in mind the risks they face if they drift into Western or post-modern waters that carry them too far from their young clients' cultural field to be able to speak to them in a language they can readily understand.[17]

One firm conviction that Huang and the other reformers of his time shared was that they and the nation's political leaders should alert the nation's youth to the dangers their country faced. As Huang made clear in his speeches and writings, however, it was not enough merely to awaken in students a patriot spirit; it was also essential to develop in them an ethos consistent with life as good citizens and cultivated human beings. Actually, this emphasis on personal moral development placed Huang well within the mainstream of Chinese reform thought in the 1920s and 1930s which, despite its emphasis on qualification for employment and socialization for citizenship, always retained a strong commitment to ethics (Curran, 2005, pp. 173–217). What made Huang unusual was his belief that in China's cultural heritage the nation already possessed a very rich resource, one to which educators should turn rather than to devote their time and energy studying the foreign models that most often drew their attention. As he told his audience in his fourth lecture at Huaxi University in 1942, 'A great joke played by Heaven' was that the Chinese had utterly lost confidence in the validity of their civilization. They had taken slavishly to following the West in all manner of behaviour, from 'worshipping foreign products' to following foreign educational trends that were poorly suited to China's needs. One consequence was that there was a wide gulf between the cultures of China's Westernizing elite and Chinese society at large. Therefore, he continued, rather than keep looking to the West for inspiration, China's educators should try to find ways to help their students re-establish contact with ethical principles that already lay within their repertoire of ancient folk traditions. Education of all kinds, formal and informal, should become a mechanism for the Chinese people to recover their self-confidence (Huang, 1944, pp. 33–7).[18]

In the final analysis, the conclusion Huang drew from his experience as a reformer was that for Chinese education to fulfil its person-making mission its leaders would first have to inform themselves about the ancient sources of the values and virtues that had made China successful in the past, and then find new ways to activate those values and virtues among the people, acting in the certainty that these wellsprings of national culture could serve well both individuals and the nation. When one considers the intellectual journey he travelled, from his flirtation in the 1910s with 'pragmatic education' to his more fully-developed argument of the 1930s and 1940s for an education aimed at cultivating a version of personhood rooted in Chinese history and culture, although the contemporary context is very different, one can reasonably propose that his life story and ideas may be of interest to reformers today who, as Huang did many decades ago, have come to expect something more from schooling than mere preparation of the next generation of employees for China's factories, offices and businesses.

Notes

1 In the same issue of *Frontiers* Prof. Zhang Huajun argues that contemporary Chinese education has come to be dominated by an instrumentalist mode of thinking that has produced an examination-oriented curriculum which neglects the cultivation of well-rounded adults (pp. 540–1), and Limin Bai argues that one of the legacies of China's turbulent twentieth century was that in their quest to master the elements of Western science and technology Chinese curriculum planners lost the balance that

centuries of Neo-Confucian education had struck between the spiritual and material worlds, only to awaken later to the 'ugly side of the imperialist West', that is, a ruthlessly competitive spirit and a Darwinist world view in which humane values such as generosity and compassion were subordinated to the law of the jungle (pp. 531–2). Elsewhere, Prof. Liu Haifeng of Xiamen University's Higher Education Research Center laments the overwhelming vulgarization of today's college education, and Beijing University's Qian Liqun lists among the six dangers facing Chinese higher education the degree to which utilitarian professional training has come to dominate it (Xie and Du, 2012, p. B05).

2 The term 'liberal' as it is used here refers to broadly focused learning that is aimed at the achievement of intellectual sophistication as well as moral and cultural refinement. In John Henry Newman's famous expression, its product is an individual who possesses 'a habit of mind . . . of which the attributes are freedom, equitableness, calmness, moderation, and wisdom' (Newman, 1907, p. 93).

3 Some of the more popular initiatives included the Guided Self-Study Method, the Group Teaching Method, the Montessori Method, the Project Method and the Dalton Plan, all of which were inspired by their founders' desire to ensure that education cultivated well-rounded, morally refined individuals.

4 At the movement's birth its leaders' declared objective was to reform curriculum and instructional methods so as to close the gap between the high demand for skilled manpower and the insufficient supply of school graduates whose training made them desirable candidates for modern sector jobs. A slogan that was displayed prominently at meetings of the private agency that did the most to promote vocational training, the Chinese Vocational Education Association, illustrates the private aspects of what was intended: 'Let the unemployed have jobs; let those who have jobs enjoy them.'

5 Huang was a member of what Schwintzer has termed a 'bridge generation', that is, men with a literati background who faced a world, indeed an intellectual universe, that was very different from that into which they were born (Schwintzer, 1992, p. 1).

6 In fact, Huang was very well informed regarding China's philosophical tradition; he had won an imperial degree (*zhuren*) in the 1902 civil service examination and during the course of his long life he wrote some two thousand poems, mostly in the classical style.

7 The inaugural manifesto issued by the Vocational Education Association in 1917, which Huang had a major hand in crafting, indicates that the society's attentions were aimed more or less exclusively at addressing the problems of unemployment and underemployment among school graduates. The three specific problems to be solved were the failure of educators to take into their planning the need to balance the supply and the demand of educated young people, the tendency of school curricula to concentrate on theory rather than practice, and graduates' own lack of practical skills sufficient to match their ambitions (中华职业教育社) ([Chinese Vocational Education Association], 1917, pp. 82–3). This tripartite set of objectives would be repeated in Huang's educational writings many times during the course of the next two decades.

8 Of particular interest to him was his impression that Euro–American societies encouraged people to develop new knowledge and technology, resulting in a tremendous record of inventions (Huang mentioned Thomas Edison, whom he had met while touring schools in the US, as an example of Western creativity).

9 For Aristotle, see *Politics*, Book One.

10 The only serious social division that Huang would acknowledge to have existed in China was that between the educated and the uneducated. 'Those who till the fields,

harvest the crops, and supply the people with food are the farmers. But their sons are not able to go to school. Those who labor to build hospitals are the workers. But when they are sick they cannot afford to go to hospitals.' Such a social arrangement as this, he admitted, might cause problems in the new China he had in mind, but even this would be minimized: 'To deal with such problems as these, is really not a difficult thing' (Huang, 1944, p. 25).

11 Guan Gong (d. 220) was an Eastern Han dynasty general who served the warlord Liu Bei 刘备 (161–223). With Guan Gong's assistance Liu broke away from the Eastern Han and founded his own state, Shu Han. Guan is remembered in Chinese folk culture as a paragon of loyalty and righteousness.

12 Zhuge Liang (181–234) was a chancellor of the state of Shu Han in the Three Kingdoms Period (220–280). He is venerated in Chinese folklore as a master military strategist and statesman.

13 Yue Fei (1103–1142) was a Southern Song dynasty general who fought a long campaign to resist a Jurchen invasion of north China. Legend has it that he was betrayed by corrupt advisers at the imperial court before being recalled and imprisoned until his death in 1142. He is remembered as a patriot and exemplar of the virtue of loyalty.

14 Cao Cao (155–220) was a chancellor of the Eastern Han dynasty who rose to power in the dynasty's final years and founded one of the states that rose from the Eastern Han's ashes in 220, the Cao Wei. He is remembered as a brilliant military commander but also as a cruel and tyrannical ruler.

15 Huang also cited counter-evidence to make his case. Chinese history, he acknowledged, included numerous examples of figures who had sought personal advantage through the betrayal of principle. Both in the official histories and in the popular mind the memory of such individuals was irredeemably tarnished. Following the Manchu conquest, for example, many former Ming dynasty officials declared their allegiance to the new Qing rulers, violating a well-established Chinese convention that officials of a doomed dynasty either follow that dynasty to their graves or withdraw from political life permanently. For centuries the Chinese people had despised such traitors, a well-known phrase, Huang pointed out, being the Confucian dictum that 'A loyal minister does not serve two masters' (Huang, 1944, p. 79).

16 Zou Zongtang (1812–1885) was a Qing dynasty (1644–1911) military leader and statesman whose service to the dynasty included the suppression of a rebellion in China's northwest, distinguished service in the civil war against the Taiping rebels (1850–1864), and leadership in China's earliest attempts to adopt Western military technology.

17 As Professor Guoping Zhao has recently put it in a rather different context, 'A successful grafting of Western civilization into Chinese civilization has proved to be difficult' (Zhao, 2013b, p. 502).

18 Referring to the well-known district in Chengdu where the city's colleges and universities were located, Huaxi Dam, he said that it was in reality a world of its own, separated by a vast cultural gap from the rest of Chengdu. 'Is it possible,' he asked, 'that this is heaven, resting above society, while China's real society is actually hell?' His own daughters and daughters-in-law, he complained, had gone to college and could speak English, sing songs and play the zither. Yet they could not cook, wash clothes or make shoes, and they were therefore not likely to be appreciated by society. Chinese education, he complained, was like a school he had once visited where students were taught to play the piano. After they left the school they would return to their homes where there were no pianos, and their training was therefore useless. It was as if they had been 'poisoned by the devil of Westernization' (Huang, 1944, pp. 36–7).

References

Aristotle (ca. 350 BCE). *Politics*.

Bai, L. M. (2013). Practicality in Curriculum Building: A Historical Perspective on the Mission of Chinese Education. *Frontiers of Education in China*, 8(4), 518–39.

Biesta, G. (2009). Good Education in an Age of Measurement: On the Need to Reconnect with the Question of Purpose in Education. *Educational Assessment, Evaluation and Accountability*, 21, 33–46.

Curran, T. D. (2005). *Educational Reform in Republican China: The Failure of Educators to Create a Modern Nation*. Lewiston, NY: The Edwin Mellen Press.

Deng, Z. Y. (2013). On Developing Chinese Didactics: A Perspective from the German Didaktik Tradition. *Frontiers of Education in China*, 8(4), 559–75.

Huang Y. P. (1916). 东西两大陆教育不同之根本谈教育杂志 [On the Basic Differences Between Eastern and Western Education]. 教育杂志 [The Chinese Educational Review], 8.1 (1). In Tian Z. P. and Li X. X. (1993), 黄炎培教育论著选 *[Selected Writings of Huang Yanpei]*, 49–51.

Huang Y. P. (1939). 我之人生观与吾人从事职业教育之基本理论 [My View of Human Life and Our Basic Theory of Vocational Education]. 重庆：国讯 [National News], 193 (January). In Tian Z. P. and Li X. X. (1993), 黄炎培教育论著选 *[Selected Writings of Huang Yanpei]*, 335–9.

Huang Y. P. (1944). 中华复兴十讲 *[Ten Lectures on China's Revival]*. 重庆：国讯书店 [Zhongqing: National News Press].

Newman, J. H. (1907). *The Idea of a University*. London: Longmans, Green and Co.

Schwintzer, E. P. (1992). Education to Save the Nation: Huang Yanpei and the Educational Reform Movement in Early Twentieth Century China. PhD Dissertation, University of Washington.

Xie, L. and Du, L. (2012). 钱理群：北大等在培养 '精致的利己主义者', [Beijing University and Other Schools are Educating 'Egotists']. 西藏法制报 *[Tibetan Legal News]*, 8 May, B05.

Zhang, H. J. (2013). Individuality Beyond the Dichotomy of 'Small Self and Big Self' in Contemporary Chinese Education: Lessons from Hu Shi and Liang Shuming. *Frontiers of Education in China*, 8(4), 540–58.

Zhao, G. P. (2013a). Introduction. *Frontiers of Education in China*, 8(4), 491–7.

Zhao, G. P. (2013b). Rebuilding the Chinese Soul: Some Considerations for Education. *Frontiers of Education in China*, 8(4), 498–517.

中华职业教育社 [Chinese Vocational Education Association] (1917). 中华职业教育社宣言书 [Manifesto of the Chinese Vocational Education Association]. In Tian Z. P. and Li X. X. (eds) (1993), 黄炎培教育论著选 *[Selected Writings of Huang Yanpei]*, 80–90.

Part III

Re-envisioning Chinese education as person-making

10 Civilizational dialogue and a new understanding of the human person

Implications for Chinese education as person-making

Guoping Zhao

Introduction

Education as a process of person-making is concerned with the full development of the human person, or the human subject, rather than with instilling skills and beliefs so that students can be used as instruments for prescribed or existing social, political and economic purposes. In other words, different from the qualification and socialization purposes of education (Biesta, 2009), education as person-making is for the flourishing of human beings, albeit what the human person eventually becomes has significant implications for social, political and economic orders. Yet, what does the flourishing of the human person mean? What is it to be a fully developed human subject? How do we understand human subjectivity? To answer these questions, education has relied heavily on profound and rich cultural and philosophical ideas from which a coherent and meaningful concept of the human person can be articulated. Education in the modern West has drawn from the modern philosophy of the subject/consciousness to articulate a rational and autonomous subject capable of critical thinking and self-realization. In Chinese history, on the other hand, education has relied heavily on Confucianism to express its concept of a moral and relational person, sometimes referred to as the Confucian man. However, in contemporary China, more than a century's gradual destruction of Chinese cultural traditions has eroded the grounds for a meaningful articulation of a Chinese person, and education has lost its foundation for the purpose of person-making (Zhao, Chapter 2). The 'shortcut' that modern Chinese reformers took to 'appropriate the "golden needle" of wealth and power from the West,' the 'politicization' of Chinese culture (Tu, 1998, p. xviii) and its gradual fragmentation in recent Chinese history, have led to the current situation, where a mixture of the psychologically deep-seated, mutated, and degenerated, cultural assumptions and the superficially adopted and transmuted modern Western expectations guide the way many Chinese live their lives and understand what it is to be a human person (Zhao, Chapter 2). Social Darwinism, Materialism and Instrumentalism run rampant and dominate the cultural landscape. The systematic and deliberative articulation, reinterpretation and reconstruction of the Chinese understanding of the human person based on Confucian, Daoist, or Buddhist insights have been deserted and education has been used only as a means of political indoctrination or, more recently, as a private means to wealth and social status.

Acutely aware of the situation, current Chinese scholars and educators have attempted to reform Chinese education largely from two directions. One is to introduce what is considered the 'new and advanced' Western educational ideas and practices to 'update' Chinese education, and the other, with a half-hearted push from the government, is to reconnect and re-appropriate what has long been lost, the deep roots of Chinese educational thinking. But I argue that the former often falls into the same trap of 'superficiality of commitment' (Tu, 1998, p. xviii) manifested in the earlier modernization period of China (Zhao, Chapter 2). In addition to the adoption of educational methods and techniques only as 'scientific' tools to modernize Chinese education, Western schools of thought have been introduced mainly because they are popular and fashionable, without a deep analysis of how they can make a meaningful connection to the Chinese condition. For example, the French thinker Foucault has been hugely popular in Chinese educational circles in recent years. While his work has found some meaningful use in analyzing certain Chinese practices, there is a lack of examination of how a line of inquiry that mainly aims to refute modern liberal societies' subtle strategies for controlling, managing and normalizing the population in the name of knowledge and freedom can be meaningfully applied to the Chinese context where the pre-modern exercise of brute power and harsh oppression is still the norm. The slogan *zou xiang shijie, zou xiang hou xiandai* 走向世界,走向后现代 (to the world, to postmodernism) captures the Chinese mentality: embracing postmodernism to catch up with the world. What is particularly missing in this new wave of 'learning from the West' is a serious engagement and dialogue with the West so a renewal of the Chinese under-standing and articulation of the human person can take place.

On the other hand, the traditionalists, the so-called 'Ruists', who have attempted to reintroduce and promote traditional Confucian doctrines and codes as a way of life for the twenty-first-century Chinese, often blindly adopt the 'tradition' without a careful consideration of its contemporary relevance. The traditionalists embrace the Confucian doctrines of the 'Three Cardinal Guides' (*sangang* 三纲) (Father being that of the son, Lord that of the subjects, and husband that of the wife) (e.g., Jiang Qing 蒋庆, in Chen and Gan, 2008), 'Familism' (*jiating zhuyi* 家庭主义) (e.g., Su Li 苏力, Sheng Hong 盛洪, in Chen and Gan, 2008), and the principle of 'Relatives Hiding Each Other' (*qinqin fuying* 亲亲互隐) (Guo Qiyong 郭齐勇, in Chen and Gan, 2008) as the founda-tion upon which to rebuild contemporary Chinese society, in order to challenge 'the Judeo-Christian,' 'modern Western' or 'liberal democratic' conceptions of family and personhood (Pfister, 2011, pp. 175, 176). Traditionalists also offer 'rites-based personhood' as an antidote to the 'naked self-interest' of the 'post-communist personality disorder, . . . exist[ing] in contemporary China' (p. 176).

But this kind of 'nativism' has long been contested (see Lai, 2009), not the least by Tu Weiming. Tu admits (1998) that, as an intellectual historian, he is fully aware of the 'dark side' of Confucian culture, 'the Confucian contribution to despotic, gerontocratic, and male-oriented practices and tendencies in traditional and contemporary China' (p. xvii). The 'filial piety' that developed from Confucianism has also been criticized, particularly by anthropologists and sociologists in the area of 'family studies' (Slote and DeVos, 1998). The easily observable underdeveloped rational capacity of some Chinese as demonstrated in daily communication and actions, internet discussion/debates, even academic discourses, can be attributed not only to the decades-long political control and indoctrination, but also to the Chinese cultural emphasis on feelings and emotions, rather than logical thinking and reasoning. There are also widespread complaints about the Chinese lack of respect for human rights, dignity and freedom, which are at the root of many of the contemporary tragedies and to which the contribution of Chinese cultural tradition seems undeniable. In addition, a four-decade long sociological survey study confirms that, living in the contemporary world where exposure to some of the more appealing outside ideas is impossible to prevent, 'most Chinese persons accepted and supported values associated with Enlightenment rationality and individual rights' rather than the 'traditional values' (Ambrose King 金耀基, in Chen and Gan, 2008). In such a situation, a naïve and uncritical 'return to the tradition' or the belief that 'the more national, the more universal and global' (*minzu de jiushi shijie* 民族的就是世界的), is unjustifiable and unattainable. All of these observations and critiques point to the necessity of a critical cultural renewal, rather than a simple return to the 'innocent' past.

In fact, if we look at how Chinese culture, or more particularly Confucianism, has evolved in history, it clearly has never been the case that some original, 'uncontaminated' ideas were completely handed down from generation to generation. On the contrary, cultural transmission is always a matter of reinterpretation and reconstruction, and each generation is faced as much with incredible insights, wisdom and inspiration as with 'obstacles, failures, limited attainment, and unfinished projects' (Cua, 2000, p. 269). For a cultural tradition to be alive, it has to be in a process of endless renewal in the face of challenges. The challenges are most daunting when they come from outside the tradition but they are also most useful, helping create fruitful cultural or civilizational synthesis, as is the case with Neo-Confucianism in the Song and Ming dynasties, when Confucianism faced the Daoist and Buddhist challenges, and the contemporary New Confucianism developed in Taiwan, Hong Kong and the US, in the face of Western challenges.

In this chapter, I briefly review the changing concept of the Confucian man in the history of Confucian evolution, particularly in Neo-Confucianism and New Confucianism, and how these concepts of the human person have been the result of deep cultural and civilizational engagement and dialogue. I then discuss recent developments in Western philosophy, the new trends in its ways of conceptualizing human subjectivity, and how these trends converge with the Chinese tradition. As a result of this discussion, I propose that by drawing upon resources from both Western post-humanist philosophy and Chinese tradition, the Chinese understanding of the human person can be revitalized, and I suggest the implications of such an understanding for education as person-making.

From Confucius to new Confucianism: the changing concept of the Chinese person

The original Confucian concept of man is formulated by Confucius in *The Doctrine of the Mean* (*zhong yong* 中庸) as benevolence, and benevolence is defined as two-men mindedness (人者仁也). Thus for Confucius, a human being is fundamentally a relation-oriented, social and moral being. In *The Analects* 论语, the collection of Confucius' sayings, the Chinese man, or the ideal person (*junzi* 君子), is described as one that is imperturbable, resolute, 'firm and decided'; 'proud but not quarrel-some'; 'dignified but never haughty' (泰而不骄, 矜而不争), but at the same time, also conciliatory, modest, humble, even mild (Morton, 1971, p. 72), expressing filial piety and fraternal submission.

The exact meanings and implications of such descriptions of the Confucian man are, apparently, subject to interpretation. Historically, the Confucian man has been interpreted as a relational person who is confined by his social conventions and devoid of autonomy and agency, but also as one who enjoys, in his unity with the Dao/Tian, a sense of spirituality beyond the social convention. While different interpretations and reconstructions have emerged in history, the two early interpretations that have had the most profound impact and left a lasting legacy are those of Mencius 孟子 in the fourth century BC and Dong Zhongshu 董仲舒 two centuries or so later. The Mencian line of interpretation underscores the moral and spiritual aspects of the human person, his innate sensitivity for others' suffering, and the role of self-cultivation in realizing the heavenly benevolence. Mencius's thought is particularly appealing for later Confucian thinkers and has been the foundation of many of the subsequent historical reconstructions of Confucianism, including Neo-Confucianism and New Confucianism. On the other hand, the Dong Zhongshu's line of interpretation has not only established the supremacy of Confucian teaching and raised its status to that of state orthodoxy, but has also codified and canonized Confucian teaching into building blocks of the social hierarchy of the next two millennia, a complex network of social and political relationships in which individuals were tightly ensnared with limited agency. Evidently, from the very beginning, the study and use of Confucius's ideas has been an active endeavour of reconstruction.

To a certain degree, Neo-Confucianism is the result of reconfiguring classical Confucianism in the face of Daoist and Buddhist challenges. The internal difficulty that has always been present in classical Confucian thought, the tension between the human and the heavenly, the unlimited trust granted to humanity and the elusiveness of the 'heavenly feeling' (Metzger, 1977, p. 199), and the tension between self-agency and the confines of social conventions was only exacerbated in the face of the challenges. With the inspiration of Daoism and Ch'an Buddhism, the sense of 'predicament' (Metzger, 1977) found its release in the realm of Tian, or the transcendent. It has been observed that the Neo-Confucians were 'preoccupied with the task of elucidating the character of the purely metaphysical realm' (p. 100). As a result of such reconfiguration, the Neo-Confucian man is much more spiritual in nature, with a much stronger sense of agency and responsibility for his own perfection. As Wang Yangming 王阳明 states, to be human is to realize one's 'heart of Dao' (*daohsin* 道心). 'If one's mind was "correct", one's consciousness became one with this "mind of the *dao*"' (Metzger, 1977, p. 100). Tu Weiming (1985) comments that Wang Yangming's thought demonstrates a combination of 'the wisdom of Ch'an Buddhism and the aesthetic sensitivity of Taoism with the humanist concerns of Confucianism' (p. 28). It is the result of cultural and civilizational engagement and dialogue.

In Neo-Confucianism, the Confucian idea of cultivating the self to bring peace to others and to the world (*The Analects*: 修己以敬, 修己以安人, 修己以安百姓) was further articulated and extended to 'a ceaseless process of inner moral and spiritual transformation' (Tu, 1985, p. 22). Deeply embedded in Heaven and Earth and myriad things, the Confucian man has the potential to break free of conventional constraints and human fallibilities and, through self-cultivation, realize his true, genuine self. For Zhu Xi 朱熹, the transformation starts with 'extending knowledge' (*gewu zhizhi* 格物致知), but for Wang Yangming, 'extending knowledge' simply signifies exercising our innate moral awareness (also see Bai, Chapter 4). Man becomes a 'creative agent who participates in the onto-cosmological process which brings about the completion of the Great Ultimate' (Tu 1971, p. 80). Such reconfiguration underlines the spirituality of the human person as connected to and affected by the divine, and underscores his openness, independence, agency and freedom, albeit not the freedom of the egoist's autonomy as pursued in the modern West.

New Confucianism, on the other hand, is the contemporary development of Confucianism in response to Western challenges. It emerged in Taiwan, Hong Kong and the US at the time when mainland China was undergoing 'down with Confucius' political movements under the Communist rule. A Chinese nationalist, Mou Zongsan 牟宗三 (1909–1995) was one of the forerunners, starting his journey before he moved from mainland China to Taiwan in 1949 and later to Hong Kong. In the context of the century-long West and East encounters and the painful realization of Chinese weakness and vulnerability in front of the West, Chinese scholars have all, to different degrees, reflected on the source of Western strengths and the ways in which Chinese culture can be transformed and made compatible with the ideas of democracy and modern science. Mou Zongsan intended a reinvigoration of Confucianism through a serious engagement with Western, especially German, philosophy. In Mou's view, the Chinese cultural tradition is strong in its inner sagehood, the moral and spiritual life of the self, but is weak in its 'outer kingship,' and that is why China lagged behind in its political and economic development. He believed the transformation has to start with drawing from indigenous Chinese resources, and while adopting and engaging closely with Immanuel Kant's philosophy, he attempted to overcome the perceived limitation of Kantian philosophy with Chinese philosophy.

Tu Weiming (1940–), a student of Mou Zongsan, is probably the most renowned New Confucian scholar and the spokesperson for this school of thought. Tu has spent most of his academic life in the US and speaks mostly to Western audiences. His main orientation in reinvigorating Confucianism, therefore, is to show the West how it can be made a complementary alternative to the Western Enlightenment culture. As he states,

> The possibility of a radically different ethic or a new value system separate from and independent of the Enlightenment mentality is neither realistic nor authentic – it may even appear to be either cynical or hypercritical. We need to explore the spiritual resources that may help us to broaden the scope of the Enlightenment project, deepen its moral sensitivity, and, if necessary, creatively transform its genetic constraints in order to fully realize its potential as a worldview for the human community as a whole.
> (Tu, 1996, p. 68)

Rather than 'deconstructing or abandoning the [Enlightenment's] commitment to rationality, liberty, equality, human rights, and distributive justice' (Tu, 1996, p. 71), Tu embraces them while noting the danger of the mindset shaped by instrumental rationality, private interests and the politics of domination. With this orientation and along the line of Neo-Confucian thinking, Tu's reconstruction of the Confucian person focuses on his/her 'ethical and spiritual dimensions' (Tu, 1996, p. 74), cosmological depth, connection to community, and agency in moral and spiritual self-cultivation – a selfhood that emphasizes 'communication, networking, negotiation, interaction, interfacing, and collaboration' (Tu, 1996, p. 74).

I argue, however, that neither Mou's strategy of keeping the Chinese inner sagehood intact nor Tu's juxtaposition of the Western and the Confucian selfhood adequately addresses many of the challenges the Western approach to the human person has mounted against the Chinese, nor have they adequately reconstructed the concept of the Chinese person to absorb the many Western strengths Tu Weiming found so appealing: the commitment to rationality, liberty, equity and human rights. For a culture to be a living tradition that provides continuity and guidance to lives today, and for the Chinese to thrive among other global citizens in the contemporary world, we need a more thorough reconfiguration of the Chinese understanding of the human person, one that sufficiently addresses our strengths and weaknesses while absorbing what we can learn from the West. The Western challenges that have devastated the Chinese for a big part of modern history can become the impetus to transform and reinvigorate the tradition. Rather than rejecting our own cultural roots in total acceptance of the 'new and the advanced' or returning to the 'unadulterated' past, I propose that we meet the challenges head on and embark upon a cultural project of renewal, particularly in reconsidering the way we understand and conduct ourselves in the world and with others – the idea of the Chinese person for the educational purpose of person-making.

At the same time, Western civilization, while it seems to have single-mindedly pursued human agency, rationality and freedom in its approach to the human subject, has only recently been moving in a direction that shows more resonance and convergence with the Chinese. The tragedies and difficulties of the last century have fundamentally altered the way Western philosophy understands and approaches human subjectivity. It seems that both the Western and Chinese cultural approaches to the human person have had their historical struggles and that both have benefited and damaged humanity in different ways. The current resonance may point to a potentially fruitful civilizational engagement and interchange, and thus the Chinese person can grow from China's own cultural roots but be transformed with new ideas from the West.

In the next section I briefly sketch the modern and postmodern development of Western philosophy regarding the subject and identify a few new trends in its approach to human subjectivity that resonate strikingly with the Chinese approach.

New trends in the Western post-humanist philosophy of the subject and its convergence with the Chinese tradition

While there has been a clear difference between the ancient Greek approach to the world and that of the Chinese, a far-reaching departure is marked by the development of modern Western thinking that centrally underscores the rational and individualistic, rather than the sensual/emotional and relational, experiences of human beings. Modern thinking is what underlines the Western advancement over the rest of the world in almost all aspects of modern life, including political systems, economic developments and developments in science and technology. The encounter with Western modernity is also what has devastated the Chinese in the last century and a half.

At the core of modern Western thinking is a humanistic conceptualization of the nature of human beings and their capacities. As early as the seventeenth century, René Descartes made the famous statement: '*Cogito ergo sum*' (I am thinking, therefore I exist) that set the groundwork for the ultimate determination of the existence of the world and ourselves in the rational thinking of the individual human subject. Human consciousness has become the definitive anchor for the objectivity of knowledge and the certainty of truth. In political theory, also in the seventeenth century, Locke and Hobbes advocated civil governments that are based on voluntary participation of free and rational individuals. Human subjects, with their capacity for reason, are conceived of as being capable of self-direction and self-realization and able to take charge of their own lives. This construction of human beings as sovereign, rational and autonomous subjects reached its apex in the eighteenth century when Kant proposed that we release ourselves from our 'self-incurred tutelage,' use our understanding 'without direction from another' (Kant, 1992[1784], p. 90), and impose order upon the world through the construction of knowledge and moral principles.

This humanist construction of the subject, however, while its purpose was to bring freedom and empowerment to humanity, is based on the idea that human beings have a fixed 'essence' that can be identified and known. Human beings should enjoy unlimited freedom because we are essentially conscious beings making decisions based on reason. As far as we allow ego and consciousness to organize our existence and allow rationality to dominate our being, we should enjoy the freedom of self-determination. The sovereign subject is to exert his egoistic and conscious power over himself, the world, and others. The world is his project and the other cannot affect him in any meaningful and substantial way. This orientation, obviously, is in direct contrast to that of the Chinese, which emphasizes human hearts/feelings instead of reason and which stresses relatedness with other human beings and the cosmos. The humanist claim for the essence of the human subject and the pursuit of individual autonomy has been pivotal in the development of modern Western education. For many educational philosophers, modern education as person-making 'is about producing rationally autonomous individuals' (Wain, 1996, p. 351) and is a process of 'liberation' that is distinguished from domination, indoctrination, or domestication.

But the whole system of modern thinking and practice has been under heavy fire in recent decades, particularly from post-structural and postmodern thinkers. The tragedies of the twentieth century – the holocaust, colonialism, imperialism and the suffering of the many 'others' – have forced philosophers to reflect on what has gone wrong with the grand modern narrative of human emancipation. Many have concluded that the source of the bloody barbarism expressed in the tragedies 'lies not in some contingent anomaly within human reasoning, nor in some accidental ideological misunderstanding,' but in the very construction of 'the famous subject of a transcendental idealism that before all else wishes to be free and thinks itself free '(Levinas, 1990, p. 63). It is also argued that colonial projects have been based on the logic of the subject's 'annexation [and] conquering, which means consuming otherness and revising it as "sameness"' (Eaglestone, 2010, p. 64).

The problem is the totalitarian logic embedded in the construction of the humanist subject, which is seen as detrimental to both the subject and to others. When the subject is construed as an all-encompassing, self-positing and autonomous being, it exercises an ontologically totalizing power that eliminates what is different from within itself and between itself and others. The self is captured in an essence, gathered, and deadened in an ideal principle (albeit a grand and appealing one), and therefore has lost all its concealment, inexhaustibility, and internal multiplicity. The self-positing subject only approaches the other in terms of comprehension and assimilation, that is, to bring the other within the domain of the self's understanding – the logic of totalizing. As Levinas argues, such a subject cannot protect the dignity of the human subject. The totalitarian thinking embedded in the philosophy of the humanist subject has been linked to political totalitarianism such as Nazism in Germany and Fascism in Italy, as well as racism, sexism, heterosexism and religious fundamentalism in contemporary political economies.

According to Biesta, the problem with such a humanist subject for education is the paradox of 'spontaneity and reproductivity' (Schleiermacher, 1983/1984, quoted in Biesta, 1998, p. 3), a constant tension between 'socialization,' or 'normalization,' and 'subjectification' (Biesta, 2010). While the subject is characterized as autonomous and self-directing, Biesta argues that the identification of the essence of the subject means there is a specific norm for 'what it means to be human *before* the actual manifestation of "instances" of humanity' (Biesta, 2010, p. 292, emphasis in the original), thus depriving students of the opportunity to become anything different or unique, to be free and creative in their own person-making. The ideal or essence of humanity, postulated as freedom and autonomy, paradoxically, takes freedom away from students and makes person-making a process of normalization.

With all these problems and difficulties with the humanist subject and the 'liquidation' of the subject in recent decades by postmodern and post-structural thinkers, several new trends in the understanding and configuration of the 'post-humanist' subject have emerged in Western philosophy.

The first trend is to consider the subject in terms of difference and multiplicity, rather than essence and presence. In the last part of the twentieth century, 'a new pattern [emerged] in the French philosophy' that can be characterized as centrally concerned with 'difference and its valorization' (May, 1997, p. 1). This 'philosophy of difference,' associated with figures such as Jacque Derrida, Emmanuel Levinas, Jean-Luc Nancy, Gills Deleuze, and to a lesser degree, Michel Foucault, argues that difference and absence are always associated with being and presence, and the subject and its identity cannot be fixed and closed, but has to be considered as open and unexhausted (Zhao, 2015b).

Related to this trend is the tendency to counter the power of ego and consciousness by appreciating the flow of the pre-ego, pre-conscious, human existential experience. The challenge does not dismiss the importance of human rationality, but particularly targets the omnipotent power granted to ego and consciousness in modern thinking.

Third, and related to the first and second trends, is the tendency to emphasize the relational experience of the subject. Rather than seeing human beings as isolated, self-positing subjects that totalize the other, the post-humanist subjects are seen as inevitably connected with each other. For example, Levinas (1998) calls attention to the pre-ego, pre-conscious connectedness of the self with others and the world.

Additionally, with the omnipotent egoist power of the subject challenged, there also appears a tendency, in the midst of a troubled modernity, to reconsider the role of spirituality in human subjectivity and society. This 'post-secular' (e.g., Blond, 1998) tendency is interested in incorporating a philosophic-spiritual dimension into contemporary human lives.

Lastly, there is the tendency to challenge the pursuit of freedom as autonomy, the hallmark of modernity. Instead, many (e.g., Levinas) are considering the possibility of a creative tension between freedom as autonomy and freedom as heteronomy.

Holding all of these tendencies together, a new, post-humanist understanding of human subjectivity is already emerging – a subjectivity that is characterized by its internal richness and multiplicity that cannot be reduced and deadened, and by its endless potential to change, to become new again in its ethical and spiritual connection with the world and beyond.

Clearly, these new trends in the post-humanist Western philosophy of the subject show striking resonance and convergence with the Chinese tradition, thus offering an unprecedented opportunity for a serious civilizational interchange. Yet as much as the post-humanist Western subject is a reflection and critique of the modern subject, the post-humanist subject is built upon, rather than a total rejection of, the modern approach. To revitalize, strengthen and transform Chinese civilization, to provide a richer, post-West/East articulation of the human person, I suggest a project of reconfiguring the Chinese person based on both the humanist and post-humanist as well as the Chinese approaches.

Reconfiguring the Chinese person based on an East–West dialogue: some considerations

A cultural project of reconfiguring the Chinese person for education's purpose of person-making can be understood as a project of 'internal reconstruction' of the Chinese traditional understanding of the human person and of the 'critical development' of this understanding based on a East–West dialogue.

In the post-humanist era, the West has struggled to conceive of the human person in the non-essential terms that defy the totalizing power of ego and consciousness and recognize the un-captured richness, difference and concealment of human subjectivity. What has come out of the struggle seems to be a notion of the post-humanist subject that emphasizes its singular existence with irreducible subjectivity and alterity, an existence that cannot be categorized, exhausted and replicated but is unique and open to the world and beyond (Zhao, 2015b).

While the West has had to struggle for a long time to reach such an appreciation and understanding of human existence, the Chinese have long approached the human person in a non-essential fashion. As Brindley (2011) notes, 'A quick survey of the Analects reveals that Confucius is most singularly concerned not with delineating fixed, inborn natures but with ascertaining the potentials of many, diverse individuals' (p. 266). When Confucius asks the question 'what is human?' rather than giving a fixed answer, he always 'pursues an account of how individuals might seek to change themselves' along moral lines (p. 266). The Daoists also conceptualize a nonbeing self (Zhao, 2015a), a self that is between emptiness/nothingness and presence/abundance, transcending all limited entities and beyond all boundaries and things. In fact, when the first post-humanist philosopher, Martin Heidegger, encountered the Daoist notion of *Wu*, the nothingness and emptiness, he thought it provided a completely different avenue to the understanding of being than that of the Western metaphysical tradition. He claimed that 'Tao could be the way that gives all ways' (Heidegger, quoted in Wohlfart, 2003, p. 52) and 'The original human dwelling . . . [can only be found] within that in which prevails the "great usefulness of the useless" ' (in Zhang, 2009, p. 80–81). Both Confucianists and Daoists, as well as the Chinese Buddhists, have tried to defy the totalizing power of ego and consciousness. As Tu (1985) points out, the 'Confucian instructions on the falsehood of self-centeredness, the Ch'an warning against egoist attachments, and the Taoist advocacy of self-forgetfulness' (p. 27) all point to the necessity of breaking free from the deadening power of ego and consciousness and going beyond it.

Thus the Chinese have long appreciated and understood the richness, the nothingness/concealment/difference-embedded, inexhaustible subjectivity of the human person. What needs to be further articulated and reconstructed from such an understanding, however, is what such an understanding of the human person implies and how to extend it. If the human subject is always in a potential state, self-cultivating in its encounter with others and the world; if it is in a simultaneous and inescapable creative tension between *you* 有 and *wu* 无, presence and absence, the human person comes as a unique individual with an irreducible subjectivity and alterity that cannot be captured and identified in a category. S/he is a subject, irreducible to an object of examination and judgement. As Levinas (1969) argues, the uniqueness and otherness of the individual entails a sense of opacity or 'secrecy' (p. 120) that cannot be penetrated by knowledge. The individual is a 'free being' (p. 73), free from conception, manifestation and reduction.

Such singular subjectivity, if it is not to be violated, calls for a human society where the subjectivity and alterity of each individual are maintained, received and respected without truncation. Such a 'Kingdom of Ends,' as Kant once imagined, is not based on the free will and rational capacity of each individual. Human dignity and respectability come from our irreducible subjectivity, from the fact that we are all 'infinite' beings, 'infinitely transcendent, infinitely foreign' (Levinas, 1969, p. 194), and infinitely beyond others' egoism and grasp. Human relations are inevitably ethical relations.

Such singular and irreducible subjects are also existentially connected with each other. Confucian thinking has long cherished the relatedness of human beings and the ethical nature of human relations. It highlights the significance of human feelings and sentiments as the key for the self to relate to others and the larger whole, the universe. As Thomas Berry (2003) comments, in Confucian thinking there is this 'consistent and all-pervading emphasis on the affective life of human beings ... The feeling, emotional aspect of life was considered of primary importance in sustaining people in a human form of existence' (p. 96). Tu Weiming (1985) also notes, 'In a comparative perspective, it seems that Neo-Confucian ontology, [is] grounded in the ultimate certitude of human sensitivity, our ability to feel, sense, and experience an ever-enlarging reality as an integral part of our selfhood' (p. 15). The Daoists further propose that it is our comparing, calculating and judging minds that have separated people and erected boundaries among us. Against the modern thinking that emphasizes free will and universal reason devoid of human emotion and feeling, recent Western philosophers such as Emile Durkheim, Harold Oliver, Martin Buber and Emmanuel Levinas have all suggested that human beings are related to each other in their pre-ego, pre-conscious existential experiences. Like the Confucianists who see the 'personal-cosmic communion' as granting a sense of sacredness and goodness to human sentiment and sensitivity, Durkheim and Levinas also accentuate the spiritual and religious dimension of our moral sensitivity. 'Whoever makes an attempt on a man's life, on a man's liberty ... inspires in us a feeling of horror analogous in every way to that which the believer experiences when he sees his idol profaned' (Durkheim, 1973, p. 46). Such a claim resonates deeply with Mencius's observation that the human heart cannot stand others' suffering.

Thus the emphasis on and appreciation of human sensitivity necessitates human relatedness, not only the moral nature of such relations but also their transcendental and spiritual dimension. If human subjectivity is understood not only as irreducible and inexhaustible, but also open and connected with the world and beyond, rather than enclosed and deadened by ego and consciousness, if we are affected and transformed with our encounters with others and the world in the 'pre-reflective,' sensible experience, we are indeed social, moral and spiritual beings, and the modern secular, totalizing and autonomous Western subject that violates the subjectivity of both the self and others is challenged.

But such an understanding of the human person does not reject the idea that human rationality is an essential part of human subjectivity. What is challenged is the absolute, totalizing and dominating power of ego and consciousness, not the appreciation and recognition that the subject also 'announces, promises' (Nancy, 1991, p. 4), becomes, and presents while simultaneously concealing and disappearing. As long as such an understanding of the human person emphasizes its richness and inexhaustibility, it underscores a creative tension between rationality and sensitivity. Particularly since the Chinese, unlike their Western counterparts, have not fully appreciated the significance and power of human rationality, it is of critical importance to emphasize and cultivate such a human capacity in the Chinese cultural context.

The understanding of the human person as an irreducible subject with internal multiplicity also implies a creative tension between human freedom as autonomy and as heteronomy. Western modernity, failing in many aspects of modern life in its attempt to bring empowerment to humanity, did liberate humanity from irrational superstitions and untenable traditional confines. With their accomplishments in political democracy and economic development and their scientific achievements, human beings are enjoying unprecedented freedom and well-being. But the historical lessons have also taught us that the moral project of freedom as autonomy has to be conditioned and dependent on an inevitable and simultaneous responsibility and heteronomy to human others. Our freedom is conditioned by our unconditional responsibility to others' human dignity, subjectivity and alterity (difference). In the face of the other, our autonomy is limited by our heteronomy to the other's call (Zhao, 2014).

In Chinese cultural tradition, freedom has been a difficult concept, and an even harder accomplishment. The Confucian emphasis on human relatedness has made the pursuit of individual freedom seemingly difficult, since personal actions have an inevitable effect on others. It has been argued that in the Chinese context there is no concept explicitly comparable to Western 'autonomy,' or freedom of self-determination. The concept of *Ziyou* 自由 (freedom) only indicates 'without constraints' and has been considered the speciality of the Daoists. But a closer reading of Confucian thought suggests that an unyielding belief in individual freedom that can be extended to an equivalent notion of autonomy is deeply embedded in Confucian thinking.

As Brindley (2011) explains, while the Confucianists stress the self's moral responsibility to others, such responsibility is not a blind submission to the other's demands, but is a responsibility to answer the call of a higher order. In other words, it is our sense of embodying and extending the Dao or Tian that is calling for our responsibility to the other. The Chinese Tian, like the Western God, is a supreme, spiritual being beyond the confine of humanity. Yet, unlike the Western personal deity, it is not a super being with will and consciousness, but a natural entity that calls for the participation of humanity for the realization of its purposes and goodness. As I elaborated elsewhere (Zhao, 2009), this particular feature of Tian, the highest being in Chinese civilization, made it inevitable that the Chinese, with all their humbleness and passiveness in front of Tian, have to bring to the fore a humanist spirit that looked to their own inner being for strength and hope. Matteo Ricci suggested that the early Chinese Tian brings a sense of natural 'reasonableness' and principles akin to the Western 'natural law' (see Tang, 1991). But in the Chinese context it leads to the idea of the unity of Tian and humanity (天人合一) – the individual's embodiment of the qualities of the universe itself. In this 'personal-cosmic communion,' Berry (2003) notes, humans see most clearly 'the meaning of their existence and the cosmic function that they [fulfil]' (p. 97). Brindley (2011) further argues,

> Far from recommending slavish conformism, Confucius advocates a Dao that never allows individuals to abandon their own autonomous faculties of judgment and choice of action. Though individuals are ultimately

encouraged to conform to the moral principles of Heaven's Dao, they can only do so if they want to, and also, if they properly apprehend the Dao in the first place. . . . Through the very act of understanding and fulfilling the Dao, individuals draw upon their own, unique, particularized contexts, with the result that they may creatively extend the Dao in some vital way.

(p. 269)

Such Confucian 'basic theme on autonomy of moral will as the defining quality of human worth,' Cheng (2006) notes, almost resonates with Kant's 'notion of the moral sovereignty of man' (pp. 3, 4). But unlike modern Western autonomy, which bequeaths the egoist self unlimited power to realize its purpose, Confucian autonomy is indeed conditioned and depends simultaneously and inevitably on the heteronomy associated with the good, which is the purpose of following the Dao. The Neo- and New Confucians' further move to the ethicoreligious dimensions of humanity only made such autonomy for the moral good even more poignant. Such an understanding of human autonomy inherently preconditioned by spirituality and ethics resonates deeply with the current post-humanist move to critique the modern pursuit of unlimited and unconstrained egoist autonomy and to precondition human freedom in the higher pursuit of the common good. The indigenous Chinese understanding of human freedom, though often buried and underdeveloped, embodies a viable element that can be further articulated to grant human beings an autonomy they can enjoy in the contemporary age.

Clearly the Chinese approach to the human person converges with many of the hard-learned lessons of the West and can be strengthened by extending and further articulating some elements that have not been fully developed and cultivated. Many of the perceived problems of traditional Chinese culture, such as lack of appreciation for human dignity, rights, capacity for reason, and individual freedom, can be traced to the underdevelopment of some already embedded elements and now is the time to re-articulate and reconstruct these elements. On the other hand, historically there has been abundant evidence that particular interpretations and uses of Confucianism have contributed to many of the problems and led to undesirable social and human conditions that we still live in, and one of them is to frame the Confucian emphasis on human relatedness in the concrete, differentiated social relations of father–son, husband–wife, lord–subject, and so on. Dong Zhongshu's 董仲舒 canonization of the 'Three Cardinal Guides' 三纲 as the organizing principle of Chinese society and the guiding principle for individual actions has been at the root of many of the problems the Chinese still have to deal with today. With such canonization, individuals are seen and treated mainly as nodes through which social networks flow and take on a life of their own. Individuals' individuality, agency, freedom and room for imagination and creativity are seriously suffocated. Concepts such as equality and individual dignity, whose seeds are deeply embedded in Confucian and Mencian thought, cannot be formulated and implemented and the modern idea of a civil society is far from a reality.

While the expected mutual care among the related parties has resulted in a strong and stable familial system in China, the submission demanded of the Chinese person to his/her superiors and the power of the superior over his inferiors have resulted in much of the oppressive experience of the Chinese.

But such an interpretation of Confucian relatedness in terms of concrete social and familial relationships is not the only development in Confucian thought. In fact, I would argue that such development has taken the Confucian moral project in the opposite direction and led many Chinese to gradually lose a sense of relatedness to anybody beyond their private lives. Precisely because of the canonization of certain familial and social relations, instead of extending relationality to an outer circle, the larger society, the environment and the world beyond, the Chinese have mostly made sharp distinctions in their concerns between the inner and outer circles. They care deeply about their families and close relatives, but often show a stunning lack of concern for strangers and society at large. In a culture that embraces the unity of *Tian* and humanity, that encourages the cultivation of the self to embrace the world and beyond, people care little about the natural environment, the animals and plants that constitute the world, and the other human beings who have no direct connection with them. What an irony and a surprising consequence for Confucius and Mencius!

As made clear in the discussion of human relationality above, in Confucian thinking, human beings are related to each other not because they have particular familial or social relationships, but because of their natural sensibility and sentiments which become sacred with the notion of 'personal–cosmic communion.' We as human beings are existential and sensitively connected with each other, and our sensitivity and our encounters with each other have an impact on our very being and our selfhood. Confucius' earlier emphasis on the father–son relation is only his way of embracing the most common and most natural human experience of his time (Zhao 2009). For the Chinese, as for many ancient societies of the time, the most natural state of man was man in relationship with parents, and the relationship between son and father signalled the difference between humans and animals; thus the most natural sentiments among people were the sentiments of parents and children. Filial piety was predominantly emphasized in many ancient societies (e.g., Moore, 1927). However, only a later interpretation made this particular relationship the essence of human relatedness; and it is a mistake, I argue, to codify the relationship into an unchangeable power/status structure.

Thus it is of critical importance to reconsider the Confucian notion of relationality for the project of cultural renewal. The Confucian emphasis on human relatedness based on our sensitivity has been shared by many post-humanist Western philosophers, who have provided phenomenological evidence and careful explications for how as human beings we are essentially social beings or 'beings-with', without plugging us into any particular social relations. We are related to each other and morally responsible to each other not because we have any particular relationship, but because of our pre-ego and pre-conscious existential connectedness and because human beings as irreducible subjects are calling for our highest respect. Expanding our relationality beyond our closed private circles to embrace strangers, the environment, and the world seems essential for a critical development of contemporary Confucianism for the flourishing of human beings.

Cultivating the Chinese subject in education

With such a cultural project of renewal and a new understanding of human subjectivity, education as person-making is no longer about producing a certain kind of person whose subjectivity is already identified and predetermined. Education must not participate in shackling young human beings by marking certain modes of existence while dismissing others, but must be prepared for the new and the unpredicted and for the possibility of the limitations of knowing. With the understanding of human subjectivity as unique, changing and uncaptured, but also relational and ethical, education must create an open and respectful space where students can come to terms with themselves as well as be challenged, interrupted and encouraged in unique ways in their never-ceasing becoming. Such an understanding of education does not mean that it ceases to be the cultivation of the human subject. It only means that the cultivation does not have a pre-set norm and end, but is for the purpose of enriching, reminding and inspiring so that students can eventually shine forth with their creativities, multiplicities and irreducibility. With this idea in mind, I propose some points of departure for the educational project of cultivating the new Chinese person for the flourishing of human beings and for a vibrant society.

The first point of departure is for education to cultivate in students an unconditional respect and responsibility for other human beings: to teach students to recognize the other as a unique and irreducible subject with inherent dignity and moral worth and to understand that others' inexhaustible subjectivity cannot be captured or identified; nor is it subject to our judgement and examination. Education should encourage students to gradually develop an appreciation that each one of us is different and unique and that while we may not understand or agree with others, we nevertheless have an unconditional obligation to respect them and to be responsible for their well-being.

The second point of departure is for Chinese education to take the cultivation of students' capacity for reason as a priority, considering the extent to which rationality has been undervalued in the Chinese context. Schools should commit themselves to opening students' eyes and minds, exposing them to different ideas and perspectives, and allowing for open and respectful discussions. Logical thinking skills and rigorous reasoning should be encouraged and taught along with cultivation of sensitivity to and responsibility for other human beings. Through the pedagogy of dialogue, debate, and open discussion, and the intro-duction of different ideas and points of view, students should be encouraged to freely think for themselves and make up their own minds, and they should be respected and encouraged in their own thinking and imagination. We need to revive the lost Confucian value for human autonomy and cultivate our natural tendency for good and kindness and our spiritual connection with the beyond.

In particular, in the Chinese cultural context, education should play a key role in interrupting and breaking down the entrenched cultural habit of regarding human beings as only threads and nodes, suffocated and judged only by their social positions, through which the web of social networks operates. It is imperative that students be led to relate to others as human subjects, as our existential companions embodying the sacred Dao or Tian, rather than only as relatives or superiors/inferiors. Reinvigorating the genuine meaning of relationality deeply embedded in Confucian and Daoist thinking is critical.

This civilizational interchange may be just the beginning of a long, strenuous cultural and educational project of renewal, and pondering, formulating, articulating and implementing it may take generations. These points of departure are only the start of a long journey, but they are necessary and may eventually lead the Chinese to a total reinvigoration and transformation of the way we conduct ourselves in the world and relate to others and the world.

References

Berry, T. (2003). Individualism and Holism in Chinese Tradition: The Religious Cultural Context. In Tu Weiming and M. E. Tucker (eds), *Confucian Spirituality*, Vol. 1. New York: The Crossroad Publishing Company.

Biesta, G. J. (1998). Pedagogy Without Humanism: Foucault and the Subject of Education, *Interchange*, 29(1), 1–16.

Biesta, G. J. (2009). Good Education in an Age of Measurement: On the Need to Reconnect with the Question of Purpose in Education. *Educational Assessment, Evaluation and Accountability*, 21(1), 33–46.

Biesta, G. J. (2010). Education After the Death of the Subject: Levinas and the Pedagogy of Interruption. In Z. Leonardo (ed.), *The Handbook of Cultural Politics and Education* (pp. 289–300). Rotterdam: Sense Publishers.

Blond, P. (1998). *Post-Secular Philosophy Between Philosophy and Theology*. London: Routledge.

Brindley, E. (2011). Moral Autonomy and Individual Sources of Authority in The Analects. *Journal of Chinese Philosophy*, 38(2), 257–73.

Chen, L. and Gan, Y. (2008). 孔子与当代中国 [*Confucius and Modern China*]. Beijing: 三联书店 [Three Links Bookstore].

Cheng, C. Y. (2006). Theoretical Links Between Kant and Confucianism: Preliminary Remarks. *Journal of Chinese Philosophy*, 33(1), 3–15.

Cua, A. S. (2000). Problems of Chinese Moral Philosophy. *Journal of Chinese Philosophy*, 27(3), 269–85.

Durkheim, E. (1973) *On Morality and Society: Selected Writings*. Chicago, University of Chicago Press.

Eaglestone, R. (2010) Postcolonial Thought and Levinas's Double Vision. In P. Atterton and M. Calarco (eds), *Radicalizing Levinas* (pp. 57–68). Albany, State University of New York Press.

Kant, I. (1992/1784). An Answer to the Question 'What is Enlightenment?' In P. Waugh (ed.), *Post-Modernism: A Reader* (pp. 89–95). London: Edward Arnold.

Lai, M. (2009). *Nativism and Modernity: Cultural Contestations in China and Taiwan Under Global Capitalism*. New York: State University of New York Press.

Levinas, E. (1969). *Totality and Infinity*, trans. Alphonso Lingis. Pittsburgh, PN: Duquesne University Press.

Levinas, E. (1990). Reflections on the Philosophy of Hitlerism. *Critical Inquiry*, 17, 63–71.

Levinas, E. (1998). *Otherwise Than Being or Beyond Essence*. Pittsburgh: Duquesne University Press.

May, T. (1997). *Reconsidering Difference: Nancy, Derrida, Levinas, and Deleuze*. University Park, PA: The Pennsylvania State University Press.

Metzger, T. A. (1977). *Escape from Predicament, Neo-Confucianism and China's Evolving Political Culture*. New York: Columbia University Press.

Moore, G. F. (1927). *Judaism*, Vol. 2. Cambridge: Harvard University Press.

Morton, W. S. (1971). The Confucian Concept of Man: The Original Formulation. *Philosophy East and West*, 21(1), 69–77.

Nancy, J. (1991). *The Inoperative Community*, trans. Peter Gonnor, Lisa Garbus, Michael Holland, and Simon Sawhney. Minneapolis: MN: University of Minnesota Press.

Pfister, L. F. (2011). Family Ethics and New Visions of Selfhood in Post-Secular Chinese Teachings. *Journal of Chinese Philosophy*, SI(38), 165–82.

Slote, W. H. and DeVos, G. A. (1998). *Confucianism and the Family*. Albany, NY: State University of New York Press.

Tang, Y. (1991). *Confucianism, Buddhism, Daoism, Christianity, and Chinese Culture*. Washington DC: The Council for Research in Values and Philosophy.

Tu, W. M. (1971). The Neo-Confucian Concept of Man, *Philosophy East and West*, 21(1), 79–87.

Tu, W. M. (1985). *Confucian Thought: Selfhood as Creative Transformation*. Albany, NY: State University of New York Press.

Tu, W. M. (1996). Beyond the Enlightenment Mentality: A Confucian Perspective on Ethics, Migration, and Global Stewardship. *International Migration Review*, 30(1), Special Issue: Ethics, Migration, and Global Stewardship, 58–75.

Tu, W. M. (1998). *Humanity and Self-Cultivation: Essays in Confucian Thought*. Boston: Cheng & Tsui.

Wain, K. (1996). Foucault, Education, the Self and Modernity. *Journal of Philosophy of Education*, 30(3), 345–60.

Wohlfart, G. (2003). Heidegger and Laozi: Wu (Nothing) – in Chapter 11 of the Daodejing, trans. Marty Heitz, *Journal of Chinese Philosophy*, 30(1), 39–59.

Zhang, X. (2009). The Coming Time 'Between' Being and Daoist Emptiness: An Analysis of Heidegger's Article Inquiry into the Uniqueness of the Poet via the Lao Zi, *Philosophy East & West*, 59(1), 71–87.

Zhao, G. (2009). Two Notions of Transcendence: Confucian Man and Modern Subject. *Journal of Chinese Philosophy*, 36(3), 391–407.

Zhao, G. (2014). Freedom Reconsidered: Heteronomy, Open Subjectivity, and the 'Gift of Teaching'. *Studies in Philosophy and Education*, 33(5), 513–25.

Zhao, G. (2015a). Transcendence, Freedom, and Ethics in Levinas' Subjectivity and Zhuangzi's Non-Being Self. *Philosophy East & West*. 65(1), 65–80.

Zhao, G. (2015b). From the Philosophy of Consciousness to the Philosophy of Difference: The Subject for Education After Humanism. *Educational Philosophy and Theory*, 47(9), 958–969.

11 Rethinking and re-envisioning Chinese didactics

Implications from the German *Didaktik* tradition

Zongyi Deng

Pedagogics (*jiaoyu xue* 教育学), or *Pädagogik* in German, refers to a distinct discipline or science of education relating to the work and practice of schooling, which is widely accepted in European countries as an important educational discipline for teacher education (Biesta, 2011). As a central component of pedagogics, didactics (*jiaoxue lun* 教学论), or *Didaktik* in German, stands for *a theory of teaching and learning* embedded in the societal, institutional and instructional context of schooling, addressing issues pertaining to state-curriculum planning, development and classroom enactment (Hopmann, 2007; also see Arnold and Lindner-Müller, 2012). Such a tradition of educational thinking was first introduced to China in the early-1900s via Japan, and fundamentally shaped in the 1950s by Kairov's pedagogics (凯洛夫教育学) imported from the then Soviet Union. Today, pedagogics is in serious crisis in China. On the one hand, it has been severely challenged by a multiplicity of educational disciplines, branches and discourses imported from the US, the UK and other Western countries (Ye, 2004; G. Wu, 1995). On the other, the field has been in danger of dissolving into various branches like *didactics, moral educational theory* and *school administration* (Ye, 2009a). Furthermore, it has been questioned for its relevance in terms of educating open-minded, critical and creative citizens for the twenty-first century (see Zhong and You, 2004). Many scholars have called for constructing Chinese pedagogics, in particular Chinese didactics, rooted in the current social, cultural and educational context of China, in light of the issues and challenges facing education in China today (see Zhou, 2011; Ye, 2004).

This chapter discusses issues concerning the development of Chinese didactics from the perspective of the German *Didaktik* tradition, which can date back to Johann Amos Comenius (1592–1670) and Johann Friedrich Herbart (1776–1814). However, it remains largely unknown to educational scholars in China even though they might possess basic knowledge of Comenius and Herbart (see Deng, 2012). The German *Didaktik* tradition is also largely unknown to North America and English-speaking countries where issues of teaching and learning are discussed within the tradition or paradigm of curriculum or curriculum and instruction (Westbury, 2000; also see Hopmann and Riquarts, 2000). This tradition, as will be argued, challenges Chinese educationists to rethink and re-envision some basic concepts of didactics if they are to reconstruct Chinese didactics with a central concern for the *subjectification* purpose of education (i.e., the making of a person, the becoming of unique individuals, with autonomy, critical thinking and creativity) – in addition to *qualification* (i.e., the acquisition of knowledge, skills and attitudes required for jobs) and *socialization* (i.e., the development of values and norms necessary for becoming members in existing social and cultural orders) (Biesta, 2009).

To provide a context of the discussion, this chapter starts with a brief historical sketch of the development of Chinese didactics, and then proceeds to elucidate the basic feature of contemporary didactics in China by examining Kairov's pedagogics. This is followed by an explanation of three basic tenets of the German *Didaktik* tradition – (1) the concept of *Bildung*, (2) a theory of educational content, and (3) the idea of teaching as a meaningful encounter between the learner and content – and afterward, a discussion of their implications for rethinking and re-envisioning the basic concepts of Chinese didactics. The chapter concludes by looking at 'life-practice' pedagogics developed by Ye Lan, which, while not influenced by the German *Didaktik* tradition, provides an instantiation of what is entailed in such rethinking and re-envisioning.

A historical sketch

The history of didactics in China began with borrowing Herbart's and Herbartian pedagogic theories from Japan at the beginning of the twentieth century. Hereafter, didactics underwent a century of ups and downs as other traditions of educational thinking found their way to China, and as China went through various political turmoils in different times. At the risk of omission and over-simplification, I present a brief historical sketch of five distinct periods characterized in terms of: (1) borrowing from Japan and Europe, (2) Americanization, (3) Sovietization, (4) Cultural Revolution, and (5) Reform and open-up (see Lu, 2001; Ye, 2004).

- *Borrowing from Japan and Europe* (1901 – 1919). The imperial civil service examination system (603CE–1905) was abolished, and the traditional school system replaced by a modern (Western) school system. The pedagogic theories of Herbart and Herbartians were introduced to China from Japan. Herbartian didactics, with its aims–means rationality and five-step method, was found to be particularly relevant; it provided practical answers to the questions of what to teach and how to teach it (X. L. Zhang, 2006; Zhou and Ye, 2006). Starting from 1912, the pedagogical theories of Pestalozzi, Montessori, and others were introduced to China from Continental Europe, and had an impact on Chinese pedagogical thinking and practice (see Curran, 2005).

- *Americanization* (1919–1949). The wave of borrowing from Japan eventually faded away as Chinese educators turned to the US for educational theory and inspiration. During the New Culture Movement (1915–1919) and the May Fourth Movement (1919), Chinese intellectuals called for the creation of a new Chinese culture largely based on American standards. With the two-year historic visit of John Dewey, American pragmatic educational philosophy became highly popular and influential in Chinese educational discourse. American curriculum and instruction theories were systematically introduced to China (G. Ding, 2001; Ye, 2004).
- *Sovietization* (1949–1960). The American influence came to a halt after the establishment of new China in 1949. Isolated by Western capitalist countries (led by the US), China turned to borrowing pedagogic theories and methods from the Soviet Union. I. A. Kairov's *Pedagogics* was translated into Chinese, together with the texts of other Soviet pedagogues. Kairov and associates were invited to give lectures in universities across the country, and Kairov's pedagogics eventually became extremely influential in China's pedagogic theory and practice. However, the Sino–Soviet split in 1960 led to a wholesale criticism of Soviet pedagogic theories (Chen, 1998; Huang, 2010).
- *Cultural Revolution* (1966–1976). Soviet pedagogic theories were completely denounced and repudiated during Cultural Revolution. This 10-year period also 'eradicated' the remnants of American influence on educational discourse and 'wiped out' the traces of Confucian educational heritage (Yang and Frick, 2009).
- *Reform and open-up* (1977–2000). The reopening of China to the world led to an influx of a variety of educational theories to the country. Comenius' *Didactica Magna*, Herbert's *General Pedagogics*, and other related works were reintroduced from Germany and other European countries. Kairov's pedagogics was revisited and revaluated, together with the works of other Soviet pedagogues. Likewise, a vast body of curriculum and instruction theory was introduced mostly from the US. Scholars in China had also endeavoured to develop Chinese didactics and curriculum and instruction theory through writing their own texts (e.g., Cai, 2000; J. Wang, 2011; Zhang and Zhong, 2003).

This brief historical sketch brings to light three main traditions of educational thinking imported to China over the last century, *German pedagogics* (represented by Herbart and Herbartians), *American curriculum (and instruction)*, and the *Soviet pedagogics* (primarily represented by Kairov). However, during the course of theory borrowing these three traditions have been treated as 'discontinuous' and 'mutually exclusive'; the embrace of one led to the rejection of another (Zhou and Ye, 2006). As a result, the German pedagogic legacy has receded to the background, overshadowed, if not completely replaced, by Soviet pedagogics and American curriculum (and instruction) – both of which have become rather influential traditions in educational theory and discourse in China.

Within the Soviet tradition, Kairov's pedagogics has exerted the most influence on the development of didactics in China, and become the 'standard' paradigm in pedagogic thinking (Chen, 1998). Most contemporary didactics texts are written largely within the framework of Kairov's pedagogical theory, and significantly shaped by its basic principles and concepts (Liu and Lin, 2008; Wei and Cai, 2002). An examination of Kairov's *Pedagogics* can reveal the theoretical orientation and basic features of didactics in China.

Kairov's *Pedagogics* and Chinese didactics

Written by Kairov and associates in the 1940s, *Pedagogics* was intended to be used by teachers as a guide for pedagogical practice, and provide a theoretical base for teacher training in the Soviet Union. As such, it was inextricably embedded in the context of the Soviet centralized school system where instructional plans and syllabi from kindergarten to college were developed by the Academy of Pedagogical Sciences under the purview of the Ministry of Education (Medlin, 1958).

A particular branch of Marxist–Leninist philosophy, *Dialectical materialism*[1] was used to establish ground rules that served to guide and inform the development of pedagogic concepts and principles. *Pedagogics* was also based on European pedagogic thinking, represented by Comenius and Herbart. Like Herbart in *General Pedagogics* (*Allgemeine Pädagogik*), Kairov attempted to establish a full-scale science of education – a comprehensive body of theory or discourse concerning the aims of education, educational policy and constitution, didactics, school administration, upbringing, aesthetics and physical education (Kairov *et al.*, 1953).

As a central component of pedagogics, didactics provides a distinct theory of teaching and learning having to do with implementing the state curriculum (instructional guidelines and syllabi) in the classroom. It was comprised of three essential components – goals, content and methods (Künzli, 1998). In Kairov's text, the purposes of teaching are: (1) the mastery of basic knowledge of physical, social and human sciences; (2) the development of cognitive skills and abilities; and (3) the cultivation of a socialist worldview. These purposes are said to be based upon Marxist theory of all-round development of individuals,[2] according to which the central aim of school education is the development of 'all-round developed persons' for the socialist society, or the 'active builders of the communist society' (Kairov *et al.*, 1953, p. 21).

Content refers to a body of knowledge, skills and abilities that provides an essential basis for the all-round development and formation of the communist dialectical worldview, attitudes and behaviours. It is prescribed and specified in instructional materials (instructional plans, syllabi and textbooks) developed by the Ministry of Education, and conveyed to students through the medium of instructional materials (Kairov *et al.*, 1953, p. 21). Methods refer to the means employed by the teacher to help students master curriculum content. The selection and development of methods is based on seven instructional principles, namely (1) students' self-awareness and self-activeness, (2) intuitiveness, (3) theory–reality connection, (4) systematicness and continuity, (5) consolidation, (6) receptiveness, and (7) individualized guidance. Furthermore, teachers are supposed to employ the so-called five-step teaching method when planning and conducting a lesson, consisting of (1) reviewing old material, (2) introducing new material, (3) explaining new material, (4) consolidating newly-learned material, and (5) giving assignments (Kairov *et al.*, 1953).

It is important to note that while Kairov's didactics was constructed in a way that follows the ends–means organizing framework of Herbart's *General Pedagogics* (Chen, 1998), it is in essence Herbartian didactics – a mechanistic, distorted version of Herbart's thinking – in that it encourages dogmatism and prescriptive practice of teaching: teachers are required to adhere to instructional principles and employ the five-step method in lesson planning and classroom teaching.

The ideological orientation and basic features of Kairov didactics are widely shared within the didactics community in China, and can be identified in many contemporary didactics texts (see Deng, 2012). Dialectical materialism is commonly held as an essential ideological and methodological base for the formation of didactic theories (Zhu and Liu, 2009; also see Li and Li, 2001; C. S. Wang, 1985). Didactics is also regarded as a central component of general pedagogics in the European pedagogic tradition (Li and Li, 2001; C. S. Wang, 1985; also see Deng, 2012). The aim of education is defined as the all-round development of individual students needed for socialist China on the basis of Marxist theory of all-round development (e.g., C. S. Wang, 1985; Li and Li, 2001; Tian and Li, 1996). Accordingly, the basic purposes of teaching include: (1) the transmission and mastery of basic knowledge and skills; (2) the development of cognitive capacities and physical strengths; and (3) the cultivation of desirable worldview and moral character (Li and Li, 2001; Tian and Li, 1996; C. S. Wang, 1985). A Kairovan notion of content can also be found in many didactics texts (e.g., Li and Li, 2001; Pei, 2007; C. S. Wang, 1985; also see Deng, 2012). Furthermore, the search for instructional principles and methods that can facilitate the transmission of content to learners has long been a preoccupation in the didactics community in China (see Li and Zhao, 2009).

In short, framed within the Kairov's framework, didactics in China is directed towards the transmission of content by means of a body of instructional methods and principles, with the primary aim of producing individuals needed for the socialist society. As such, Chinese didactics is directed to the qualification and socialization aims of education, producing citizens and workers for the political and economic needs of the country. A concern for subjectification in terms of the formation of the self or cultivation of the unique individual is largely lacking.

Like Kairov's didactics, didactics in China in essence is a kind of Herbartian didactics that encourages prescriptive and procedural practice of teaching in view of the social and political aims of schooling (also see L. Y. Wang, 2009). As such, it is indeed a far cry from the vision of didactics purported in Herbart's

General Pedagogics – in which the central purpose of teaching is the formation of the moral and intellectual character of the child according to his or her 'natural liveliness' (Hilgenheger, 1993), achieved not through the employment of formulaic pedagogical methods and techniques, but through 'an inviting unlocking of contents which stimulates understanding, and consequently elevates a child's *dialogue* with his or her world' (Krüger, 2008, p. 227).

In this junction, the German *Didaktik* tradition becomes particularly relevant and meaningful for rethinking and re-envisioning Chinese didactics. Standing for a reconceptualization of Herbartian didactics, this tradition was developed out of a criticism of Herbartianism near the end of the nineteenth century, together with a revisiting of the original thinking of Herbart and Kant (Hamilton, 1999; Hopmann and Riquarts, 2000; Kansanen, 1999). As alluded to earlier, the original thinking of Herbart has become lost during the process of theory borrowing in the twentieth century. Recently, there have been attempts to rediscover the significance of Herbart's general pedagogics for educational theory and practice in China (see B. X. Zhang, 2006). However, the German *Didaktik* tradition remains largely unknown to the Chinese educational community. Yet in this tradition, as will be seen below, the three essential aspects of didactics – purposes, content and methods of teaching – are primarily conceptualized in the subjectification domain, with a central concern for the formation of the unique and free individual with the capacity for independent and critical thinking, and with a sense of social responsibility and commitment. It therefore can address the issues and problems facing didactical theory in China today.

The German *Didaktik* tradition

There exist many traditions or branches of didactics in Germany, such as *Bildung*-centred *Didaktik* (*Bildungstheoretische Didaktik*), Berliner *Didaktik*, and Psychological *Didaktik* (H. Meyer, 2013; also see Arnold and Lindner-Müller, 2012). This chapter only deals with *Bildung*-centred *Didaktik* which, also called the German *Didaktik* tradition, was established in the 1960s primarily by Wolfgang Klafki (born 1927). It is 'the main tradition of didactics and has had the longest and most profound impact' (Gundem, 2000, p. 242) and has been 'at the center of most school teaching and teacher education in Continental Europe' (Hopmann, 2007, p. 109).

In this tradition didactics is positioned within the realm of human sciences (*Geisteswissenschaften*) rather than natural science (*Naturewissenschaften*), with the employment of a hermeneutic approach to understanding and theorizing educational phenomena. Its philosophical underpinning consists in the thinking of European Enlightenment associated with Kant, Herder, Goethe, Schiller, Pestalozzi, Herbart, Schleiermacher, Fichte, Hegel, Froebel and Diesterweg. Underpinning this thinking is the image of 'the responsible and socially aware person contributing to his or her own destiny and capable of knowing, feeling, and acting' (Gundem, 2000, p. 242).

The tradition provides a theory of teaching and learning pertaining to implementing the state curriculum in the classroom. All German states have a well-articulated state curriculum framework, the *Lehrplan*, which lays out school subjects and their content to be taught in school. However, it does not specify the educational meanings of the content, which are to be interpreted by teachers in their classroom situations (Hopmann, 2007). In this connection, teachers have a high degree of professional autonomy to interpret the state-mandated curriculum in classroom settings; they are viewed as reflective professionals 'working within, but not directed by' the state curriculum framework, informed by the idea of *Bildung* and the didactics way of thinking (Westbury, 2000). Three basic tenets are fundamental to the German *Didaktik* tradition: (1) the notion of *Bildung*; (2) a theory of educational content; and (3) an idea of teaching as a meaningful encounter between the learner and the content.

Bildung stands for the German ideal of education or what it means to be educated. In essence, it refers to the process of self-formation, which entails the development of intellectual and moral powers, the cultivation of sensibility, self-awareness, liberty and freedom, and the dignity of the individual (Hopmann, 2007; Humboldt, 2000). The process also requires the unification of oneself within the broader society and culture. An educated person is one who

> has succeeded in establishing a certain degree of order in the whole of his existence, in the wide variety of gifts, opportunities, drives and achievements he incorporates, linking the one to the other in the appropriate relationship, guarding against over-emphasis, but also against suppression of the particular. However, a person can never, never create order within himself, unless he has regulated his relations to the world in an appropriate manner.
> (Litt, 1963, cited in Klafki, 2000, p. 146)

Thus, to achieve *Bildung*, the individual seeks to 'grasp as much [of the] world as possible' and to make contribution to humankind through developing his or her own unique self and intellectual and moral powers (Humboldt, 2000). Evidently, *Bildung* is centred on the subjectification function of education – that is, on the life-long process of personal development rather than training in gaining certain knowledge and skills.

In German *Didaktik* content is viewed as 'a potential stimulus for human development' and 'a means of expressing, exercising and intuiting powers,' and therefore, must be 'used in the service of intellectual and moral *Bildung*' (Lüth, 2000). As such, it is an important cultural resource for *Bildung* (Klafki, 2000). Content, characteristically defined by curriculum designers as the content of education (*Bildungsinhalt*), is the result of special selection and organization of the wealth of the conceivable knowledge, experiences and wisdom for *Bildung*. The content of a particular school subject is construed as comprising *educational substance* (*Bildungsgehalt*) – *essential* elements, aspects or structures – that could contribute to *Bildung* (Klafki, 2000). Such content, by virtue of its educational substance, has the 'formative potential' or the 'possible value-laden impact' on the mind of the becoming person. In other words, it can lead to *fundamental* experience (Krüger, 2008). These four interrelated concepts, *content of education, educational substance, essential* and *fundamental*, together constitute *a theory of educational content (Theorie der Bildungsinhalte)* – a theory of what content is, what educational value and significance content possesses, and how content is selected and organized for educational purposes.[3]

Accordingly, teaching is largely conceived in the subjectification domain, having to do with human formation through participating in the world and culture (von Humboldt, 2000; also see Lüth, 2000). At the heart of teaching is a 'fruitful encounter' between content and the learner (Klafki, 2000). Teachers are to understand the content of a school subject – more precisely, the theory of content – embedded in the *Lehrplan*. They are to be centrally concerned with analyzing and unpacking the educational meaning, value and significance of content from the perspective of *Bildung*, when engaged in instructional planning in a classroom setting. As Künzli (1998) explained,

> A didactician looks for a prospective object of learning . . . and he asks himself what this object can and should signify for the student and how the student can experience this significance . . . All other questions and problems – other than the significance of the learning content – such as class management, individual and social learning, learning control, individual learning speed, appropriate representation, etc. – are subordinate to this central concern and gain significance only when the question of educative substance (*Bildungsgehalt*) is at issue.
>
> (pp. 39–40)

In other words, teachers need to disclose the educational potential inherent in content through conducting *Didaktik* analysis. Klafki formulated a five-step set of questions that assists teachers in exploring educational potential:

1. What wider or general sense or reality does this content exemplify and open up to the learner? What basic phenomenon or fundamental principle, what law, criterion, problem, method, technique, or attitude can be grasped by dealing with this content as an 'example'?
2. What significance does the content in question, or the experience, knowledge, ability or skill, to be acquired through this topic, already possess in the minds of the children in my class? What significance should it have from a pedagogical point of view?
3. What constitutes the topic's significance for the children's future?
4. How is the content structured (which has been placed in a specifically pedagogical perspective by questions 1, 2 and 3)?
5. What are the special cases, phenomena, situations, experiments, persons, elements of aesthetic experience, and so forth, in terms of which the structure of the content in question can become interesting,

stimulating, approachable, conceivable or vivid for children of the stage
of development of this class?

(Klafki, 2000, pp. 151–7)

Questions 1 to 3 explore the essential ingredients, features and significances
that constitute the educational potential of the content. Questions 2 and 3
necessitate an analysis or unpacking of the educational meaning and significance
of those essential elements – an analysis which is crucial for disclosing the
educational potential inherent in the content. By discerning the essential
elements of the content and elucidating their possible manifestations or aspects,
didactics analysis unlocks the 'organic power' contained in the content that could
bring about fundamental experience leading to *Bildung*.

However, it is important to note that German *Didaktik* is not without issues
and problems. Historically, the notion of *Bildung* has long been 'charged' with
the interest and sentiment of the middle class, the utopian hopes of enlightenment and the realization of those hopes (Hansen, 2008). It a humanist version
of liberal education that defines the aim of education exclusively within the
subjectification realm, with a strong tendency to overlook the extant social,
cultural and political expectations and demands on the qualification and
socialization functions of education. As a result, the German *Didaktik* tradition
has been under severe challenge particularly in the context of globalization,
standards and accountability (also see Hopmann, 2007, 2008). These issues
need to be kept in mind when we draw on the tradition to rethink and re-
envision the development of Chinese didactics

Rethinking and re-envisioning basic didactic concepts

The three tenets of the German *Didaktik* tradition carry important implications
for the development of Chinese didactics. They invite and challenge Chinese
educationists to rethink and re-envision what education is for, how content
should be conceived, selected and organized, and what teaching entails with
attention to the subjectification function of education – in addition to the
qualification and socialization functions.

With its foregrounding of the subjectification purpose of education, *Bildung*
is fundamentally different from the notion of educational aims in Chinese
didactics construed for socialization and qualification purposes, in terms of
preparing individual students for the social and economic needs of China.
Bildung privileges self-formation over qualification and socialization. This
resonates with the Neo-Confucian idea of self-cultivation concerning the
development of self-worth, self-respect, self-understanding and individual
powers vis-à-vis fulfilling one's social responsibilities and functions. As de Bary
(1996) observed,

> The Four Books with Zhu Xi's commentary gave the individual a sense of
> self-worth and self-respect not to be sacrificed for any short-term utilitarian

purpose; a sense of place in the world not to be surrendered to any state or party; a sense of how one could cultivate one's individual powers to meet the social responsibilities that the enjoyment of learning always brought with it – powers and responsibilities not to be defaulted on.

(p. 33)

Such self-cultivation is the essential precondition for developing the critical and creative potentials of the individual and enabling him or her to fulfil social responsibilities and functions (de Bary, 1996; also Bai, Chapter 4, this volume; Zhao, Chapter 2, this volume). As such, it is inextricably connected with the task of making a contribution to the family, the community and the nation. Like *Bildung*, self-cultivation is achieved through the interactions with the physical and cultural world, entailing the investigation of natural and social phenomena and the advancement of knowledge (Bai, Chapter 2, this volume; de Bary, 1996). However, self-cultivation is different from *Bildung* in that the former attaches greater significance to the community or society of which one is seen as an organic part rather than (as does the latter) the individual as an almost independent and self-sufficient entity (de Bary, 1996).

If learning to be human, either in the sense of *Bildung* or of self-cultivation, is to be taken seriously, Chinese educationists would have to rethink and re-envision the basic meanings and purposes of education. What constitutes self-worth, self-understanding, self-respect, intellectual power and moral dispositions? How could/should self-worth, self-understanding and self-respect be developed? How could/should individual intellectual powers, moral dispositions, social responsibilities be cultivated vis-a-vis the development of self-worth, self-understanding and self-respect? What role do scientific, natural, cultural and historical resources play in such cultivation or development, and how? How could/should the purposes of education be re-conceived to facilitate the process of learning to be human?

The idea of a theory of educational content in German *Didaktik* provides an important way of thinking about issues pertaining to content selection, organization and framing for educational, social, cultural and pedagogical purposes – issues that are essential to curriculum making at the programmatic level. As already noted, unlike in Chinese didactics where content is largely taken as a body of steady, ready-made knowledge and skills for acquisition and mastery (see Deng, 2012), in German *Didaktik* content is construed as the indispensable resource for *Bildung*, with inherent educational potential to be disclosed and realized in classrooms (Klafki, 2000; also see Deng, 2011). Accordingly, content is selected, organized and framed in a way that supports and facilitates classroom teachers to interpret and transform content so as to bring out manifold educational opportunities in classroom for the formation of self and cultivation of intellectual and moral powers and capacities. To this end, teachers are seen as professionals with sufficient autonomy to interpret and enact the state curriculum (Hopmann, 2007).

Yet in Chinese didactics discourse the theory (or theories) of content (if any) is largely constructed for the tasks of qualification and socialization (Deng, 2012). The educational potential inherent in content for the formation of self and the development of intellectual and moral powers is far from being adequately recognized. What should constitute the content of teaching and learning in view of the need to help students develop self-understanding, intellectual and moral powers? What educational value and significance does content possess with respect to the subjectification purpose of education – apart from the qualification and socialization purposes – in the current social, economic and educational context of schooling in China? How could/should content be re-conceived, selected, organized and framed in a way that not only contributes to the qualification and socialization aims but also facilitates the subjectification process of individuals? How could/should content be organized, arranged and framed in a way that ensures teachers have sufficient professional autonomy and the leeway necessary for cultivating students' self-understanding, self-worth, intellectual and moral powers through disclosing the educational potential of content in a classroom setting?

The third tenet, the notion of teaching as a learner–content encounter, invites Chinese educationists to rethink the essence of classroom teaching from the perspective of subjectification. As indicated above, in German *Didaktik*, teaching is not viewed as in terms of transmitting knowledge, skills, abilities and attitudes per se. At the heart of teaching is a 'meeting' between learners and content initiated by the classroom teacher – an 'encounter' that can give rise to the unfolding of the self and cultivation of intellectual and moral powers (Hopmann, 2007). This is a stark contrast to current pervasive pedagogical practice in classroom in China which is largely driven by qualification and socialization purposes, which, as Levine (2010) observed, 'focuses on the mastery of content, not on the development of the capacity for independent and critical thinking.' Yet, to a certain extent, the *Didaktik* notion of teaching is consonant with the Confucius vision of teaching rediscovered by Wu Zongjie, based on his analysis of *The Analects* – an image in which the teacher engages students in a 'heart-to-heart' dialogue necessitated by an in-depth engagement with the meaning of a classic text (Z. Wu, 2011).

How should classroom teaching be reconceived and re-envisaged in light of the subjectification purpose – apart from the qualification and socialization purposes? How could/should a teacher analyze and unpack content in terms of educational potential for person-making or subjectification? How could/ should a teacher ascertain the meaning and significance of a particular topic from the students' perspective and for their future? How could/should students' voices be taken into consideration in the process of analyzing content for the purpose of person-making? How could/should a teacher and a group of students jointly plan and enact instructional events in a particular classroom setting? How could/should a teacher facilitate the 'encounter' between students and content in a way that renders manifold opportunities for not only the acquisition of knowledge, skills and competences but also the cultivation of freedom, inner worth, agency and intellectual and moral powers?

In short, the German *Didaktik* tradition invites and challenges educationists in China to rethink and re-envision the purposes, content and methods of teaching. This rethinking and re-envisioning is essential if they are to construct Chinese didactics with a concern for the subjectification purpose of education – in addition to qualification and socialization purposes. How might such a construction look in China? What might the rethinking and re-envisioning entail in the current social, cultural and institutional context of schooling? As an illustration, I now look at the development of 'life-practice' pedagogics by professor Ye Lan and colleagues at East China Normal University – an undertaking that entails a fundamental rethinking and re-envisioning of many basic didactic concepts pertaining to the subjectification purpose of education. The rethinking and re-envisioning, while not informed by the German *Didaktik* tradition, in many respects resonates what is implied in the three tenets outlined above.

The case of 'life-practice' pedagogics: an illustration

As a new paradigm or school of thought, 'life-practice' pedagogics was constructed by Ye Lan and associates over the course of planning and implementing 'New Basic Education' – a reform programme directed towards reforming elementary and secondary schools in the midst of profound social, economic and educational transition undergoing in China at the turn of the twenty-first century – caused by globalization, a fast-growing market economy, the emergence of information technology, etc. The reform was motivated by the concern for developing students' abilities to self-regulate, judge and think reflectively, and cultivating their self-confidence and courage to face challenges (Ye, 2009a, 2009b; also see Bu, Xu and Deng, Chapter 12, this volume). 'Life-practice' pedagogics was also envisioned as a response to critical issues facing pedagogics in China, discerned by Ye Lan based on her critical reflection on the historical development of the field – issues having to do with its undue reliance on imported Western theories, its adherence to political ideologies, its preoccupation with transmitting disciplinary knowledge, skills and attitudes needed for the society, and (as a result) its overlooking of the developing individual, among others (Bu, 2011).

In 'life-practice' pedagogics Ye Lan attempts to redirect the concern for transmitting content (knowledge, skills and attitudes) to the one for cultivating *individuals* who possess intellectual, moral and spiritual potentialities – actively developing individuals. Accordingly, the central aim of education is re-envisaged as cultivating individuals with the 'self-consciousness of life' – the 'inner power' for realizing the value of life (Ye, 2009a). It is 'to help people to "own" their consciousness and ability to lead their own destinies' (Ye, 2009b, p. 562). This aim is essential to New Basic Education reform that 'attempted to cultivate future citizens with the qualities of independent thinking and independent personalities, and to also instill in them a sense of collective [social] responsibility'

(Ye, 2009b, p. 584). In other words, the cultivation of self-consciousness is seen as the necessary precondition for achieving the qualification and socialization purposes of education. This is largely compatible with what is implied in *Bildung* and in the Neo-Confucian notion of self-cultivation outlined above.

Like in German *Didaktik*, in 'life-practice' pedagogics content is held as an important 'resource' and 'means' for cultivating individual learners rather than a body of knowledge and skills for mere transmission or mastery (Ye, 2009a). A distinction is made between *explicit content* and *implicit content*. The former is embodied in instructional frameworks, syllabi and textbooks, consisting of the outcomes of human experience and practice selected and organized for the purposes of providing students with opportunities to understand and interact with the real world, developing their intellectual and moral abilities, and cultivating their self-consciousness of life. The latter is further differentiated between *implicit 'process' content* – pertaining to the process and practice through which knowledge was developed and formulated by human beings – and *implicit 'relational' content* – concerning knowledge relationships in and across school subjects These three notions are essential for recognizing and appreciating the educational values and significance inherent in content – in terms of developing students' self-understanding, intellectual capacities and social responsibilities (Ye, 2009a). They can be seen as constituting *a theory of educational content* envisioned by Ye Lan and colleagues.

Furthermore, Ye Lan envisions classroom teaching as a 'dynamic' and 'generative' process organized around content and directed towards cultivating the life-consciousness, intellectual and moral potential of the active individual (Ye, 2009a). Like in the German *Didaktik* tradition, in 'life-practice' pedagogics teaching is seen as involving an active 'interplay' between learners and content which could bring about a profound impact on learners. To facilitate such an interplay, classroom teachers necessarily analyze and explore the educational value and significance inherent in content in terms of explicit content, implicit 'process' and 'relational' content, with attention to who students are, their interests, knowledge backgrounds and experiences. Teachers are to reorganize, frame and transform content in a way that allows the educational value and significance to be realized in the classroom (Ye, 2002, 2009a). Furthermore, classroom teaching is envisioned as an important phase of the 'life journey' for both the teacher and students, which can have an impact on their current and future lives. It is not only a way of contributing to the development of students, but also an arena where teachers realize their life value, self-development and self-fulfilment (Ye, 1997).

Overall, the above brief discussion of 'life-practice' pedagogics illustrates what is entailed in rethinking and re-envisioning the aim of education, content, and the practice of teaching within the current social and cultural context of schooling in China, with a primary concern for the subjectification aim of education. This rethinking and re-envisioning, albeit not informed by the German *Didaktik* tradition, bears significant resemblance to what is implied in the three tenets of the German tradition.

Concluding remarks

Primarily framed within the framework of Kairov's pedagogics, Chinese didactics has been developed to serve the qualification and socialization purposes, with little concern for person-making or the subjectification purpose of education. Through expounding the three basic tenets of the German *Didaktik* tradition – (1) the concept of Bildung, (2) a theory of educational content, and (3) the idea of teaching as a learner–content encounter – this chapter challenges Chinese educationists to rethink and re-envision the purposes, content and methods of teaching. Such rethinking and re-envisioning is essential if they are to reconstruct Chinese didactics with a central concern for person-making in the current age.

Nevertheless, as mentioned earlier, the German *Didaktik* tradition is fraught with problems caused by the utopian notion of Bildung and the inherent tendency to ignore the existing social and economic expectations and demands for education, and the challenge of translating those demands and expectations into the curriculum and into classroom practices. Such problems can be addressed if Chinese didactics is to be (re)constructed within the current social, cultural and educational context of schooling in China, with close attention to the expectations and demands on the subjectification, qualification and socialization purposes of education in today's world. A thorough understanding of these expectations and demands calls for, on the part of Chinese educationists, extensive theoretical and empirical investigations. Furthermore, apart from the German *Didaktik* tradition, other theoretical sources need to be eclectically brought to bear on the task of theory development. This way of constructing didactical theory can, on the one hand, take account of the insights and contributions of the German *Didaktik*, and on the other, overcome their (inherent) issues and limitations. In short, a new paradigm of Chinese didactics can be established when theory development is grounded in a sophisticated and thorough understanding of the demands and challenges facing today's Chinese education, together with an embrace of eclecticism that allows a variety of theories – Western, Eastern or Chinese – to be brought to bear on theory development in a productive manner (see Deng, 2012, 2013).

Notes

1 Dialectical materialism, the 'official' interpretation of Marxism–Leninism, was formulated in the 1930s by Stalin and his associates. It is a theory about the organization and evolution of complex natural and social forms. Blakeley (1975) explains:

> This whole series of forms (mechanical, physical, chemical, biological and social) is distributed according to complexity from lower to higher. This seriation expresses their mutual bonds in terms of structure and in terms of history. The general laws of the lower forms of the motion of matter keep their validity for all the higher forms but they are subject to the higher laws and do not have a prominent role. They change their activity because of changed circumstances.

Laws can be general or specific, depending on their range of applicability. The specific laws fall under the special sciences and the general laws are the province of diamat.

(p. 29)

2 According to Marx, a communist society presupposes that all individuals be fully developed in all dimensions, intellectual, physical, moral, social, relational, and so forth, and it is only in a communist society that such a full development can be possible (Kairov *et al.*, 1953).

3 For issues concerning a theory of content, interested readers can be referred to Doyle (1992a, 1992b) and Deng (2009, 2011).

References

Arnold, K.-H. and Lindner-Müller, C. (2012). The German Tradition in General Didactics. *Jahrbuch für Allgemeine Didaktik (JfAD – Yearbook for General Didactics)*, 2, 46–64.

Biesta, G. (2009). Good Education in an Age of Measurement: On the Need to Reconnect with the Question of Purpose in Education. *Educational Assessment, Evaluation and Accountability*, 21(1), 33–46.

Biesta, G. (2011). Disciplines and Theory in the Academic Study of Education: A Comparative Analysis of the Anglo-American and Continental Construction of the Field. *Pedagogy, Culture & Society*, 19(2), 175–92.

Blakeley, T. J. (ed.) (1975). *Themes in Soviet Marxist Philosophy*. Dordrecht: Reidel.

Bu, Y. H. (2011). 叶澜 '生命.实践 '教育学创建的思想路径 *[The Ideological Path of Ye Lan's Pedagogics of 'Life and Practice']*. 高校理论战线 [Theoretical Front in Higher Education], (9), 19–28.

Cai, B. L. (2000). 传统教学论的产生及发展历程 [The Genesis and Development of Traditional Didactics]. 教育研究 *[Educational Research]*, (6), 60–65.

Chen, G. S. (1998). 重评凯洛夫《教育学》 [Reevaluating 'Kairov's Pedagogics']. 河北师范大学学报（教育科学版） *[Journal of Hebei Normal University (Educational Science)]*, 1(1), 42–8, 78.

Curran, T. D. (2005). *Educational Reform in Republican China: The Failure of Educators to Create a Modern Nation* (Vol. 40). New York: Edwin Mellen.

de Bary, W. T. (1996). *Confucian Education in Premodern Asia. In Weiming Tu (ed.), Confucian Traditions in East Asian Modernity* (pp. 21–37). Cambridge: Harvard University Press.

Deng, Z. (2009). The Formation of a School Subject and the Nature of Curriculum Content: An Analysis of Liberal Studies in Hong Kong. *Journal of Curriculum Studies*, 41(5), 585–604.

Deng, Z. (2011). Revisiting Curriculum Potential. *Curriculum Inquiry*, 41(5), 538–59.

Deng, Z. (2012). Constructing Chinese Didactics: (Re)Discovering the German Didactics Tradition. *Jahrbuch für Allgemeine Didaktik (JfAD – Yearbook for General Didactics)*, 2, 108–28.

Deng, Z. (2013). The Practical and Reconstructing Chinese Pedagogics. *Journal of Curriculum Studies*, 45(5), 652–67.

Ding, G. (2001). Nationalization and Internationalization: Two Turning Points in China's Education in the Twentieth Century. In G. Peterson, R. Hayhoe and Y. Lu (eds), *Education, Culture, and Identity in Twentieth-Century China* (pp. 161–86). Hong Kong: The University of Hong Kong Press.

Doyle, W. (1992a). Constructing Curriculum in the Classroom. In F. K. Oser, A. Dick and J. Patry (eds), *Effective and Responsible Teaching: The New Syntheses* (pp. 66–79). San Francisco: Jossey-Bass.

Doyle, W. (1992b). *Curriculum and Pedagogy. In P. W. Jackson (ed.), Handbook of Research on Curriculum* (pp. 486–516). New York: Macmillan.

Gundem, B. B. (2000). Understanding European Didactics. In B. Moon, M. Ben-Peretz and S. Brown (eds), *Routledge International Companion to Education* (pp. 235–62). London: Routledge.

Hamilton, D. (1999). The Pedagogic Paradox (or why no Didactics in England?). *Pedagogy, Culture & Society*, 7(1), 135–52.

Hansen, L-H. (2008). Rewriting *Bildung* for Postmodernity: Books on Educational Philosophy, Classroom Practice, and Reflective Teaching. *Curriculum Inquiry*, 38(1), 93–114.

Hilgenheger, N. (1993). Johann Friedrich Herbart. *Prospects*, 23(3–4), 649–64.

Hopmann, S. (2007). Restrained Teaching: The Common Cores of Didaktik. *European Educational Research Journal*, 6(2), 109–24.

Hopmann, S. (2008). No Child, No School, No State Left Behind: Schooling in the Age of Accountability. *Journal of Curriculum Studies*, 40(4), 417–56.

Hopmann, S. and Riquarts, K. (2000). Starting a Dialogue: A Beginning Conversation Between Didaktik and Curriculum Traditions. In I. Westbury, S. Hopmann and K. Riquarts (eds), *Teaching as a Reflective Practice: The German Didaktik Tradition* (pp. 3–11). Mahwah, NJ: Erlbaum.

Huang, S. G. (2010). 凯洛夫《教育学》在中国的理论辐射与实践影响 [The Theory Radiation and Practical Influence of I. A. Kairov's Pedagogics in China]. 复旦教育论坛 *[Fudan Education Forum]*, 8(3), 42–7.

Humboldt, W. von. (2000). Theory of Bildung. In I. Westbury, S. Hopmann and K. Riquarts (eds), *Teaching as a Reflective Practice: The German Didaktik Tradition* (pp. 57–61). Mahwah, NJ: Erlbaum.

Kairov, I. A. and Associates (1953). 教育学 *[Pedagogics]* (trans.), 北京：人民教育出版社 [Beijing: People Education Press].

Kansanen, P. (1999). The Deutsche Didaktik and the American Research on Teaching. In B. Hudson, F. Buchberger, P. Kansanen and H. Seel (eds), *Didaktik/Fachdidaktik as Science(-s) of the Teaching Profession. TNTEE Publications*, 2(1), 21–35.

Klafki, W. (2000). Didaktik Analysis as the Core of Preparation. In I. Westbury, S. Hopmann and K. Riquarts (eds), *Teaching as a Reflective Practice: The German Didaktik Tradition* (pp. 139–59). Mahwah, NJ: Erlbaum.

Krüger, R. A. (2008). The Significance of the Concepts 'Elemental' and 'Fundamental' in Didactic Theory and Practice. *Journal of Curriculum Studies*, 40(2), 215–50.

Künzli, R. (1998). The Common Frame and the Places of Didaktik. In B. B. Gundem and S. Hopmann (eds), *Didaktik and/or Curriculum: An International Dialogue* (pp. 29–45). New York: Peter Lang.

Levine, R. C. (2010). Top of the Class: The Rise of Asia's Universities. *Foreign Affairs*, May/June 2010. Available online at: http://foreignaffairs.com/articles/66216/richard-c-levin/top-of-the-class (accessed 7 June 2013).

Li, B. D. and Li, D. R. (2001). 教学论 *[Didactics]*. 北京：人民教育出版社 [Beijing: People's Education Press].

Li, S. and Zhao, X. (2009). 20 世纪中国教学论的重要进展和未来走向 [The Important Development and Future Direction of 20th Century's Chinese Didactics]. 教育研究 *[Educational Research]*, 30(10), 42–8.

Liu, H. M. and Lin, D. (2008). Difficulties and Outlets: On Paradigm of China's Pedagogy. *Frontiers of Education in China*, 3(2), 163–77.

Lu, J. (2001). On the Indigenousness of Chinese Pedagogy. In R. Hayhoe and J. Pan (eds), *Knowledge Across Cultures: A Contribution to Dialogue Among Civilizations* (pp. 249–53). Hong Kong, China: Comparative Education Research Centre, The University of Hong Kong.

Lüth, C. (2000). On Wilhelm von Humboldt's Theory of Bidung. In I. Westbury, S. Hopmann and K. Riquarts (eds), *Teaching as a Reflective Practice: The German Didaktik Tradition* (pp. 63–84). Mahwah, NJ: Erlbaum.

Medlin, W. K. (1958). Soviet Pedagogical Academy and the New School Plans. *Comparative Education Review*, 2(2), 12–14.

Meyer, H. (2013). Crisis and New Orientation of General Didactics in Germany. In X. M. Peng (ed.), *Sino-German Dialogue on Didactics: Post Graduate Academic Forum* (pp. 16–24). Shanghai, China: East China Normal University.

Pei, D. N. (2007). 教学论 *[Didactics]*. 北京：教育科学出版社 [Beijing: Educational Science Publishing House].

Tian, H. S. and Li, R. M. (1996). 教学论 *[Didactics]*. 河北: 河北教育出版社 [Hebei: Hebei Education Press].

Wang, C. S. (1985). 教学论稿 *[Didactics Manuscript]*. 北京:人民教育出版社 [Beijing: People's Education Press].

Wang, J. (2011). 论中国特色的教学论学派 [On Schools of Chinese didactics]. 华中师范大学学报（人文社会科学版）*[Journal of Huazhong Normal University (Humanities and Social Science)]*, 50(1), 140–7.

Wang, Y. L. (2009). '目中无人': 凯洛夫《教育学》核心概念批判 ['Care For No One': A Critique of the Core Concepts of Kairov's Pedagogics]. 全球教育展望 *[Global Education]*, 37(4), 18–25.

Wei, X. M. and Cai, B. L. (2002). 教学论的困境与出路 [The Dilemma and Resolution of Didactics]. 教育研究 *[Educational Research]*, (6), 54–9.

Westbury, I. (2000). Teaching as a Reflective Practice: What Might Didaktik Teach Curriculum. In I. Westbury, S. Hopmann and K. Riquarts (eds), *Teaching as a Reflective Practice: The German Didaktik Tradition* (pp. 15–39). Mahwah, NJ: Erlbaum.

Wu, G. (1995). 论教育学的终结 [The End of Pedagogics]. 教育研究 *[Educational Research]*, 7, 19–24.

Wu, Z. (2011). Interpretation, Autonomy, and Transformation: Chinese Pedagogic Discourse in a Cross-Cultural Perspective. *Journal of Curriculum Studies*, 43(5), 569–90.

Yang, J. and Frick, W. (2009). Will the Leadership of Chinese Education Follow the Footsteps of American Education? A Brief Historical and Socio-Political Analysis. *Journal of Thought*, 44(3, 4), 23–48.

Ye, L. (1997). 让课堂焕发出生命活力 – 论中小学教学改革的深化 [Let Classrooms Exhibit Life Power: On Deepening Instructional Reform in Elementary and Secondary Schools]. 教育研究 *[Educational Research]*, 9, 3–7.

Ye, L. (2002). 重建课堂教学价值观 [Reconstructing Value Beliefs About Classroom Teaching]. 教育研究 *[Educational Research]*, 5(3–7), 16.

Ye, L. (2004). 中国教育学发展世纪问题的审视 [The Development of Pedagogics in China: A Review of Century-Long Issues]. 教育研究 *[Educational Research]*, 7, 3–17.

Ye, L. (2009a). 基础教育改革与中国教育学理论重建研究 *[Research on Basic Educational Reform and the Reconstruction of Chinese Pedagogic Theory]*. 北京：中国人民大学出版社 [Beijing, China: Economic Science Press].

Ye, L. (2009b). 'New Basic Education' and Me. *Frontiers of Education in China*, 4(4), 558–609.

Zhang, B. X. (2006). 重新掀开被湮没的历史, 正确认识被曲解的传统 [Reopening a Forgotten History, Rediscovering a Misinterpreted Tradition]. 教育学报 *[Journal of Educational Studies]*, 2(5), 3.

Zhang, H. and Zhong, Q. Q. (2003). Curriculum Studies in China: Retrospect and Prospect. In W. F. Pinar (ed.), *International Handbook of Curriculum Research* (pp. 253–70). Mahwah, NJ: Lawrence Erlbaum.

Zhang, X. L. (2006). 赫尔巴特教育学在中国的传播 (1901–1904) [The Introduction and Spread of Herbart's Pedagogics in China (1901–1904)]. 教育学报 *[Journal of Educational Studies]*, 2(5), 36–41, 57.

Zhong, Q. Q. and You, B. H. (2004). 发霉的奶酪 – 《认真对待'轻视知识'的教育思潮 [Moldy Cheese: Review of 'A Critical Reflection on the Thought of "Despising Knowledge" in Chinese Basic Education']. 全球教育展望 *[Global Education]*, 33(10), 3–7.

Zhou, G. P. and Ye, Z. J. (2006). 赫尔巴特教育学在中国: 一个跨越世纪的回望 [Herbart's Pedagogy in China: Review of the Study in the Past Century]. 教育学报 *[Journal of Educational Studies]*, 2(5), 29–35.

Zhou, Y. (2011). Reflections on Modern China and the Progressive Power of Educational Studies. *Frontiers of Education in China*, 6(2), 167–81.

Zhu, C. K. and Liu, H. M. (2009). 教学认识论的审思与勾画 – 历史唯物主义思维向度的检视 [Reflection and Construction of Teaching Epistemology: An Examination of the Thinking Orientation of Historical Materialism]. 高等教育研究 *[Higher Education Research]*, 3, 13–18.

12 The new basic education and the development of human subjectivity

A Chinese experience

Yuhua Bu, Jing Xu and Zongyi Deng

During the last two decades, the Chinese school system has developed dramatically. Reforms have taken place at all levels, from educational policy and discourse, through curricula and programmes, to schools and classrooms. Among many efforts at reforming Chinese schooling, the New Basic Education (NBE) (*xin jichu jiaoyu* 新基础教育) is one of the most influential and has developed its own theory and practice. Born in the 1990s, NBE was envisioned as an answer to the call for a way to deal with challenges facing education in a new era characterized by the emergence of a market economy and accompanying rapid social and cultural transition. Initiated by Ye Lan 叶澜, a professor of education at East China Normal University, NBE is a whole school reform programme aiming at the development of active, self-aware human beings. This chapter discusses the historical background against which NBE is developed, the theoretical underpinning upon which NBE is based, and the translation of NBE's theory into school and classroom reform.

Background

The early-twentieth century saw the introduction of the Western school system to China and the accompanying importation of a variety of educational theories – ranging from the school system and management to curriculum and instruction – from the West. In the Republic (1912–1927) and Nationalist (1928–1949) eras, efforts were made to reform the school system and modify imported educational theories in view of the domestic situations of China. However, these efforts were frustrated and thwarted during the War of Resistance against Japanese Aggression (1937–1945) and the ensuing full-scale civil war (1946–1950) (Curran, 2005). In the first eight years after the founding of the People's Republic of China in 1949, educational reforms were mainly of a political nature, oriented towards the making of the socialist new person (also see Zhao, Chapter 2; Law, Chapter 3). The school structure and educational theories were borrowed from the then Soviet Union. Then in the 1960s and 1970s, the Cultural Revolution (1966–1976) disrupted the normal function of schooling, and all Western educational theories were eradicated.

As a result, when China's reform and opening up began in 1978, Chinese school patterns were largely the same as those in the Soviet Union and the broader industrialized world. As Ye Lan observed,

> Schools in China had the characteristics of education in an industrial era. Schools were built to serve industrialization and mass production and teachers were known as 'engineers of human souls'; there was a unified purpose, a uniform basic curriculum and unified textbooks; classrooms were as orderly and uniform as production lines and school timetables strictly regulated the duration of classes, the teaching cycle and the progress of teaching; everything had to be in accordance with the regulated education and teaching process.
>
> (Ye, 2006, p. 231)

This was indeed similar to the education in Europe at the beginning of the twentieth century (Ye, 2006).

For a hundred years, classroom teaching in China had been shaped by the Herbartian approach in two different forms. In the first half of the twentieth century, teaching was strongly influenced by Herbartian didactical theories borrowed from Japan for training teachers to teach in the modern school system (also adopted from Japan). From the 1950s until the start of the Cultural Revolution, classroom teaching was then under the powerful impact of Kairov's didactical theory – a Soviet form of Herbartian theory (see Deng, Chapter 11). As a result, Herbartian teaching ideas had found deep roots 'in the daily teaching habits and behaviors of millions of Chinese teachers even in the 1980s when China reopened itself to the world (Ye, 2006, p. 246). Teachers focused only on how to transfer knowledge contained in instructional plans to students, with no concern for nurturing students' awareness and ability to reason through knowledge acquisition. Classroom teaching was teacher-centred, directed towards the transmission of knowledge and for the sake of knowledge, whereas students passively absorbed what teachers taught, without any dynamism or sense of enjoyment. The challenges and inspiration that derived from learning knowledge as human wisdom were literally inexistent in classrooms.

With the implementation of reform and opening-up, China entered a period of radical change triggered by economic reform. A new market economic system was established, and people's social values became more diverse as they adapted to the changing social and economic environment. Such a new era calls for the development of human subjectivity through education. Ye explained:

> A society undergoing radical change urgently needs timely changes in education. This is not just a matter of human will to change, but calls for us to consciously understand the requirements of the times and take positive action to move forward in response to those times . . . The core spirit of the contemporary times is a call for the development of human subjectivity.
>
> (Ye, 1999b, p. 10)

NBE was born in this era, as a response to the urgent need for proactive individuals in a rapidly changing society. Society 'needs individuals who can control their own destinies and search for their own directions in this changing world; society needs to rely on such individuals to create the future' (Ye, 1994, p. 4).

The problems of China's basic education had also become evident in light of such an urgent need. The majority of school administrators lacked initiative; they tended to simply respond to requirements laid down by educational ministries and departments. Traditional patterns of school management, educational organization and classroom activity inherited from the industrial age remained intact. Although there have been reforms in China's basic education since the 1980s, 'the focus has been on updating educational content and reforming teaching methods', with the former ensuring that 'the educational content can reflect new technological developments', and the latter that 'students can have better access to knowledge' (Ye, 1994, p. 5). Students were not regarded as living individuals and neither was school life seen as co-constructed by the lives of students. As a result, reforms could not meet the expectation and demand of the new era, which called for the development of a new type of individual who is self-aware and proactive and capable of making life decisions.

Resonating with Karl Marx's dictum, 'The philosophers have only interpreted the world, in various ways; the point, however, is to change it' (Marx 1976 [1886], p. 64), Ye Lan believes that she can enrich her understanding about education through a practice that changes education. In 1994, she started her initial cooperation with one primary school, and from there she took steps to initiate the exploratory stage of NBE, and subsequently launched a campaign for NBE which lasted for nearly 20 years. We now turn to outline the theoretical foundations of NBE developed by Ye Lan.

Theoretical underpinnings

Our discussion of the theoretical underpinnings of NBE focuses on addressing four questions: What is the decisive factor in the development of a person? What is the central goal of education in the new era? What are the relationships between theory and practice as theory bears on intervention into school practice? How is the theory of NBE translated into school reform, classroom practice and school management?

Life-practice and the development of a person

The first question has long been an important one not only in education but also in philosophy, psychology, sociology and other social sciences. In China, the question became an essential concern among scholars in the field of education in the 1980s. There have been heated debates over which of the three factors – genetic, environmental and educational – is fundamental in the development of an individual.

In her article 'On factors in the development of an individual and the dynamic relationship between these factors and the individual,' Ye provided an answer to the question:

> We must shift from a biological position to a humanistic one, regarding the subject's life-practice as the most important factor in his or her personal development, and we should realize the dynamic relationship between the person and the factors affecting the process of human development, because it is the person who has a self-awareness and the capacity to dynamically transform and build both an outside world and their own internal spiritual world.
>
> (Ye, 1986, p. 86)

The notion of life-practice foregrounds the ability of an individual to make decisions in life which can be developed through education. '[O]ur fates,' according to Ye (2009), 'are determined by our own decisions, and the important task of education is to give people the power to take control of their own destiny, awareness and the capacity to act' (p. 145). Dietrich Benner (2001), a contemporary German educator, expressed a similar view: 'only humans can be educated, and can be asked to be active' (p. 59). Educators need to think about how to associate themselves with the initiative of the learner all along, in that only with initiative can a man become a real man. 'Education is accomplished when a learner becomes active without external demands' (p. 68). 'Only educational practices are based on presupposing their own ends' (p. 68).

The central goal of education

The purpose of education is therefore to foster the development of the subjectivity or 'life quality' of individual students – that is, the development of the self-awareness and ability to make decisions. Ye (2009) explains,

> individual's life quality is the biggest concern of education, and educators should focus on how to develop individual students' awareness and capacity. Up to the present, this is what I know, hope and judge to be the basic foundation and frame for education.
>
> (p. 145)

In short, achieving self-awareness and an enhanced sense of life is the ultimate goal of education. NBE aims at fostering students' self-awareness and helping them to achieve an enhanced sense of life. Each student is envisioned as an individual who has an awareness of self and the surrounding environment, with the personality and self-confidence to be involved in the transformation of the environment, who allows himself or herself to be renewed through interactions with the environment.

Theory and practice relationship

NBE is a research programme carried out by university professors together with primary and secondary school teachers. When it comes to methodology, the key issue is how to deal with the relationship between theory and practice, with professors working on the theory and school teachers working on the practice of teaching. There are three steps, according to Ye Lan.

In Step One, theory takes precedence over practice, while the two are closely related. As mentioned earlier, NBE is directed towards school reform in the midst of the significant social and economic transition underway in China. In reality, the impetus for change or reform may not come from schools; it is usually not possible for school practitioners to come up with a coherent theoretical system for school transformation based on their experience. However, educational change or reform needs theory to give impetus and direction. The final formation, legitimacy and feasibility of a theoretical position, on the other hand, need to be tested in practice.

In Step Two, theory and practice become intertwined and interdependent, as university researchers (working on theory) and school practitioners (doing practice) communicate and interact with each other. As reform moved on, Ye Lan realized that school practitioners became not only implementers but also makers of theory and analysts of educational issues by means of theory. Accordingly, university researchers were asked not to try to guide school practitioners, but to try to understand how to change or modify the existing 'theory' of school practitioners, prompting them to develop new educational theory for their new practices. According to Ye Lan,

> The relationships between theory and practice within an individual are integral and interactive, which is different from an individual's words and deeds. Words and deeds may not be consistent. Words can be contrary to deeds, whereas deeds can conceal the real meaning of words. The relationship between words and deeds can be very complex. However, in natural circumstances, sustaining the daily patterns of interaction between theory and practice within an individual are consistent.
>
> (Ye, 2009, p. 145)

Therefore, university professors should not simply disseminate and apply the existing theories and believe that as long as they have appropriate theory, they would be able to guide practice. Likewise, school practitioners should not be mere implementers who neglect the responsibility to criticize and reconstruct theories.

Step Three is characterized by a stage of increased complexity as reform has a transformative impact on practice. In 2004, the NBE programme reached a stage of implementing reform at the school level in which the units of research and analysis (having to do with the interplays of students, teachers and curriculum content within a particular cultural and institutional context) became much more complex. It called for a new way of reasoning – informed by the complexity theory of Mitchell Waldrop (1995) and the works of Edgar Morin – to be used in analyzing the process, and a series of transformations occurred during NBE reform. As Ye explained,

> If reformers want to achieve the goals of the reform, they cannot just depend on random factors that emerge. Instead, they should create new factors, and consciously adopt a variety of measures to strengthen and develop their self-organizational capacity in order to bring about the final completion of the system of transformation.
>
> (Ye, 2009, p. 181)

It is necessary to point out that these three steps of theory and practice relationship do not negate one another, nor do they substitute one another; rather, they complement and enrich one another.

Translation into school reform, classroom practice and school management

The translation of NBE theory into reality and practice in schools can be discussed in terms of (1) a whole school reform, (2) three basic reform tasks, (3) school management reform, and (4) interventional research in schools and classrooms.

A whole school reform

In NBE school reform is both systemic and transformational. It is *systemic* in the sense that changes are required in all aspects of the school system, including value orientation, relationship of elements (such as classroom teaching, class management, teacher development and school management, etc.) within the school system, the overall framework of the system, and its management and operational mechanisms. It is *transformative* in the sense that the reform 'does not merely make adjustments to the existing system, or simply eliminate unsuitable aspects from the original system, but rather it is a task of rebuilding' (Ye, 2013). More specifically, the reform involves the following aspects of change:

- *Goal and content of teaching*: There needs to be a shift in the goal of teaching from mainly transferring knowledge to developing students' initiatives, awareness and capacity so as to allow them to develop their own potential in a variety of scenarios and situations (Ye, 2002). To this end, curriculum content includes not only subject knowledge required for higher education entrance examination, but also knowledge pertaining to students' life experience, the vocational needs around them, science and technology, and communication skills for life.

- *Decentralizing and empowering schools*: A central task of NBE is to empower teachers and students and enable them to fully display their enthusiasm and initiative. Schools need to be committed to the development of active, healthy students, and laid down a solid foundation for their life-long learning and development. Schools should also empower teachers and students to 'be involved in democratic decision-making, and form mechanisms for the democratic supervision of school management.' (Ye, 2006, p. 328.)
- *An open structure*: Schools should be an open system, connected to the internet, media, the community, society and other schools; internally, the management of schools should also be open to teachers and students, while teaching should be open to all the possibilities for student development.
- *A mutually interactive process*: The life of the school should consist of interactions that involve multiple elements, multiple levels, multiple orientations and multiple clusters, all moving towards raising the quality of education and producing a comprehensive set of penetrations which inspire initiative and creativity in students and teachers.
- *Developing internal dynamics*: This means a school should be a self-organizational system, 'forming its own built-in development needs, motivation and mechanisms' to drive it forward.

(Ye, 1999a, pp. 331–42)

Three basic reform tasks

Based on the understanding of the nature of transformational reform, the NBE team worked for 20 years to fulfil three basic tasks: *classroom teaching reform*, *the reconstruction of classroom life*, and *the revitalization of school management*.

1 Classroom teaching reform

Classroom teaching has a direct influence on students' basic quality of school life. Therefore, during the course of the reform, the NBE team put a tremendous effort into reforming classroom teaching. Unlike the pervasive, dominant model of classroom teaching in China in which teachers are responsible mainly for transmitting knowledge contained in textbooks, the teaching philosophy of NBE holds that 'teachers should promote the active and healthy development of the new generation in contemporary society' (Ye, 2006, pp. 123–4). The primary purpose of classroom teaching is to cultivate students who 'take initiative in the development of their life' (Ye, 2006, p. 234). This is achieved through the teaching of various school subjects in the curriculum. Three aspects are vital for classroom teaching reform.

The first aspect is to conduct in-depth research into the rich educational value or potential of each specific school subject. This is defined in the following way:

Each subject has its value for the development of students. In addition to the knowledge of the field, there are values at the deeper level: to provide students with the ability to know, elaborate on, feel, understand, and change their way of life, and encourage constant interaction with the rich and colorful reality of the world of theoretical resources; to provide students with the opportunity to develop and realize their own purposes; to provide unique paths and unique perspectives on the learning of different subjects by finding out methods, strategies, special symbols and logical tools; to provide students with a special capacity and experience which enable them to discover the unique beauty of a particular subject.

(Ye, 2006, pp. 231–7)

In teaching a school subject, teachers need to think about how they can use what they teach to promote students' well-being in life, what educational potential the content has for fostering students' self-awareness and abilities to make decisions, and how their instructional approaches contribute to the realization of the value in life as well as enhance the value of life.

The second aspect is to conduct an analysis of the needs of student development in relation to the teaching of various school subjects. In China, under the framework of the national curriculum, curriculum content is mainly organized according to the logical structures in the system of knowledge, with little reference to the needs of students of various ages. As a result, curriculum content and students' daily experience are often disconnected, and students tend to have no motivation to learn. In NBE's reform, a significant entry point of classroom teaching is to connect teaching with the experiences of students by tapping into their curiosity, aspirations, interests and potential capacity and exploring the educational potential of curriculum content for students' growth and development.

The third aspect is to reconstruct the 'logic' of the process of classroom teaching and to promote the active and healthy shaping of students' life in the classroom. In China, educators have been torn between two opposite perspectives – one centred on how teachers teach and the other on how students learn. In NBE researchers see the relationship between teachers and students in the teaching process as an interpersonal one, and the relationship between teaching and learning as an organic whole. 'It is a process in which students and teachers, aiming to achieve instructional objectives, influence each other and promote teaching activities in a dynamic, generative way, through participation, dialogue, communication and cooperation centering around curriculum content' (Ye, 2006, p. 268).

2 Reconstructing classroom life

Classroom life has been given considerable attention in NBE reform. In China, the classroom is the basic organizational unit of teaching. Maintaining discipline and dealing with conflicts among students are two important issues in managing a class, and the majority of students in the class live within the framework of class organization. Under such a traditional management pattern, teachers tend to focus on the management process and ignore students' autonomy, inhibiting students' participation in classroom life. For this reason, NBE attaches great importance to classroom life because of the unique influence it has on the growth of students. Classroom life is reconstructed by organizing students in small groups and providing them with a wide range of learning activities – such as service learning, cooperative learning, role-modeling, problem-solving and project work – that contribute to the development of students' overall quality and, in particular, self-awareness and abilities to make decisions. In NBE, there is a slogan for the reconstruction of classroom life: 'Give the classroom management to students, and fill it with fresh air for growth.' This is in sharp contrast to the traditional mode of class-building which aims at the transmission of content, with listening to teachers' talks as the primary activity (Li and Chen, 2013).

Revitalizing school management

In NBE, school management reform is vital for systematic, transformative school reform, as how a school is managed has a direct impact on the soul and direction of school changes in various aspects. Management reform is also essential for teaching reform and the reconstruction of classroom life.

In fact, due to the many levels of management (national, provincial, regional or local, etc.) in China's centralized system, the management of schools is basically a kind of top-down decision making where school personnel tend to have low motivation and enjoy rather limited autonomy. To address this problem, NBE reform has focused on efforts to release the power within school authorities, trying to raise their sense of responsibility as leaders, so that they can inspire creativity in school teachers and encourage them to explore various issues concerning school organization, the school system, operational mechanisms, school culture and leadership. The goals of school management reform include: to bring the locus of management down to individual schools; make the organizational structure efficient; get more people involved in the leadership; provide more democratic channels for participation; reduce school administrative hierarchies and job divisions; and increase overall productivity and vitality.

In addition, NBE attaches considerable importance to changing the concept of the school leadership (including the headmaster). NBE stresses the consistency between 'personal fulfillment' and 'fulfillment of one's professional objective for the school'. 'Fulfillment of a person is made in the fulfillment of their objectives', and these two forms of fulfilment are mutually reinforcing (Ye, 2006, p. 245). This principle is relevant to various dimensions of school work, particularly the development of teachers and students. In the process of change, people are the most important and decisive force for sustaining the development of revitalized schools.

Interventional research in schools and classrooms

In the NBE, school reform includes two related aspects of research. The first involves interaction and open sharing between university researchers and school practitioners, and the second entails specific changes in educational practice at the school level as the result of research.

NBE is a research programme that requires multidimensional communication between ideal and reality, theory and practice, objectives and results, university researchers and school teachers, with individuals drawing on their inner resources as they interact. What kind of research can contribute to the realization of such a complex process? Evidence shows that most of the teachers are attached to their own ideas, and tend to have a risk avoidance mentality; when they face change, they respond by reinforcing their own thoughts and behaviour patterns. They lack the capacity for critical self-awareness, and do not have what is needed to face the challenges of the new era. For this reason, when researchers enter into schools, their intention is not to simply apply a theory of school reform, but to stimulate theoretical thinking among the teachers, and inspire them to embrace change. Ye explains:

> we act not only as outside observers, but as partners, going directly into the classroom, listening to classes, and intervening in teachers' teaching and their educational research processes. This involves choosing teaching values and goals, re-structuring teaching content, doing research on class design, inquiry into the relevance and reasonableness of the teaching–learning process, student analysis, the development of educational resources, analyses of teaching effectiveness and consideration of how teachers achieve their own development in the practice of teaching.
>
> (Ye, 2006, p. 181)

In this process, as university researchers clarify the problems in practice, they pay more attention to changing teachers' educational concepts and ways of thinking. Teachers, in turn, generate new ideas and new ways of thinking to guide their creative practice, which constantly opens space for researchers and their new educational thought. Over and over, university researchers and school teachers nourish each other in this symbiotic interaction between theory and practice.

In addition, NBE's ultimate goal is to achieve inner power for development, and thus ways of changing school leadership and cultivating wisdom in these leaders is one of the important objectives in NBE. A full description of the measures for empowering school leaders is beyond the scope of this chapter. Interested readers can find additional information in Bu and Li (2013).

Concluding remarks

NBE was born in the 1980s when Chinese society was experiencing a tremendous transformation in areas including economy, culture, ideology and way of life. Its primary mission is to nurture human beings with subjectivity to welcome this new era. At the same time, it also looks to the future and future possibilities, hence the building and rebuilding of ideals. Informed by the educational standpoint of potentiality, possibility and malleability, the focus is on creating a new future of education rather than complaining about the present status. In this regard, this study adopts a Confucian humanistic approach and promotes Professor Ye's idea that 'Education is the business of heaven, earth and human beings, life and self-consciousness should be nurtured'. This idea, as the core of the educational concept of NBE, may suggest a key difference between NBE and the work of other contemporary scholars whose research tends more towards criticizing the present world.

Acknowledgements

This research was supported as part of the Key Project for Humanities and Social Sciences and approved by the Ministry of Education of PRC (11JJD880034): Basic Education Reform and the Development of Innovative 'Life/Practice' Educational Research. The researchers are grateful for the translation by Dr. Yao Zhen Jun. They would also like to thank Professor Ruth Hayhoe for her selfless help and support in revising and polishing the translation.

References

Benner, D. (2001). 普通教育学: 教育思想和行动基本结构的系统的和问题史的引论 *[General Pedagogy: A Historical Introduction to the Issue of the Structure of Thought and Action]*. 上海, 中国: 华东师范大学出版社 [Shanghai, China: East China Normal University Press].

Curran, T. D. (2005). *Educational Reform in Republican China: The Failure of Educators to Create a Modern Nation*. Lewiston, New York Edwin Mellen.

Li, J. C. and Chen, J. (2013). Banzhuren and Classrooming: Democracy in the Chinese Classroom. *International Journal of Progressive Education*, 9(3), 89–106.

Marx, K. (1886/1976). Theses on Feuerbach. In F. Engels (ed.), *Ludwig Feuerbach and the End of Classical German Philosophy*. Beijing, China: Foreign Languages Press.

Waldrop, M. M. (1995). *Complexity: The Emerging Science at the Edge of Order and Chaos*. New York, NY: SDX Joint Publishing.

Ye, L. (1986). 论影响人发展的诸因素及其与发展主体的动态关系 [On Factors in the Development of an Individual and the Dynamic Relationship Between These Factors and the Individual]. 中国社会科学 *[Social Sciences in China]*, 3, 83–98.

Ye, L. (1994). 时代精神与新教育理想的构建 – 关于我国基础教育改革的跨世纪思考 [The Spirit of the Times and the New Basic Education: The Cross-Century Thinking of the Basic Education Reform in China], 教育研究 *[Educational Research]*, 10, 3–8.

Ye, L. (1999a). 把个体精神生命发展的主动权还给学生 [Giving the Students the Initiatives for the Individual Spiritual Life Development]. In K. M. Hao (ed.), 面向21世纪我的教育观 *[My View on Education in the 21st Century]*. 广东, 中国: 广东教育出版社 [Guangdong, China: Guangdong Education Publishing House].

Ye, L. (1999b). 面向21世纪的新基础教育 [New Basic Education for the 21st Century]. 新华文摘 *[Xinhua Digest]*, (10), 163.

Ye, L. (2002). 实现转型：世纪初中国学校变革的走向[J] (Transition: The Trend of China's School Reform at the Turn of the Century). 探索与争鸣 *[Exploration and Free Views]*, (7), 10–14.

Ye, L. (ed.) (2006). '新基础教育' 论: 关于当代中国学校变革的探究与认识 *[The 'New Basic Education' Theory: On Contemporary Chinese School Changes]*. 北京: 教育科学出版社 [Beijing: Educational Science Publishing House].

Ye, L. (2009). 个人思想笔记式的15年研究回望 [Personal Thinking and Notes on Education in the Past 15 years]. In L. Ye and Z. T. Li (eds), *NBE 研究史 [The Research History of NBE]* (pp. 143–204). 北京: 教育科学出版社 [Beijing: Educational Science Publishing House].

Ye, L. (2013). Spirit and Wisdom in the Tradition of Chinese Philosophy. Paper presented at the 69th Annual Meeting of the Philosophy of Education Society. 14–18 March, Portland, Oregon.

Index